THE SELF-SUFFICIENT KITCHEN

SMOKING FOODS

CHEF TED READER

Publisher: Mike Sanders
Editor: Christopher Stolle
Book Designer: William Thomas
Cover Designer: William Thomas
Compositor: Ayanna Lacey
Proofreader: Georgette Beatty
Indexer: Jessica McCurdy Crooks

First American Edition, 2021
Published in the United States by DK Publishing
6081 E. 82nd Street, Suite 400, Indianapolis, IN 46250

21 22 23 24 25 10 9 8 7 6 5 4 3 2 1
001-322405-NOV2021

Library of Congress Catalog Number: 2021931004
ISBN 978-0-74402-920-8

Note: This publication contains the opinions and ideas of its author. It is intended to provide helpful and informative material on the subject matter covered. It is sold with the understanding that the author and publisher are not engaged in rendering professional services in the book. If the reader requires personal assistance or advice, a competent professional should be consulted. The author and publisher specifically disclaim any responsibility for any liability, loss, or risk, personal or otherwise, which is incurred as a consequence, directly or indirectly, of the use and application of any of the contents of this book.

Trademarks: All terms mentioned in this book that are known to be or are suspected of being trademarks or service marks have been appropriately capitalized. Alpha Books, DK, and Penguin Random House LLC cannot attest to the accuracy of this information. Use of a term in this book should not be regarded as affecting the validity of any trademark or service mark.

DK books are available at special discounts when purchased in bulk for
sales promotions, premiums, fund-raising, or educational use. For details, contact:
DK Publishing Special Markets, 1450 Broadway, Suite 801, New York, NY 10018
SpecialSales@dk.com

Printed and bound in the United States of America

Reprinted and updated from
The Complete Idiot's Guide® to Smoking Foods

For the curious
www.dk.com

Contents

Introduction

As I'm writing this, we're in the midst of a global pandemic. We're all living through some tough times. Lockdown is very real. I know it's crazy, but I've had fun every day of this. I've decided it's time I share the fun I have every single day. With everybody. Even my miserable neighbor Bruce should be able to find fun in these pages. There's something amazingly comforting and warm about pulling a pork shoulder out of the smoker, shredding it into succulent, juicy threads, and piling it high on a bun with maybe some sauce. I defy you not to smile at each other while you mow into that pile of deliciousness. Good smoking could stop wars!

When I was a kid, my father built his own smoker/barbecue. I was his helper. From a very early age, I was fascinated by the smell of smoke off a carefully built fire. I doubt my dad realized he was inspiring me in ways he could only imagine. Watching him grill the perfect steak on a home-built oil drum barbecue pinged the deep recesses of my tiny mind. On top of my dad's love of the outdoors, my mother is Latvian. My brothers and I lived for the several visits a month from our grandparents. These always involved magical smoked meats and sausages and even cheeses. Every visit included a visit to one or another of their favorite Eastern European delis. We were eager for those Sunday afternoon feasts. As I grew, I began to want to know how these flavors came to be.

Fast-forward 50 years. I've somewhere around 100 smokers and grills in my backyard. I've got a firepit and a full-sized wood-fired brick oven. There's a pellet grill and a pizza oven in the garage (aka my office). I've got a tree full of hanging spatulas. And to top it all off, there's a hot tub! The whole neighborhood knows the smoke coming from my house is all good. My backyard has seen some pretty stupendous parties. Some of my chef buddies and I have fired up more than one of those units and turned out some awesome eats for anyone who happens along. Sitting around the firepit after eating slow-smoked beef or pork or chicken or even whole pineapple is the best feeling.

What you need to understand is that smoking isn't my hobby. It's not my job either. It's my vocation. If you dropped me on a desert island with meat and matches, I'd find a way to dig a pit. I'd find me some banana leaves to wrap that meat and bury it with hot rocks. The point I'm trying to make is, you can smoke anywhere and you don't have to have one of those fancy expensive rigs I'll discuss in this book. Nice to have if, like me, you literally light it 7 days a week. If you aren't that crazy, read on. I'll tell you how you can even smoke on a hibachi or right in your oven. Curiosity and passion have pushed me in multiple directions over the years but never far from my rig. There's always smoke!

#itbetasty has become my well-known catchphrase. I live for this thrill ride of deliciousness. I'm a barbecue guy. Always have been, always will be. I've been obsessed with food, fire, and smoke almost my whole life. I've grilled and smoked my way through a crazy variety of foods—from chocolate to cheese to whole prime ribs. Almost nothing has gotten past my gaze. Not even Twinkies. What can I say? I'm a curious guy!

I attended culinary school at George Brown College in Toronto—back when the culinary campus was smack in the heart of one of the oldest open-air markets in North America. We were free to roam through the spice shops, cheese shops, and, especially, butcher shops of Kensington Market. Back then, there was even an old kosher shop where you could choose a live bird and wait for it to be killed, blessed, and dressed to take home. The freshest product possible. Then there were Spanish shops with serrano hams, sausages, and smoked meats hanging from the ceiling. The Ukrainian and Polish shops were filled with kielbasa, sausages, hams, hocks, chickens, and all sorts of oily fish. All these shops had one thing in common: an old smoker pumping out rich, oily smoke.

I'm a meat guy. I just am. Which is why, as my culinary career progressed, I found myself drawn to the grill and then to the smoker. At one point, I reached the lofty position of corporate chef for one of the largest grocery chains in Canada. I was sent all over the world to research suppliers, learn about various cooking methods, and attend culinary events. While on the job, I ate brisket that was to die for at Franklin Barbecue in Austin, Texas—it was so moist, your napkins needed napkins. I researched the most incredible smoked duck at R.U.B. BBQ, Paul Kirk's former barbecue joint in New York City. I studied many a sausage in Texas and had the satisfying job of eating brisket, ribs, and beans at The Salt Lick in Driftwood, Texas. Oh, it be tasty!

I'll smoke anything, anyway, anywhere, anyhow.

As my career grew, I discovered research and development. I worked for meat guys all over North America, developing pretty much any smoky product I was approached about. Using the great industrial smokers in these plants taught me that much more about refining technique on my own smokers. Smoking is as much a science as it is an art. You work with the food scientists responsible for quality control and you gain an incredible amount of knowledge about the proteins I love so much. It's only right I share some of that knowledge. I'm a sharing kind of guy!

It was because of all the business trips that I began to look into this phenomenon further. It's been close to 30 years and there's no stopping now. I've become known as the "Godfather of the Grill" far and wide, but the smoking aspect of barbecue is my real passion. There's absolutely nothing I won't put in a smoker.

This is just a bit of my story. I hope this book is the beginning of your own story. It doesn't have to turn you into a pro or a fanatic, but it might. To me, smoking food is about spending time in the great outdoors and preparing some outrageously delicious food. My wife and my kids play too. It's not a solitary activity. The pit world is a social world. In these rough times, this is just what you need to get to know your family all over again. The thing I most want you to get from this book is that smoking foods isn't hard! My kids have been helping me since they were old enough to understand HOT!

I'll take you through every step of smoking by offering you the basic principles. I'm not going to lie: There will be times when you'll have to figure a few things out for yourself. Because every smoker is different and every situation is different, I can only predict and troubleshoot so much for you. Then you need to let your natural instincts kick in. Years ago, a wise old chef told me the way to really judge a chef was by how well they could make their mistakes look like they meant it. I believe this book will give you the tools you need to be prepared for most of the smoking obstacles that might come your way.

The most important piece of advice I can give you is that smoking foods with success requires one thing above all others: patience. Low and slow wins the day. If you don't think you're someone who can patiently tend to a fire for 12 hours or wait up to 3 days for the perfect meal, then this book might not be for you. All I can say is, give it a shot. I hope you'll not only like it but will also genuinely fall in love with it. I know I did!

How This Book Is Organized

I've divided this book into four parts to make it easy to follow:

Part 1: Where There's Fire, There's Smoke separates facts from misconceptions when it comes to smoking foods. You'll learn it really isn't difficult—and it doesn't take a lot of money or equipment—to get started on your adventure. In these chapters, you'll get all the details on choosing the right fuel, buying a smoker and accessories, and more. I finish with my 10 commandments to help make the experience successful—and fun!

Part 2: Layering the Flavor shows you how to use brines, marinades, rubs, and cures to make your meat more flavorful, tender, and moist. I share my favorite recipes for basic marinades, cures, rubs, spritzes, and more.

Part 3: Meat, Meat & More Meat … & Fish gives you information on different cuts of beef, pork, chicken, and other meats as well as a rundown on fish and shellfish so you know what to ask for when you head to your butcher or grocery store. The recipes in these chapters are some of my favorites—they're sure to make your mouth water!

Part 4: Starters, Sides & Sweets fills you in on some of the more unusual things you can smoke, such as side dishes, desserts, and even a cocktail. Expand your smoking repertoire and have fun trying these more unconventional recipes. You can truly smoke just about anything, as you'll see in these chapters!

I also include two helpful appendixes in this book that are geared toward the novice smoker: a glossary of terms I use throughout the book and a list of recommended books and websites for those who wish to continue their smoking adventure.

About My Barbecue & Social Media Friends

Since I first wrote this book, social media has busted out big! There just isn't anything you can't find through social media. Everybody is there. Everybody. Some of it's indispensable and some of it isn't worth your time. Everybody thinks they're an expert these days. This is a list of my go-to buddies. If I don't have the answer, they do!

Ray Lampe, known as Dr. BBQ, is a member of the Barbecue Hall of Fame. Along with Suzanne and Roger Perry, he owns Datz Restaurant Group and runs the Dr. BBQ restaurant in St. Petersburg Florida. Find him on Facebook (@drbbq), Instagram (@realdrbbq), and Twitter (@drbbq).

Myron Mixon is known as the winningest man in barbecue and a fixture as a judge on more than one barbecue competition on TV. He's also a member of the Barbecue Hall of Fame. Find him at www.myronmixon.com, on Facebook (@LordofQ), on Instagram (@myron.mixon), and on Twitter (@Lord_of_Q).

Paul Kirk is known as the Kansas City Baron of Barbecue and he's a member of the Barbecue Hall of Fame. Find him at www.baron-of-bbq.com and at www.langbbqcookingclass.com/chef-Paul-Kirk.html.

Steve Raichlen is an author, journalist, lecturer, and TV host who's often referred to as the man who reinvented modern barbecue. He was the host of three seasons of *Project Smoke*, the first program entirely devoted to the art of smoking. He's authored more than 30 books and he's another Barbecue Hall of Famer. Find him at www.barbecuebible.com/blog, on Facebook (@stevenraichlen), on Instagram (@stevenraichlen), and on Twitter (@sraichlen).

Mike Zaborsky is someone I met at the 2004 Grey Cup in Ottawa. After he finished bowing to me, calling me King of the Q, I joined him for a few pints to discuss the fine arts of football and barbecue. We've been fast friends ever since. Find him on Facebook (@mike.zaborsky).

Danielle Bennett, known as Diva Q, has a passion for barbecue that knows no boundaries. She lives, breathes, and eats barbecue. She's won numerous barbecue awards and multiple grand championships, and she's a former world pork champion and a former world bacon champion. Like me, she's a native Ontarian. Find her at www.divaq.ca and on Instagram (@dicaqbbq).

Mel Chmilar, of Dark Side of the Grill, has you covered with an electric personality and a character that makes cooking fun again! He's part of the pro team at Big Green Egg and he's a certified judge for the Kansas City Barbeque Society. Find him on YouTube (darksideofthegrill) and Instagram (@darksideofthegrill).

Matt Crawford, of Sasquatch BBQ, is pretty much as obsessed as me. I swear! He's big on Traeger pellet smokers and open flames. Find him on Facebook (@sasquatchbbq) and Instagram (@sasquatchbbq).

Craig Tabor is known as Big Green Craig. He's a chef playing the role of a backyard barbecue warrior. His slogan "There isn't anything I won't grill" is a dead-on representation of how he approaches outdoor cooking. Find him at www.craigtabor.com and on Instagram (@craigtabor).

Rob Tuzi of Barbecue Break is a Canadian grill master. He calls himself "just a backyard griller," but I'm here to tell you, he's the man. He's also the creator of the Tuzi Challenge. Rob is a man possessed—much like me! Find him at www.bbqbreak.ca, on Facebook (@BBQBreak), and on Instagram (@bbqbreak).

Roel Westra, of Pitmaster X, is a Dutch barbecue champion who constantly inspires people. Find him at www.pitmasterx.com, on YouTube (@Pitmaster X), on Facebook (@BBQPitmasterX), and on Instagram (@pitmasterx).

Marco Greulich is a world barbecue champion and one of the most successful grillers in Europe with over 40 titles. He's the only guy in Europe producing original rubs and seasonings. Find him at www.don-marcos-barbecue.de, on Facebook (@DonMarcosBBQ), and on Instagram (@donmarcosbbq).

Acknowledgments

Pamela, you're my heart and soul and the foundation of our beautiful family. You're the very best—I love you!

Layla and Jordan, my wickedly delicious little eaters, your smiles bring me sunshine and inspiration every day.

My dearest friend, Wendy Baskerville, thank you for coming to my rescue to help me with this book. We've shared many great times together. You're a part of our family and my children love Aunty Wendy. Your knowledge and talent with food is truly passionate. Thank you. I love ya!

Thank you to the world of barbecue, those I've touched, and those who've touched me—including all the barbecue chefs, fanatics, grill masters, and smoke masters. Thank you all for your continued support. Your passion for the world of smoke and barbecue fuels my fire. You're my inspiration. Keep it sticky and always make it delicious! #itbetasty

I'd also like to thank the following companies for their kind help in providing me with smokers for the testing of this book. Thank you so much for your support.

- Big Green Egg
- Bradley Smoker
- Napoleon Gourmet Grills
- Weber
- Traeger
- Pit Barrel

Where There's Fire, There's Smoke

Many people are under the impression that smoking is a lot harder than it actually is. And to the untrained eye, smoking food can seem daunting. There's all the equipment needed, the length of time it takes, and the countless fuel and wood combinations. But don't let the unknown deter you from taking up this great activity. (I didn't, but I now suffer from a serious illness—one that occasionally drives my wife a little crazy. It's called OCBD, or Obsessive-Compulsive Barbecue Disorder.)

The fact is, you don't need to buy a lot of equipment to smoke a great meal. I'll cover all the details on choosing the right fuel, buying the best smoker and accessories, and more in these chapters so you know what you're in for when you finally decide to start smoking.

For the Love of Smoked Foods

Chapter 1

Through the centuries, our eating habits have undergone an amazing evolution as we've adapted to our surroundings as well as the ingredients and tools available to us. Different cultures have developed their own unique culinary traditions. For example, at some point in history, some of us figured out how to use a fork, while others invented chopsticks and created a whole class of etiquette around eating with our hands. Depending on where you live, you might eat yak, zebra, camel, or buffalo. To round out our meals, we learned to cultivate grains, such as rice, which is a cornerstone of many cuisines today. And fortunately, we also learned that the roots under those pretty potato flowers are delicious when boiled and mashed with butter and roasted garlic.

Everybody smokes food. Examples exist everywhere: smoked tea eggs in northern China, glorious *churrasco*-style meats in Spain and Portugal, cured and smoked meats in Eastern Europe and Italy, and the quintessential oily smoked whitefish of Lake Baikal in Russia. Let's also not forget that peat is burned to dry and smoke the barley malt used to make whiskey in Scotland. Recently, archeologists in South Africa found the remains of a firepit in Wonderwerk Cave estimated to be 1 million years old.

In Paraguay and Argentina, they have the *asado*. This is practically a religious ceremony. The preparation takes easily as long as the long, slow cook. The *asador* spends a good deal of their time burning the wood until it's the perfect heat and the smoke is rich and ready to impart its flavor to whatever's being cooked. The tradition of asado can be found all over South America and is often a cultural event attended by whole towns. In Brazil, they follow the tradition of churrasco, which is a *gaucho* method of cooking over an open fire still followed today out in the vast pampas.

Then there's the relatively new approach to smoking food: American barbecue! This particular art of smoking really gets me excited. Firing up the smoker awakens my inner caveman. I'm almost hypnotized by the fire. Give me a cool fall day, a few beers, and a big hunk of meat or maybe some nice slabs of ribs—and I'm in the zone.

A Brief History of Smoking

Smoked food has been around nearly as long as humans have been cooking over fire. Smoking was the first way to preserve meat. Archaeologists have discovered that Neanderthals might have smoked strips of meat to make primitive jerky that was carried on long hunts and stored to feed them over cold and snowy winters. They didn't have salt yet and I don't suppose they knew about marinating, brining, and inventive seasoning rubs, but there's evidence they might have used certain herbs and woods to make things taste better. Humans have always had a yearning to play with their food and I'm quite sure that, even back then, there were good cooks and not-so-good cooks. I'll bet there was plenty of bragging going on around that big fire—just like today.

It was our cave-dwelling ancestors who first started cutting fish into nice, thin strips to hang over the fire. This early smoking process would draw all the moisture out of the flesh and stop bacterial growth. Our ancestors weren't concerned about bacteria. They just knew if they hung fish over a fire for a certain amount of time, they'd have food to sustain them over long distances. No doubt much like the discovery of fire itself, smoking foods guaranteed the survival of humans.

In the Middle Ages, all manner of foods were heavily smoked and salted to get people through the winter—until early spring, when new crops came in and the hunt began again. One notable example: Heavily salted red herring were smoked for up to three weeks in a kiln. Those herring never went bad. I'm not kidding. Smoked red herring has been found in archaeological digs in modern times and, when tested, still didn't show any bacterial activity. (Something tells me that even though they might technically be safe to eat, they're probably not very tasty.) These smoked fish were perhaps one of the first exported food products because they were sent all over the world on trade and exploration ships.

Without refrigeration, meat and fish had to be cooked and eaten quickly after slaughter or go through a spicing process or smoking period to preserve the meat. The spicing process used large amounts of salt to fully dehydrate the meat. The lack of water slows the growth of microorganisms and bacteria that cause food to spoil. Smoking was a popular preserving method during this time because it offered the same effect as salting but didn't require such huge amounts of salt. This meant that the meat didn't require soaking to remove the extra salt before it could be eaten. Another common technique to preserve meat was cold-smoking, where the meat was dried by exposure to the sun and then preserved by the addition of smoke. (I discuss cold-smoking later in this chapter.)

Hot burning lump charcoal

Smoking foods for preservation wasn't exclusive to meats and fish because fruits, especially berries, were also often smoked. Cheeses were also smoked using the cold-smoking method. The original purpose was for preservation, but along the way, people began to acquire a taste for the dusky flavor of smoked foods. Appearing on tables in castles everywhere, smoked foods were a mandatory part of a good old-fashioned banquet. Smoked hams and sausages became standard fare in every larder and maintained their popularity until the arrival of refrigeration.

When the first Spanish explorers arrived in the Caribbean, the native people were preserving meat in the sun. To drive away bugs, they built small, smoky fires and then placed the meat on wooden racks built over the fires. The smoke kept away the insects, and although they weren't sure why it helped, it preserved the meat. The Spaniards and the natives called—and still call—this process *barbacoa*. Some believe this is the genesis of the word "barbecue," but there is much debate on that topic. Another place the modern word "barbecue" could be derived from was French-speaking pirates who referred to Caribbean roasted pork as *"de barbe à queue,"* which means "from beard to tail" or "snout to tail." The hog was the most versatile animal and could be eaten from the tip of the snout through the end of the tail.

As Europeans and Africans started to populate the southern United States, this style of smoking continued to evolve. The Europeans brought pigs and cattle, which became the primary meats consumed in the New World. Pork was the meat of choice in the South, mainly because pigs can thrive with little care. The racks they used to dry the meat were replaced with pits and later smokehouses. It's not certain how pits became a fixture throughout the Caribbean, although it's known that pit-smoking was a technique used for hundreds of years by Polynesians. Another way pit-smoking could have come to the Caribbean was from enslaved and indentured Africans, whom the British began importing in the 1700s.

The early American Black population brought with them many delicious cooking traditions. Blacks were typically left with all the worst cuts of the animals. Given the poor quality of the food, the low and slow gentle smoking of the pit was the only thing they could do to make the toughest cuts on the animal not only edible but also enjoyable. Their method transformed "waste cuts," such as brisket, ribs, pork belly, and so on, into yearned-for delicacies. Sauces were created that further enhanced these meats. Women would fill bean pots with sauces and slowly bake them in the pit to pick up subtle smoky notes. These delicious smoked foods began to make a jump into the main houses sometime in the late 1800s.

After the Civil War, many of the former enslaved Blacks found that one of the quickest ways to begin making a living was to offer their delicious smoked food for sale. Soon, every small town had some sort of pit-style roadhouse. Legends grew around the various communities and different regions began to be known for particular dishes or styles. Everyone knew that for beef, you wanted to go to Texas; Kentucky became famous for lamb; and the Carolinas were the home of awesome succulent pork.

In the late 1800s, the world began to industrialize an infrastructure for the rapid delivery of perishable foods, such as seafood and produce. The need for heavily preserved foods began to wane, but people still longed for the smoky flavors they were accustomed to. It's at this time we begin to see the growth of smoking on a different plane: lightly smoking foods for added flavor without the heavy salting of the past. The modern foods we know so well, such as smoked salmon and sliced bacon, were born.

For many years, the pit traditions were a local fixture in small towns of the southern United States, but with the upwardly mobile 1950s and 1960s, leisure time made barbecuing a new phenomenon. Barbecue grills became a must-have for every backyard in America. We were simply fascinated with the whole grilling concept.

As the profile for this hobby grew, diehards wanted to experience the true, smoke-filled tradition of barbecue and recreate it in their backyards. Small obscure companies became larger as they recreated equipment they had been supplying to the food-service market for backyard applications. As fun as it was to have a shiny barbecue grill, it became even cooler to have your own smoker.

Humans have a relentless way of investigating a subject until it's completely exhausted, but smoking foods continues to open up new vistas. The number of ingredient combinations—not to mention wood mixes, flavoring agents, techniques, and more—is limitless. Every weekend somewhere in the world, someone with a great imagination is trying out some crazy combination of meat, flavoring, and wood under the dome of a smoker—maybe not even realizing how old an art it actually is. In fact, more than 15 million grills and smokers are sold in the United States every year—now that's a craze! Having visited Franklin Barbecue in Austin, Texas, I can't deny that smoking has infiltrated every aspect of North American culture. Once you get to the front of the line, you might find yourself sitting next to a biker or a CEO. I think a pit-smoked barbecue could hold the key to world peace!

The Current Smoking Craze

The current smoking craze owes a fair bit to the rising celebrity of chefs in general and to the world of competitive barbecue specifically. Television has been a major force in inspiring new interest in smoking foods. Programs like *BBQ Pitmasters* and Steven Raichlen's *Project Smoke*, along with documentaries on such events as the Memphis in May World Championship Barbecue Cooking Contest and the Jack Daniel's World Championship Invitational Barbecue in Lynchburg, Tennessee, have made our mouths water.

Then we have the Kansas City Barbeque Society, a nonprofit organization dedicated to promoting and enjoying barbecue. It's the world's largest organization of barbecue and grilling enthusiasts, with more than 20,000 members worldwide. KCBS sanctions more than 500 barbecue contests across the globe—from volunteering to actual event production. A whole new generation of smokers has been created literally worldwide.

The number and diversity of attendees at some of the contests and shows I've attended have grown by leaps and bounds in the last 10 to 15 years. For those who just want to eat, authors like Jane and Michael Stern have created travel guides that feature great pits as must-see destinations. Some travel agents will help you plan a trip around the legendary establishments you want to visit.

Smoking vs. Grilling

Simply put, *grilling* is the act of cooking meat (or other foods) by setting it on a grate over a heat source, such as a gas flame or hot coals. Tender cuts of meat as well as seafood and vegetables are best suited for this cooking method. Grilling is sometimes done covered, but it's always at relatively high heats: anywhere from 350°F (175°C) up to 800°F (425°C) in the case of some kamado-style grills or barbecues with infrared pads.

Smoking is generally done over charcoal or wood, and although it's not as common, gas can also be used. It might involve fully cooking the food because its main purpose is to infuse smoke flavor into the item being smoked. Smoking always happens in a closed (lid-down or doored) atmosphere. The phrase "low and slow" was coined to describe the relatively low temperatures used for smoking and the lengthy amount of time it takes to infuse and cook the food. The temperature for smoking typically sits between 180°F (85°C) and 225°F (110°C).

Smoking must be viewed as much as science as it is an art. Smoke is produced as a side effect of combustion. You light your fuel and then oxygen combines with your fuel to create combustion. Smoke is the result. A semi-technical explanation: The fuel burns and creates chemicals within the smoke that attach themselves to your meat, hopefully flavoring them in some manner. It's important to understand just this: Don't burn something that isn't certified food safe. For example, don't use treated wood. Whatever chemicals are present on your fuel will end up in some form on your food.

I'm not gonna be that guy who tells you that grilling is better than smoking or that smoking is better than grilling. I will tell you, though, that they have a place in your cooking repertoire. I say, if you can afford it and have the space, get yourself a smoker and a grill. If you can only have one, look for the best unit available that will do both. Smoking and grilling can accomplish essentially the same thing—namely, making good and tasty food.

A grill provides you with a quick and convenient way to cook outdoors and it doesn't make a huge mess. It sits out there and all you have to do in most cases is trot out, turn on the gas, scrape the grate, and start cooking. Within 30 to 45 minutes, you're eating something tasty. Even if you have a charcoal grill, you'll likely be eating in an hour or so. A smoker can't really be called convenient. With a smoker, you have to plan ahead. Mind you, I don't necessarily feel that way in my own life. Then again, not everybody has six to nine grills and a half-dozen smokers set up in their backyard at any given time— it's my job!

There have been studies done on differences in taste reactions of food cooked on various grills. Studies show that unless you have an amazing palate, you won't be able to tell the difference between burgers cooked over gas, charcoal, or electric grills. Even grilling over charcoal doesn't add a whole lot of smoke flavor. (Of course, you do get some—and we all know how good a charbroiled steak can be.) However, when you take it up a notch and go to the smoker, you're literally forcing smoke into the food. The whole point of the process is to impart that flavor.

Preparing a meal on a smoker requires some planning. Even if all you want to do is smoke a steak, you need to be sure you can afford a couple hours to wait for your dinner. The average person might not try smoking a steak because let's face it, some people love immediate gratification—but you're missing out on a really good thing if you don't try it. Low and slow can challenge those who are used to fast results on a grill, but the end results will be worth the effort.

Learning the art of managing a fire takes patience and practice. If you can learn the patience required to control the temperature, you'll find yourself eating undeniably great food. If one of your goals is to find that delicious smoky note in your meat, then the smoker is the way to go. All you need is a good chunk of time, some patience, a lot of beer (if you're like me!), and a large appetite!

The Different Types of Smoking

While countless types of smokers are on the market—with seemingly endless accessories and gadgets to accompany them—really only two ways exist to smoke food. Both add that sweet flavor we all yearn for, but each has a different purpose: one cooks the food with heat from fire and the other cures the food. *Curing* can refer to various types of preservation and flavoring processes. It might include the addition of a combination of salt, nitrates, nitrites, or sugar. Some curing processes also involve smoking because the added flavor is desirable. Either way, the purpose of curing is to prolong food's stability by drawing out as much moisture as possible so bacteria can't breed and spoil the food.

Cold-Smoking Foods

Cold-smoking is the process of applying smoke flavor to foods without necessarily cooking them. Cold-smoking generally occurs at temperatures in the range of 80°F to 100°F (25°C to 40°C) and certainly no higher than 120°F (50°C). At times, it can be as low as 40°F (5°C), although getting your smoker to that temperature can be tricky and isn't recommended for the average home smoker.

Examples of cold-smoked foods include bacon, sausage, country ham, fish, and cheese. Some foods—like smoked salmon—can be eaten straight out of the cold-smoker, but most—like bacon or sausage—will require further cooking at a higher temperature. Cold-smoking is a curing process more than a cooking process. Some foods can be exposed to the smoker for as long as a week, which is the case for some sausages and hams. Properly prepared cold-smoked foods never reach a temperature above 80°F to 100°F (25°C to 40°C). In the case of fish, it would be unusual to go over 80°F (25°C).

Technically, cold-smoked fish is raw but cured, so it's safe to eat. It's similar to the principles of *ceviche*, where the proteins in the fish are "cooked" by acid (usually from citrus juices). Smoked salmon gets a long soak in saturated salt brine, causing its proteins to denature (which means it modifies the structure of the flesh). In a real and safe sense, you've cooked it by way of a chemical process. Then the salmon goes into the cold-smoker to infuse it with flavor at low temperatures.

Hot-Smoking Foods

Hot-smoking is smoking in an enclosed atmosphere in the presence of heat and smoke. Heat is used to cook the meat and the smoke provides the flavor. Successful smoking requires food to be cooked slowly and at a constant temperature ranging from 180°F to 230°F (85°C to 100°C). The flavor imparted to the food comes from the types of wood used to create the smoke. The smoking process not only cooks and flavors the meat, but it can also help preserve it. The term "low and slow" is used often throughout this book because it's the basis for the entire concept of smoking food. Cooking this way is like cooking a pot roast in a slow cooker for 8 or 9 hours.

With hot-smoking, food is placed inside the smoker so it's entirely surrounded by smoke. There should be a thick stream of smoke around the meat at all times. The smoking process is intended to give the smoke enough time to sink in and naturally tenderize the meat. Slow-cooking gives tough connective fibers in heavily exercised muscles time to break down and become tender by dissolving. This is an integral part of smoking. Collagen, which is the tough connective tissue in meat, breaks down into several types of sugars when cooked slowly. Some tougher cuts are actually made sweeter by the smoking process.

Although I said smoking is a science, I believe smoking food is truly an art. And like many good things, practice and patience are required in large doses. You'll read the word "patience" over and over in this book. Heed it well, my friends, and you'll become the artist you yearn to be. Low and slow be the way to go, y'all.

Smokers & How They Work

Smoking foods can be a lot of hard work or it can be fairly easy. Although some purists feel that only hardwoods and charcoal can create a true smoke flavor, that kind of smoking can require a lot of effort for some people. At the end of the day, because you're the one who has to do the work, there's no shame in getting one of the newer-style pellet smokers. If the authentic flavor and smoking experience are what you're really striving for, then going for a more advanced smoker is worth the extra effort.

Selecting your first smoker can be tricky. You have many things to consider. You need to know what your options are and what each of those options is capable of. In this chapter, I outline the most popular smokers on the market, how each smoker works, and what needs to be done to operate it properly and safely. There are specific guidelines for each smoker, although some rules apply to every smoker:

- READ THE MANUFACTURER'S MANUAL COVER TO COVER!

- Always follow the manufacturer's recommendations for the initial setup and firing of the smoker.

- Select a wood fuel based on the manufacturer's recommendations.

- Before you start smoking, ensure you have enough fuel to complete the job.

- Never move a hot smoker.

- Thoroughly clean every part of the smoker after every use. A clean smoker is a healthy smoker.

- For your first time, start with a forgiving and inexpensive cut of meat, such as a pork shoulder. (Because it smokes for a prolonged amount of time, it will allow you to figure out all the quirks of your new smoker.)

- Recognize that you'll fail. Maybe not the first time, but there will be failures. I fail very occasionally (hardly ever), but every failure is a learning experience.

It's important to understand how each smoker works and just how much effort you'll have to put into operating it before you buy one. Even if it looks all sweet and shiny in the showroom, it might end up being more trouble than you bargained for.

Smokers for the Novice

For all those first-time smokers out there, I recommend starting out nice and easy. You can smoke foods without too much fuss in your backyard using a gas grill or an inexpensive charcoal kettle grill. Experimenting with smoking on these units is pretty simple. The upside is that because it's just another application for your existing grill, you don't have to find a home for multiple units in your backyard like I do.

If you've decided that a dedicated smoker is the way to go, manufacturers have designed many electric units that are easy to use. These smokers need less tending and monitoring than traditional models because they're automated. You just have to set the temperature, add the wood, and get your food smoking.

Gas Grill

Any gas grill with a lid can be used to smoke food. The two keys to success are indirect heat and temperature control. If your gas grill doesn't have a temperature gauge on the lid, you can pick up gauge kits at most stores that sell grills. You can use an oven thermometer, but it isn't ideal because you'll have to open the lid to check the temperature, which will result in losing heat and smoke.

To achieve a temperature low enough for smoking, you can use indirect heat. Just place the food item over a burner that isn't lit and the remaining lit burners will produce the heat that will smoke and cook the food. The actual smoke itself can be produced by using wood chips loosely wrapped in aluminum foil to make a pouch, a metal wood chip box, or a prepackaged smoking can (a small metal can filled with hardwood chips). Other options for producing smoke include external smoke generators, such as the SmokePistol system. Because most gas grills aren't insulated, the outdoor temperature and wind will have a significant impact on the internal temperature of the grill. You'll find more instructions for smoking on a gas grill in Chapter 4.

Smoking on a gas grill with a charcoal tray and charcoal briquettes

Charcoal Kettles

One of the most popular backyard grills is a charcoal kettle grill. Smoking on one of these units is also accomplished by using indirect heat: Charcoal is placed on one side and food on the other side. You'll need to monitor the temperature carefully. If your kettle grill doesn't have a temperature gauge installed on the lid, install a gauge kit or use a metal pocket thermometer or electronic probe thermometer and rest it in one of the vent holes in the lid.

A water pan needs to be placed to one side of the lower grate (charcoal tray)—disposable aluminum pans from the supermarket work well. The water pan serves two purposes: It catches meat drippings and adds humidity to the cooking chamber. Hot charcoal is placed in the kettle next to the water pan and the temperature is controlled using the air vents on the kettle's base and lid. Opening and closing the air vents on the kettle's base will have the greatest impact on the internal temperature.

Smoke production is achieved by using good-quality hardwood lump or briquette charcoal. If more smoke is desired, use wood chips loosely wrapped in an aluminum foil pouch. Rest it on the coals or place soaked wood chips directly on the coals. (See Chapter 3 for more about soaking wood.) Controlling the temperature, humidity, and airflow is the key to success, even when using a beginner smoker.

Electric Smokers

The methods I've just discussed are the best way to start smoking and not break the bank. Because being a beginner might seem a little challenging and daunting, not wanting to spend a ton of cash right off the bat makes sense. However, once you've had a little practice, you might want to move on to an electric smoker.

Electric smokers create smoke by burning wood with an electrically powered heat element. For the most part, the type of fuel is governed by the type of electric smoker being used and the manufacturer's recommendations. Basic electric smokers will require you to add wood chips manually during the cooking process. On higher-end models, the wood fuel is fed to the heating element automatically. Different smokers do this in a variety of ways. Many pellet smokers use an auger system to feed pellets into the burn pot. Wood puck smokers mechanically feed pucks to the heating element at timed intervals. (See Chapter 3 for more on wood chips, pellets, and other fuel options.)

Portable electric smokers are available in a wide array of shapes and sizes, such as kettle, vertical box, and barrel shape. Electric smokers with insulated cooking chambers can maintain more stable temperatures in adverse weather conditions.

The type of electric smoker being used governs the type of heat created. Some heat the wood fuel only to a smoldering point, then use a separate electric heating element within the cooking enclosure to achieve the desired temperature. Other models heat the wood fuel until it catches fire and then control the fire (and therefore the cooking temperature) by using forced ventilation and a precision-controlled fuel feed.

Even if your smoker has an electronic-control unit, it's not as simple as loading the unit with the required wood fuel and setting it to the desired temperature. You'll need to consider the conditions outdoors, especially on a particularly hot, cold, or windy day. The smoker needs time to build up to the desired temperature, and if it doesn't make it there or overshoots it, you'll need to adjust as you smoke. For electric smokers without a control unit, you can control the temperature by monitoring the thermostat and adjusting the vents and (to a lesser extent) the amount of wood fuel added.

Here are some things to keep in mind when using an electric smoker for the first time:

- Check the amperage of the plug you intend to use to ensure it can handle the power requirements of the smoker.

- Although some electric smokers have fully enclosed electronic elements, not all do. Because water-resistant isn't the same as waterproof, be sure to check the weather forecast before starting.

Top left: digital-electric vertical box smoker with smoking pucks
Top right: electric-coil smoker
Bottom: electric horizontal pellet smoker

- Because there's no such thing as "set it and forget it," keep an eye on your smoker. Grease flares, short circuits, and temperature-control issues can happen with even the best electric smokers.

- Look for thick gray or black smoke. This is an indicator that a grease fire is burning inside the smoker.

- If your electric smoker has a water pan, fill it to the required level. If it's not designed for a water pan, don't use one because the added humidity can damage sensitive electronic components.

- If your smoker has adjustable vents, use them to control the internal temperature and the smoke flow within the unit.

Smokers Best Suited for Adventurous Amateurs

You're probably asking yourself, what exactly is an adventurous amateur? To me, this is a person who says: "I think I can, I think I can, I think I can"—and does! And it's that attitude that sets an adventurous amateur apart from a beginner. An adventurous amateur isn't afraid to experiment and will happily try again even if the first attempt didn't have perfect results. They always want to improve upon what they smoked before. It's also for the person who wants more of a challenge and who's ready to graduate from smoking on their gas or charcoal grill. This isn't to say that smoking on an electric smoker isn't exciting, but it isn't as much work as smoking with charcoal and hardwood.

Moving on to new challenges means you'll want to get another piece of equipment. So now I'll guide you through the smoking world of vertical box smokers, water smokers, offset barrel smokers, kamado-style grills, drum smokers, and pellet smokers. These smokers work primarily with hardwood charcoal, hardwoods, or prepared hardwood pellets. I'll review the basics of what these smokers entail and which smoker might be best for your needs. In addition, I'll share my tips and tricks on how to operate each smoker to help you get the best results.

Vertical Box Smokers

A vertical box smoker is a box-shaped cooking chamber with a heat source in the bottom. Higher-quality box smokers will have a separate firebox—either underneath or on the side of the box—which allows heat and smoke to flow into the cooking chamber. Separating the firebox from the cooking chamber allows for better temperature and smoke control. Box smokers can be charcoal-, electric-, or propane-fired. Some use hardwood chips to create smoke, while others have wood pellet- or puck-feed systems to create smoke and generate heat.

Box smokers on the market today range from simple charcoal-fired, thinly walled cabinets with a couple vents to fully insulated, microprocessor-controlled, gas-fired cabinets with ultraprecise temperature and smoke controls. Insulated cabinets provide a more consistent temperature than uninsulated boxes, particularly in wet or cold weather. Each type of box smoker has distinct advantages and disadvantages. As I already mentioned, electric box smokers are convenient but need a power outlet. Basic models use a thermostat, but more advanced models use onboard computers to control the temperature. Propane box smokers are more portable—no outlet is required unless your smoker has an electrically powered pellet- or puck-feed system.

Charcoal-fired box smokers are generally the least expensive and most portable type, but they require careful attention to maintain the fire and smoke temperatures.

For basic propane-fired and electrically fired box smokers, controlling the temperature is as simple as adjusting the thermostat (electric) or flow of propane until the desired internal temperature is reached. There might not be an adjustable lower vent on these smokers because the heat source doesn't rely on a variable supply of oxygen to control the temperature. On advanced models, the internal temperature and fire are controlled by an onboard microprocessor.

In charcoal-fired box smokers, adjustable vents primarily control the temperature, but the type of charcoal and how it's arranged also play a part. Once the charcoal is lit and the desired internal temperature has been reached, adjust the vents toward the closed position. Keep an eye on the temperature gauge and make final adjustments to the vents until you've achieved a steady smoking temperature for 20 minutes.

If you're using wood chips, soak them before putting them in the chip box or chip bowl or onto the charcoal. Where you put them depends on the model of the smoker. The wood chips shouldn't have a large impact on the internal temperature because the goal is to keep them at a slow smolder (not flaming) during the smoking process. Box smokers with automatic pellet- or puck-feed systems remove the need to replenish wood chips. Depending on the smoker model, these pellets and pucks can be burned at higher temperatures to create heat and smoke or simply heated to a smoldering point to create smoke. Pellets and pucks are never presoaked with these box smokers because they'll absorb moisture, disintegrate, and not work with your smoker.

The weather will have an impact on the internal temperature of all box smokers, although well-insulated boxes will be affected to a lesser degree. Adjust the controls as needed to reach and maintain the desired temperature—and always use a thermometer to check the internal temperature of your smoker. If you attempt to "set it and forget it," you might not get to the temperature you need on a cold day or you might overshoot the temperature on a hot day.

Water Smokers

These have primarily two shapes: box and upright drum. They can be fired by charcoal, electric, or propane, and like other smokers, they use soaked hardwood chips or charcoal to create smoke. The key difference is that a pan of water is placed directly over the chip box and heat source and underneath the food being smoked.

Adding water to the smoking process has a couple key advantages: The steam created within the cooking chamber keeps the food moist and any drippings from the food fall into the water pan instead of on the fuel, reducing the chance of flare-ups or snuffing out the fire. Perhaps more importantly, the temperature within a smoker is much more stable and easier to maintain with a water pan in place. Be sure not to overfill the water pan, but also keep an eye on the water level and replenish it as necessary. The weather will also have an impact on the internal temperature of water smokers. On cold days, it's a good idea to start with hot water in the water pan. Temperature control for water smokers is achieved using the same techniques as vertical box smokers.

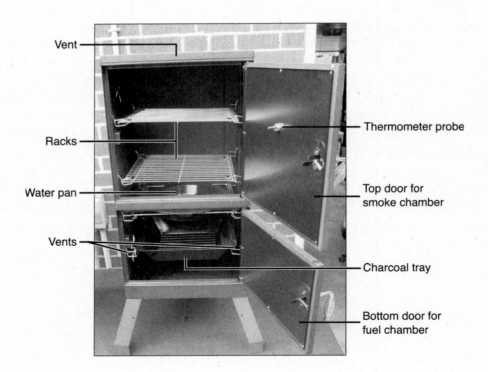

Vertical water smoker

Thermometer probe

Chimney with vent control

Heavy-duty lids

Door with vents

Smoking chamber with racks

Firebox

Offset barrel smoker

Offset Barrel Smokers

An offset barrel smoker (also known as a stick burner) is a relatively recent invention. Its origins are in Oklahoma and west Texas, where inventive and industrious oilmen decided to use materials on hand to replicate the brick-and-mortar pit smokers from back home. Using heavy-gauge oil pipe and the skills of local welders, these men put together the very first offset barrel smokers. The basic design hasn't really changed since. While they might vary widely in size and quality, every offset barrel smoker has three primary components: an offset firebox, a cooking chamber, and an exhaust flue.

The temperature in the cooking chamber is controlled using adjustable intake- and exhaust-vent dampers located on the firebox and atop the exhaust flue. Minor improvements over the years have included baffle and tuning plates to improve heat flow and distribution as well as vertical smoking chambers on the end opposite the firebox. The traditional fuel used in an offset smoker is dried hardwood logs, although lump hardwood charcoal can be used either as an alternative to or in combination with the logs. Humidity can be introduced to the offset barrel smoker by placing a pan of water directly over the firebox's baffle plate inside the cooking chamber. Offset barrel smokers are among the most labor-intensive of the bunch, requiring frequent tending of the fire and careful control of the vent dampers to maintain a steady temperature in their smoking zone. But done right, the results are beyond comparison.

Airflow in and out of your offset barrel smoker is the primary method used to control the cooking temperature. Environmental factors will also heavily influence the cooking chamber temperature. Managing the fire on a beautiful, warm, and sunny day will be a different challenge from maintaining the temperature on a cold, wet, and windy day.

Adding a water pan in the cooking chamber has a benefit beyond adding moisture to the cooking process. It acts as a secondary heat baffle for the firebox and helps regulate the temperature. Keep in mind, however, that it will take longer for the smoker to initially reach the cooking temperature when a water pan is in place.

The best offset barrel smokers are precision-welded, with excellent fit and finish, high-quality gaskets, and carefully designed heat baffles and tuning plates. If you fire up your smoker and notice smoke escaping from around the chimney or through the closed cooking chamber door, purchase heat-resistant gasket material and putty to seal things. A properly sealed cooking chamber and exhaust flue make a huge difference in the ease of maintaining a steady temperature. As an aside, I've found that the heavier the smoker is, the better it cooks.

Here are some things to keep in mind when using an offset barrel for the first time:

- Most barrel smokers need a good burn-in to eliminate chemical residue left from the factory before the first use. Heat the smoker according to the instructions.

- Lower-priced models are often better for charcoal instead of hardwood logs.

- If your smoker has a drain valve, either make sure it's closed (if you plan to drain after cooking) or set a heatproof container directly underneath to catch drippings.

- Because most cuts of meat will benefit from added humidity, use a water pan near the firebox baffle in the cooking chamber and regularly check the water level.

- Airflow through the firebox vent damper has more of an effect on the internal temperature of the cooking chamber than the exhaust flue-vent damper.

- These smokers need TLC to get the job done right. Check the cooking chamber temperature and the fire regularly, and add logs or charcoal as needed.

- After cooking, completely close the vent dampers to snuff out the fire. Or open the firebox and dampers to let the remaining wood or coal burn off at a high temperature. (This method will also "season" the inside of the cooking chamber.)

Kamado-Style Smokers

The kamado-style smoker originated in Japan, where domed, circular clay ovens have been used for centuries. In fact, the word *kamado* is Japanese for "stove." Modern kamado-style smokers have the same design elements as those clay ovens. They include thick walls with excellent thermal properties, a domed lid (usually hinged) resting on a round- or oval-shaped pot, an internal grilling surface, and vent dampers on top and bottom to control the airflow in and out of the cooking chamber.

While kamado-style smokers constructed of clay or cement are still available, most modern kamado-style smokers are constructed of high-fire ceramic, terra-cotta, insulated steel, or other more suitable materials. Traditional clay kamados are more prone to developing cracks, particularly when exposed to the elements and high temperature fluctuations.

Kamado-style grills and smokers

Kamado-style smokers are capable of reaching and maintaining internal temperatures of up to 750°F (400°C), which is excellent for quickly searing a steak but much too hot for smoking food. But with the right fuel (such as lump charcoal) and careful control of airflow, they're also one of the best smokers available. Maintaining temperatures in the smoking zone can be done with ease when using these smokers.

The airflow is what will determine the internal temperature. Airflow is controlled by adjusting the vent dampers at the top and bottom of the grill. The wider the damper is opened, the more air will reach your coal and cause it to burn hotter. For smoking, we want to allow just enough air into the smoker to maintain a steady low temperature and to keep the coals burning slowly and evenly.

If you're using a temperature-control device, attach it to the lower vent damper before lighting the coal. Put a couple pounds of lump charcoal onto the fire grate in your kamado-style smoker and form it into a mound. Be careful not to block the airway from the lower damper with little pieces of coal and then completely open up the lower-vent damper. Only light a few pieces of coal in the center of the pile. If your smoker comes with a heat diffuser, put it in place. Once the coal in the center of the pile has ignited, put the grill grate in place, close the domed lid, and fully open the upper-vent damper.

If you're adding wood chips, place them around the perimeter of the coal pile before you close the lid. Let the coals burn until the internal temperature has reached 350°F (175°C), then close both vent dampers nearly completely—leaving only a ¼-inch (0.5cm) opening at the top and bottom. While this temperature is too hot for smoking, reaching 350°F (175°C) will help ensure your fire burns throughout the entire smoking process.

After opening the domed lid and placing your food inside the kamado for smoking, the internal temperature will drop considerably. Within a few minutes of the lid being closed, the temperature will rise and then settle. If it's too hot, close the dampers completely for a few minutes. Once the kamado reaches the ideal temperature, open the top- and bottom-vent dampers ⅛ inch (3mm) and keep an eye on the gauge. These small adjustments can have a dramatic effect on the internal temperature.

As with other smokers we've discussed, these kamado-style smokers require a bit of work, a lot of patience, and a small amount of good luck and instinct. Once you learn how to manage the fuel with the dampers and become a temperature-control expert, the results will be well worth the effort.

Here are some things to keep in mind when using a kamado-style smoker the first time:

- A kamado-style smoker is designed to retain moisture in the food being cooked, but even a splash of water inside a hot ceramic unit can crack and ruin your grill. Don't use a water pan or water to put out the coals.

- Airflow through the bottom-vent damper has more of an effect on the internal temperature than the top-vent damper.

- Always open a kamado lid slowly. The gust of moist, hot air from a quickly opened lid can be a painful learning experience.

- When the kamado has cooled completely, clean out the cold ash and any remaining charcoal. Be sure to pay particular attention to the inside opening of the lower-vent damper.

Drum Smokers

Drum smokers had their genesis as homemade smokers made out of old oil drums. Burning charcoal at the bottom of the drum produces heat and smoke. The hot air and smoke rise to the food and cook it before escaping from a vent at the top. As the air rises, it pulls in more air through a small vent at the bottom. The temperature inside the drum is controlled by adjusting the size of the vent on the bottom. You can still find DIY instructions on the Internet, but you can also buy drum smokers ready to use.

Pellet Smokers

Pellet smokers are outdoor cookers that combine elements of smokers, charcoal and gas grills, and ovens. They use 100% all-natural hardwood pellets as the fuel source and they allow for direct or indirect heat. Wood pellets are poured into a storage container called a "hopper." Those are fed into a cooking chamber by an auger that's powered by electricity. Through combustion, the wood pellets ignite, heating the cooking chamber. Air is then brought in by intake fans. Heat and smoke are then dispersed throughout the cooking area. Pellet smokers and grills have precise temperature controls, usually from 180°F to 500°F (85°C to 260°C), allowing you to cook "low and slow" or searing hot.

Consider which smoker will work best for you. Keep in mind who you're cooking for, how much you're cooking, how hard you want to work, and how much fun you could have. Because that's what this is about: making some good food to enjoy with others and having a good time while you do it. Expect it to take a while to get the hang of your new smoker and remember that you're going to have frustrating moments. You're an adventurous amateur—you can do this. I know you can, I know you can, I know you can!

Smokers Best Suited for Experienced Pros

Because most experienced smokers want to show off a little bit, they enter barbecue smoking competitions, and whether they're regional or national, this puts them into the professional category. They're also always on the hunt for a new smoker or they might even build one on their own. I suggest starting with a trash can smoker, which I'll describe in a moment. It's not fancy or hard to put together, but it'll get your feet wet and give you some serious bragging rights. The other must-have for a pro is the infamous big rig. Whether it's for smoking in a competition or catering a party, the problem with most small smokers is they don't hold enough meat.

Homemade Smokers

A quick Internet search for "homemade smoker" will turn up thousands of articles, plans, videos, and discussion forums—some with well-made smokers and others with downright dangerous contraptions. One person's idea of a homemade smoker might involve copious amounts of welded heavy steel, while another might decide outfitting an old refrigerator with electric hot plates will do the trick. From trash can smokers to full-sized outdoor smokehouses, your ability, budget, and experience will determine which type is the right (and safe) one to build.

There are many reasons to build a smoker at home. Whether you're doing it to save money, impress your friends, or "kick it old school," a properly constructed homemade smoker can sometimes outperform commercial smokers. Homemade smokers must operate using the same principles as store-bought smokers with reliable heat and smoke, stable temperatures, and controlled airflow.

The easiest homemade smoker to build is the trash can smoker. While some people make these smokers using electric hot plates as the heat source, this one is designed to use lump hardwood charcoal. Your local hardware store should have everything you need to get started. You'll need the following tools and materials:

- A power drill with ³⁄₁₆-inch (4mm), ⁵⁄₁₆-inch (8mm), ⁷⁄₁₆-inch (11mm), and 1-inch (26mm) metal drill bits
- A set of small adjustable wrenches
- A sharp knife
- A small metal file
- A felt-tip permanent marker
- A 30-gallon (240-pint) galvanized steel trash can with lid
- 16 fully threaded ³⁄₈-inch × 3-inch (1cm × 7.5cm) galvanized steel bolts, with flat washers, lock washers, and nuts
- A generic replacement barbecue lid thermometer with a ¼-inch (0.5cm) diameter probe, with nut and lock washer
- A round cooking grate with handles (such as Weber model #7433)
- A stove-gasket replacement kit (such as Rutland 96N-6)
- 2 cinder blocks
- A 1-quart (1-liter) metal bowl
- A 5-quart (4.75-liter) stainless-steel colander
- A steel pizza pan (without perforations) that's larger than the top of the colander
- 8 tapered corks or silicone bottle stoppers that are 1¼-inch (3cm) diameter at the wide end

After you've assembled your materials, it's time to get building! The first thing to do is to mark and drill all the required holes in the trash can and lid. Because the cooking grate will rest on the six steel bolts, make six evenly spaced, level marks around the perimeter of the can about 8 inches (20cm) below the lip and drill ⁷⁄₁₆-inch (11mm) holes. Flip the can over (bottom side up), then mark and drill a single ⁷⁄₁₆-inch (11mm) hole in the bottom 2 inches (5cm) from the edge of the can. This is the drain hole.

Next, drill the lower air vents. These are four 1-inch (2.5cm) holes drilled horizontally along the bottom of the can, with 1-inch (2.5cm) spaces between the holes. The holes need to be 1 to 2 inches (2.5 to 5cm) above the metal floor of the can so air can flow from outside to inside.

Drill upper air vents in the lid as close to the center as possible but not under the handle—two holes on each side of the handle spaced about 1 inch (2.5cm) apart works well. The final hole to be drilled is for the thermometer. This will also be drilled in the lid, using a 5/16-inch (8mm) bit. Use the metal file to remove rough or sharp edges from around the 1-inch (2.5cm) ventilation holes. Install the six bolts using flat washers on the outside and locking washers on the inside of the can, and install the thermometer through the 5/16-inch (8mm) hole in the lid.

The next step is making a lid gasket with the gasket kit. Set the lid in place on top of the can. Take the rope gasket and wrap it snugly around the can just underneath the lid without stretching the rope. The goal is to have a gently snug—not tight—fit between the lid and the gasket during smoking. Cut the rope a few inches (centimeters) longer than the circumference of the can. (Wrapping the rope with a piece of adhesive tape will keep it from unraveling when you cut it.) Mark the can just above and below the rope gasket in a couple spots. Run adhesive tape around the circumference of the can and press the gasket in place. As you finish, cut the gasket to the exact size so it touches end to end. Let the gasket sealant dry for 24 hours before using your new smoker.

Controlling the airflow (by plugging and unplugging the vent holes with the corks) controls the temperature. However, the type of charcoal and how it's arranged also play a part. Once the charcoal is lit and the desired internal temperature has been reached, plug two vent holes on the top and bottom, then keep an eye on the temperature gauge. Plug or unplug the vent holes as needed until you've achieved a steady smoking temperature for 20 minutes. Place soaked wood chips directly on the chip tray (pizza pan) in a single layer. The weather will have a direct impact on the internal temperature because the trash can smoker isn't insulated around the cooking chamber.

Keep these in mind when using your homemade smoker for the first time:

- Put your trash can smoker on top of cinder blocks and place the bowl on the ground directly under the drain hole.
- Leave all vent holes unplugged—top and bottom.
- Fill the steel colander with charcoal halfway, place it inside the smoker, and light the charcoal.
- Soak your wood chips before putting them on the chip tray (steel pizza pan).
- Once the charcoal is burning, put the chip tray on top of the coal colander, drop in the cooking grate, and put the lid on the smoker.

- When the internal temperature reaches 250°F (120°C) or higher, plug two of the bottom holes and two of the top holes with tapered corks (or bottle stoppers).

- Safety is paramount. Use heatproof gloves and tongs to lift out the chip tray and colander from the hot smoker.

- Plan to fire up your smoker without food the first time to season it, check for smoke leaks or temperature fluctuations, and just learn about your smoker.

- To season the smoker for the first time, add charcoal as needed until the smoker has run for 12 hours at steady smoking temperatures. The smoker is now ready for regular use.

The Big Rigs

I remember getting my first rig. I still have it 10 years later. It's not the biggest of the big rigs and it's not the smallest, but for me, it's just right. It's a 10-foot-long (3m) offset barrel smoker trailer fired by hardwood and charcoal. It can smoke 60 racks of ribs or 150 pounds (68kg) of brisket and pork butts. It has three charcoal/propane grills on the side and a rocket burner on the front. Weighing in at a cool 3,500 pounds (1,600kg), it goes anywhere—including the lake!

Big rigs are the smokers used by many professional barbecue teams that need to cook up large amounts of food day after day on the road. They can be used anywhere anytime. Manufacturers such as Ole Hickory, Backwoods, and Southern Pride build full-sized, commercial-grade smoker trailers designed to deliver excellent electronic temperature, smoke, and moisture control in a road-worthy, extreme-duty design.

Each manufacturer recommends a fuel type to achieve the best results, but most of the top-quality big rigs are fired with a combination of hardwood logs and gas (propane or natural). The internal cooking chamber and the manner in which the result is achieved differ among manufacturers. Some have rotating racks, while others use a sophisticated airflow management system to achieve an even smoke. These rigs are built for frequent and rugged use, and they're priced accordingly.

This is my barbecue rig—tasty and sweet!

Industrial Smokers

Modern industrial smokers are highly automated, efficient, high-capacity units that can be permanently installed or are semiportable. These smokers will outperform residential-type smokers in virtually every aspect and most are designed with simplicity of use for the end user in mind. They're available in a wide range of sizes (physical size and internal capacity) and the manufacturer determines the type of fuel. Some use hardwood logs fired with natural gas, while others might be electrically powered and use proprietary hardwood-sawdust compounds to create smoke. Many offer precise control of the humidity within the cooking chamber. Because industrial smokers have specific requirements and maintenance costs, they might not be the best option for the smoking hobbyist.

Fuel + Wood = Smoky Deliciousness

Now that you know more about smokers and the different types and styles available, there's one more thing you should consider before going out to buy one: what type of fuel source you want to use. Many varieties of fuel options are available for smokers. You should base your decision on how often you plan to use your smoker and how much food you're going to smoke at one time.

Why all the fuss about fuel? Because fuel is just as important as the smoker itself. The fuel you choose can affect the overall flavor of the food you smoke. Electricity and gas versus charcoal and hardwood can be a very *heated* debate among enthusiasts. Electricity and gas offer wonderful convenience and they're very easy to use. Charcoal and hardwoods do a great job of heating your smoker and add a ton of flavor to the food, but they're more work to maintain.

What's right for you? Let's find out.

Propane & Natural Gases

Propane and natural gases are convenient ways of heating your fire. Because natural gas burns just as hot as propane gas and both maintain a constant temperature, they're equally capable to fuel your smoker. All in all, gas is an easy and efficient way to run your smoker. The only downside is that gas doesn't offer any flavor to the food you're smoking.

Many barbecue enthusiasts will say you're not truly barbecuing if you're using gas, which isn't at all true. It's the perfect option when you're short on time and you have a lot of food to smoke.

Pros & Cons for Using Propane & Natural Gases

Pros	Cons
• It's economical and readily available.	• Fuel explosions can occur but normally don't when proper storage and handling procedures are followed.
• Propane is portable, allowing you to travel with your smoker.	• Rising fuel prices might affect affordability.
• Gas burns efficiently.	• Hoses and valves need to be maintained regularly.
• Gas is easily controlled with the temperature adjustments found on the grill's burners.	• If a tank runs out and you're not prepared with a backup, it could be "game over."

Always keep a full backup tank on hand so you don't run out of fuel halfway through your cook. The best fuel tanks have gauges that indicate the level of gas remaining in the tank. This way, you won't waste your fuel by returning what you think are empty tanks but are really half-full tanks.

Electricity

Many styles of smokers are powered with electricity. Electricity is efficient and relatively easy to use—except when you're in the outback without an electrical outlet or in the middle of a power outage.

Electricity offers a constant heat source to keep your smoker running smoothly. Most electric smokers use electricity to heat a burner, which slowly heats hardwood smoke pellets or wood-style pucks that in turn create the smoke. An electric smoker needs to be close to an electrical outlet because using an extension cord will cause a drop in voltage that will result in a lower output of heat, leading to longer smoking times and less efficiency.

Pros & Cons for Using Electricity

Pros	Cons
• Electricity is an affordable resource.	• You need to have close access to an electrical outlet.
• It's super convenient—just plug in your smoker and you're ready to go.	• Electric smokers can't be used in the wilderness.
• Electricity is pure and free of the by-products sometimes found in combustible fuels.	• Electricity doesn't work during a power outage.
• Electricity is good for the production of supplementary heat as well as for producing smoke.	• Electric smokers can be dangerous. The external generator must be kept out of the rain to prevent water damage or short circuits that could cause shock or even a fire.

Electric smokers make great cold-smokers. And because of the heat and smoke controls, electricity allows you to monitor your heat more efficiently, which saves money and time.

Charcoal

When it comes to barbecue and smoked foods, charcoal rules as the king of all fuels because low and slow is the way to go. Nothing else is more primal or more adventurous or produces more delicious food. Most folks think working with charcoal is too hard and frustrating, but in reality, it doesn't need to be difficult and it adds wonderful flavors to your food even without the addition of wood.

Selecting the right charcoal is as important as the food you're smoking, and because not all charcoal is created equally, choose wisely. Look for charcoal made from 100% all-natural hardwoods—no softwoods should be in there. Hardwood charcoal burns more efficiently, lasts longer, and has no added chemicals. Let me say it again: You want to purchase *100% pure hardwood charcoal*.

Types of Charcoal

You're probably already familiar with some charcoal, but let's take a closer look at some you might not know about.

Lump

This is random-sized pieces of hardwood charcoal. It's just wood that's been turned into charcoal—nothing more. Lump charcoal will burn at a higher temperature—about 800°F (425°C)—but it doesn't burn for long. That's why it's normally used for grilling foods rather than smoking foods. Some die-hard barbecue cooks say lump charcoal gives a better, more natural flavor than briquettes. Use 100% hardwood lump charcoal.

Briquette

This is typically pillow-shaped and usually made from leftover pieces of lump charcoal. Processors take the leftover pieces, grind them to a consistent size, and use corn, wheat, or potato starch as a binding agent. Briquettes burn at a lower temperature—about 600°F (315°C) to 1000°F (535°C)—for a longer period of time, which makes them ideal for smoking foods. Look for 100% all-natural briquettes.

Hardwood

This comes in many varieties. Some are from one type of wood, such as 100% maple hardwood charcoal. Others are made from a blend of woods to create a unique smoke flavor. For example, blends might combine hickory and maple or oak and mesquite. Talk to your local barbecue retailer or supplier to ask what types of charcoal they carry.

Fast-lighting

This is a briquette that has fire-starting fuel in or on it. This makes for speedy lighting of your coals, but the overall flavor isn't desirable for smoking foods. I suggest saving these fuel-infused coals for simple, quick grilling.

Hardwood Charcoal Flavoring Guide

All types of charcoal are available. I like to mix and match different types of charcoal to create new flavors. Creating a blend sometimes gives you the ultimate fuel that produces an even heat and lasts a good long time—those are the things you want from your charcoal for maximum efficiency. Make your own unique recipes and blends to find out what flavors you like best. Just keep in mind that some charcoal smokers work better with a certain type of charcoal. The key is to have fun, enjoy experimenting, and make some tasty food.

Here are some of the available charcoals.

Coconut

For thousands of years, people have been using coconut shells to fuel their fires. It burns hot and offers a sweet, nutty, and robust flavor to food. Coconut charcoal isn't made from the coconut tree but from the shells. It's a medium-flavored charcoal and is best used with poultry, pork, fish, and shellfish. It's produced in Indonesia.

Hickory

Hickory is the most common wood used for smoking foods. This hardwood burns hot, lasts a long time, and offers a rich, sweet, and strong flavor to foods. It's best used with pork shoulder, ribs, bacon, and ham as well as turkey and chicken. It's produced in the United States.

Kiawe

Kiawe charcoal is a Hawaiian-style charcoal made from the *Prosopis pallida*, or kiawe tree, which is a relative of mesquite. This charcoal burns very hot because of its density and lasts a very long time. It has a very sweet, aromatic, smoky flavor as well as a spicy finish, and it's wonderful with just about any meat—beef, pork, poultry, lamb, game, and seafood. It's produced in Mexico.

Maple

Maple trees are a great source for hardwood charcoals. They burn hot and offer a sweet, buttery, and nutty flavor to foods. It's great for use with poultry, ribs, steak, lamb, and game meats. It's produced in the United States and Canada.

Mesquite

Mesquite is a very hard wood with a full flavor. This charcoal burns very hot because of its density and lasts a very long time. It has a sweet, aromatic, smoky flavor as well as a spicy finish. It can be used to smoke virtually any meat—beef, pork, poultry, lamb, game, and seafood. It's produced in the United States and Mexico.

Oak

Oak is a very hard wood that's best used on red meats. Brisket smoked with oak is a Texan's delight. It burns hot and lasts a good long time. Oak smoke has a medium to heavy flavor that's not too overpowering and has a buttery and nutty smooth finish. It's great with beef, lamb, and bison. It's produced in the United States and Canada.

Orange

Orange wood charcoal is made from 100% citrus orange trees. This charcoal offers a tangy citrus note to foods and has a mild to medium flavor. It's great for smoking seafood, fish, and chicken. It's produced in Mexico.

South American

We're beginning to see many really fine hardwood charcoals from South America—especially Cuba and Argentina, where the smoking tradition runs long and deep. These hardwoods are well worth the price if you have an adventurous spirit and a healthy wallet. I like to make sure they're from responsible, sustainable resources.

Ted's Homemade Charcoal Blends

I'm not kidding when I say secrets are huge in the barbecue world. No one ever lets their secrets slip. But I thought I'd be a pal and get you started with a couple of my own secrets—but don't tell anyone!

Brisket Lump Blend

I like to use a mixture of 2 parts oak charcoal with 1 part mesquite charcoal. I find oak produces a nice, smooth smoke but lacks sweetness. That's where the mesquite comes in, lending its sweet smoke to the mix. Because it's an extremely hard wood, mesquite works well with oak to make a great combination for burn length and overall flavor.

Ribber's Secret Recipe

If you ever have the pleasure of going to a smoking competition, you'll soon find that many things are kept a big secret. The rub, the sauce, even the wood is a secret. Well I'm here to blow the top off this secret and give you the winning charcoal blend for ribs: Try 1 part fruitwood-based charcoal, 2 parts hickory charcoal, and 1 part maple hardwood charcoal. Hickory provides heat and the body of flavor; maple gives you length of flavor (to give balance throughout eating); and fruit adds a bit of sweetness.

General Tips for Buying & Working with Charcoal

The sheer number and varieties of charcoals available can be overwhelming. Just keep it simple in the beginning and buy whatever sounds good. Here are a few other tips to keep in mind when shopping for charcoal:

- Look for briquette charcoal that's been infused with hardwood smoking chips (hickory, mesquite, maple, oak, or apple). This saves you from adding woods.

- When buying lump charcoal, avoid the little pieces. These burn up too quickly and they'll leave you frustrated and out of fuel. Look for charcoal with larger chunks that will burn longer and offer the most flavor.

- Always buy more charcoal than you need because as long as you have charcoal, you have a fuel source.

- Remember, less is more. You don't need a lot of charcoal to create enough heat for your smoker. Start out with a little and add more as you need it. It's easier to build your fire than to take it away.

- Never add cold charcoal to hot charcoal. Always add hot coals to your smoker because that keeps the temperature constant rather than losing valuable heat by adding cold coals. (See Chapter 4 for information on how to preheat charcoal.)

- Keep in mind that the more oxygen you allow into your smoker, the hotter the fire—and the more heat that will be produced.

Hardwoods

Hardwoods are the most traditional way to create fire—whether it's in a firepit, grill, or smoker. At times, there's nothing better to flavor your food than creating heat from 100% natural hardwood. You start a fire with hardwood and burn the wood down to homemade charcoal. Fueling your smoker with these hot coals creates the ultimate 100% pure wood flavor. It's a lot more work to keep your fire hot and it needs constant attention, but the result is 100% authentic barbecue. Look for hardwoods that are clean and dry. Wet woods don't burn hot enough and tend to go out. You can leave the bark on or strip it off. (See the section "Bark vs. No Bark" later in this chapter.)

Hardwood vs. Softwood

Hardwoods produce a better smoke flavor than softwoods. They burn longer and cleaner, and they have less resin. The resin from softwoods burns quickly and produces a bitter smoke flavor. The smoke from some softwoods can be toxic—horse chestnut, for example. When shopping for woods, if the wood comes from some kind of hardwood tree, it's good to go. Soft is a no!

The wood you burn needs to be cured and well dried. Never cut down your own wood. This wood has a high water content and will produce steam when you burn it. Off-gases from fresh wood can even cause health issues.

Sawdust, Chips, Chunks, Pellets, Pucks & Logs

The key to smoking isn't the form in which the wood comes but the smoke that's created from the wood used. The type of smoking equipment usually determines the form of wood needed. Let's take a look at some of the kinds of woods used for smoking.

Sawdust

Sawdust is a relatively inexpensive raw material to use for smoking. It produces a nice, even smoke and burns efficiently. However, you'll find it needs to be replenished fairly often. Always work with dry sawdust because it won't burn if it's soaked.

Wood Chips

Wood chips are about 1 to 3 inches long (2.5 to 7.5cm) and 1 to 2 inches (2.5 to 5cm) wide. They come in a variety of flavors and they're readily available in most barbecue supply stores and specialty grocers. The key with wood chips is to starve the wood of oxygen so it smolders and smokes. You don't want your wood chips to burn because that produces a bitter smoke.

I recommend soaking wood chips because they'll smoke longer and make the flavor of the smoke a little more pungent. Soaking also keeps them from burning too quickly. Wood chips are traditionally used for adding smoke to your gas grills by using a smoker box or foil pouch. They can also be directly applied to hot coals for charcoal smokers.

Wood Chunks

Wood chunks are larger pieces of wood ranging in size from 2 to 5 inches (5 to 12.5cm), which eliminates having to replenish the wood as often. Chunks are too large for smoker boxes or foil pouches. They're best for longer periods of smoking. You can use wood chunks dry or they can be soaked. Both methods work well with this size of wood.

Wood Pellets

Wood pellets are made of ground wood or sawdust that's pressed into small pellets and are held together by some kind of food starch (corn, rice, or tapioca). They're available in a wide range of flavors, such as alder, apple, black walnut, cherry, hickory, whiskey barrel, mesquite, oak, orange, pecan, savory herb, garlic, sassafras, sugar maple, and many more.

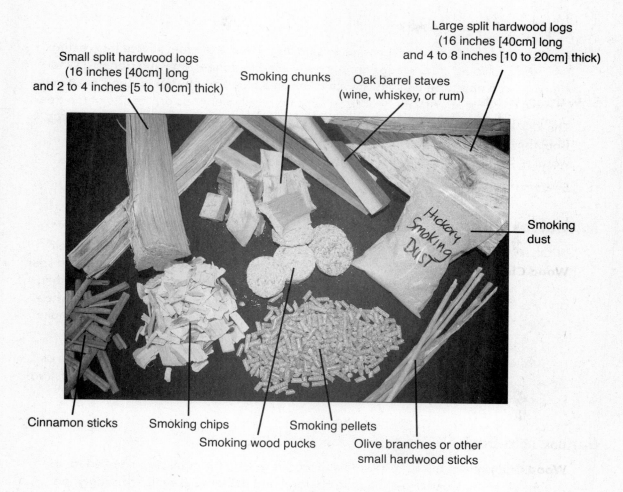

Small split hardwood logs
(16 inches [40cm] long
and 2 to 4 inches [5 to 10cm] thick)

Smoking chunks

Oak barrel staves
(wine, whiskey, or rum)

Large split hardwood logs
(16 inches [40cm] long
and 4 to 8 inches [10 to 20cm] thick)

Smoking
dust

Cinnamon sticks

Smoking chips

Smoking wood pucks

Smoking pellets

Olive branches or other
small hardwood sticks

A variety of smoking woods

Wood pellets are very easy to use and best when used in smokers designed for them, but they're also great to use in charcoal smokers. There's no need to soak them—just add a handful of pellets to the hot coals.

Pucks

Pucks are compressed wood shavings that are held together with some kind of good starch (corn, rice, or tapioca). They're available in a wide range of flavors.

Logs

Logs pull double duty when it comes to smoking: They're the fuel source for creating heat and providing smoke. Logs are normally used for longer smoking periods. When smoking with logs, wait until the smoke takes on a blue tinge before putting meat in the smoker. Logs come in a variety of sizes, which typically depends on the size of the tree the wood came from. Logs from fruit trees are smaller in size compared with logs cut from maple, oak, and hickory.

Whatever option you choose, be sure to store your smoking woods—sawdust, chips, chunks, pellets, pucks, and logs—in a cool, dry place.

To Soak or Not to Soak?

When it comes to using natural hardwoods for smoking, some folks like to soak their wood and others don't. You can buy green wood, which is naturally wet, or you can soak dried wood in water before smoking. Wet wood is going to produce more smoke than dry wood, which isn't necessarily a good thing. Certain foods don't perform well when smoked with wet wood. For example, when cold-smoking cheese, you want the smoke to be dry and not carry any humidity.

I typically don't soak logs because water doesn't really penetrate into larger pieces of wood. But if you prefer to soak logs, it should be done overnight at least. However, I do soak chips and chunks—1 to 2 hours usually does the trick.

Bark vs. No Bark

Some people claim the bark on smoking woods gives a bitter taste to smoked foods, so they remove all bark from their logs beforehand. Others believe bark adds good flavor to smoked foods, so they keep the bark on.

I've found that bark does affect the flavor of foods. It produces a stronger smoke flavor but not necessarily a bitter smoke (although I've found it to be bitter on occasion). It's just more pronounced and I find it too intense.

Most chips and chunks come without a lot of bark, but logs tend to have bark, so I order clean wood—bark removed—or I find myself peeling the bark from fire logs. It comes down to personal preference, so experiment and determine what works best for you.

A Wood Flavoring Guide

Most people can't identify the type of wood used to smoke their food, but the choice does affect the flavor. Smoking is an art, not a science, so choose whatever wood speaks to you.

Wood	Characteristics
Alder	Fragrant and delicate with a sweet yet musky smoke that's the perfect complement for fish, especially salmon
Almond	Imparts a nutty, sweet flavor that's good for beef, pork (ribs or ham), poultry, and game
Apple	The most pungent and fragrant of all fruitwoods and an excellent choice for poultry, ribs, pork, sausage, and ham
Apricot	A mild and sweet fruitwood that's good for seafood, pork, and poultry
Ash	Fast-burning with a light smoke flavor that's good for beef, pork, and poultry
Beech	Mild wood with a delicate smoke flavor that's good for beef, pork, ribs, ham, seafood, and poultry
Birch	Similar in flavor to maple but a little softer and burns much faster; good for pork, poultry, seafood, and cheese
Black walnut	An intense smoke that has a slightly bitter flavor; pair it with stronger-flavored meats, such as beef, ham, lamb, game, and turkey
Cedar	Great for plank-smoking but not for low-and-slow smoking; best with salmon and other seafood but also works well with cheese and vegetables
Cherry	Distinctive and flavorful with a sweet smoke that's great for beef, lamb, game, poultry, and ham
Chestnut	Slightly sweet, nutty smoke flavor that complements beef, pork, and game
Citrus (orange, lemon, lime, grapefruit)	A sweet and fruity smoke that isn't overpowering and works well with more delicate foods, such as seafood and poultry

(continues)

Wood	Characteristics
Grapevine	An aromatic and tart fruitwood that burns quickly and is wonderful for chicken, turkey, seafood, and pork
Hickory	The most popular hardwood; has a rich and full-bodied, sweet flavor, especially when used for smoking bacon—my favorite; also great for beef, ribs, pork, ham, sausage, game, poultry, seafood, and cheese
Maple	A wood that burns hot, with a spicy and earthy smoke; great for poultry, pork, ham, bacon, and cheese
Mesquite	An extremely hard wood that's milder and sweeter than hickory and is best used with beef, ribs, pork, lamb, poultry, and game—a Southwest smoker's delight
Oak	A great wood for all types of meat and for smoking larger cuts for longer periods of time; imparts a medium to heavy flavor, which is why it's the brisket smoker's wood of choice
Olive	Smoky flavor similar to mesquite but much lighter and best used in Mediterranean-flavored dishes with lamb, poultry, and seafood
Peach	Slightly sweet fruitwood; delicate in flavor and complements seafood and poultry
Pear	Sweet and woodsy flavor that's similar to apple and great for poultry, game birds, and pork
Pecan	Similar to hickory with a sweet, buttery flavor and great with brisket as well as other cuts of beef, pork ribs, ham, bacon, and poultry; also works beautifully with cheese

In addition to wood flavor-makers, let me share a few other trade secrets for adding more flavor.

Cinnamon Sticks

Unsoaked cinnamon sticks produce a nutty, sweet, rich flavor that adds a warm and complex layer of flavor when added to other woods. It really complements oak, hickory, maple, apple, and whiskey barrel.

Coffee Beans

These are one of my favorite flavorings, especially for beef. You don't want to throw them directly on your heat source because they burn too quickly. Often, I'll place a layer of beans over a plank and then set my meat on top. Oh #itbetasty!

Corn Cobs

Corn cobs have been used for centuries as a smoking medium for meats, fish, and poultry. Smoking with corn cobs produces a thick white smoke and compares with hickory wood in flavor and color. They're great for when you want a mild smoke flavor. There are products available on the market that include corn cob pellets. Or you can dry out your own and use them as you would with wood chips on your charcoal.

Dried Spices

Star anise, fennel seeds, and peppercorns add a hint of flavor when added to the fire.

Fresh Herbs

Rosemary, thyme, or lavender leaves are great ways to enhance your smoke flavors. Rosemary added to hickory or oak wood when cooking a beef brisket brings out a sweet, aromatic smoke.

Licorice Wood

Similar to grapevines, licorice wood produces a mild, nutty flavor that's great for lamb and game as well as beef and poultry.

Whiskey Barrel

Leftover or used whiskey barrels from distilleries are infused with the bold, sweet flavor of whiskey. Tennessee or Kentucky bourbon and whiskey barrels are prized for the sweet smoke they produce and they're often the secret ingredient at smoking competitions. They're great with all meats, poultry, seafood, cheese, and vegetables.

Plank-Smoking: All the Flavor in Less Time

Plank-smoking is a hot, fast way of smoking foods on your gas or charcoal grill. It's not the real art of smoked foods, but it adds a true, natural smoke flavor to your foods in a short period of time.

The key to good plank-smoking is presoaking the wooden planks. Before placing the plank on your grill, soak it for at least 1 hour—or up to 24 hours—to reduce the chances of it catching fire. You can soak planks in a variety of liquids: water, juice, soda, wine, or even beer. Just place the plank in a large container with your choice of liquid and weigh it down with something heavy so it stays submerged. Soak the plank for at least 4 hours to allow the flavor to penetrate the wood. Never brush planks with any type of oil—this is literally adding fuel to a piece of wood that can potentially ignite.

Woods for Plank-Smoking

Much like woods used to fuel a fire, the type of wood used when plank-smoking affects the flavor of foods. Semi-hardwood or hardwood (western red cedar, maple, and oak) are most suitable for plank-smoking because they have less sap and don't burn as quickly as softwoods. Avoid using softwoods, such as pine, because they tend to produce a bitter smoke.

Alder

Soak the planks in water, chardonnay, sauvignon blanc, Riesling, pinot noir, apple juice, lager, or ale. Alder is great for cooking vegetables, salmon, halibut, arctic char, pork, chicken, and fruit.

Apple

Soak the planks in water, apple juice, apple ale, apple wine, apple cider, chardonnay, pinot noir, or pineapple juice. Use apple planks for poultry, fish, shellfish, pork chops and pork tenderloin, veal, and assorted vegetables and fruits.

Cherry

Soak the planks in water, pinot noir, Shiraz, sauvignon blanc, chardonnay, cherry whiskey, cherry cola, or cherry juice. Cherry planks are perfect for venison, beef, turkey, pork chops, pork tenderloin, cheese, and fruits.

Hickory

This is a hardwood with a bold flavor from the southern United States. Hickory can be difficult to find, so when you do find it, buy a ton of it. It works really well when slowly plank-grilling a large cut of meat over low heat. For soaking, use water, beer, bourbon, ginger ale, cola, apple juice, pineapple juice, or cabernet sauvignon. These planks are ideal for pork (ribs, chops, and bacon), turkey, ham, steaks, game (venison, ostrich, buffalo, and pheasant), and portobello mushrooms.

Maple

Soak the planks in water, apple juice, chardonnay, cabernet sauvignon, honey brown lager, or even maple-flavored lager. Use for plank-grilling poultry (chicken, turkey, duck, and quail), trout, salmon, arctic char, pizza, and steaks.

Mesquite

Mesquite is great for long cooking times because of its thickness. Soak the planks in water, cider, pineapple juice, lemonade, or ginger ale. Because mesquite is a strong flavor, it works best with beef, pork, and poultry.

Pecan

Soak the planks in water, strong dark beer (such as Guinness stout), cabernet sauvignon, merlot, chardonnay, apple juice, or ginger ale. Pecan is awesome for plank-baking desserts, fruits, vegetables, mushrooms, quail, chicken, turkey, and pork.

Red Oak

Soak the planks in water, cabernet sauvignon, merlot, India pale ale, grape juice, cranberry juice, or orange juice. Grill beef, game, poultry, cheese, and desserts on red oak planks.

Western Red Cedar

Soak the planks in water, chardonnay, hard cider, pilsner, Dr Pepper, or cherry juice. This wood complements salmon, seafood, cheese, poultry, game meats, beef, pork, veal, and lamb. Cedar is even great for fruits, vegetables, and desserts.

Plank Size Matters

Planks are available in different sizes and thicknesses. Thickness is the most important thing to consider when buying planks. The thinner the plank, the less amount of time it can stay on the grill.

Use small planks for small portions, wider planks for roasts, and longer planks for longer items, such as whole sides of salmon. Recipes with a quick cooking time can get by with a thin plank, but a longer cooking time will need either a regular or thick plank. Every recipe in this book will specify what thickness of plank to use, but the following table gives you an idea of what thickness plank to use with what food.

Types of Planks

Thickness	Maximum Cooking Time	Best Used For
Thin (¼ to ½ inch [0.5 to 1.25cm])	15 to 20 minutes	mashed potatoes, vegetables, garlic
Regular (¾ inch [2cm])	20 to 60 minutes	salmon fillets, fish fillets, steaks, pork loin, ribs, tuna, roast chicken, game
Thick (1+ inch [2.5+cm])	60+ minutes	turkey, prime rib, veal roast, pork loin roast, whole fish

Thin planks tend to warp when heated—and that could lead to your food rolling into the grill. To avoid this, place the plank over high heat (without food) for a couple minutes, turn the plank over, and place the food on the lightly heated side. Hardwoods are less likely to warp than semi-hardwoods, but take this easy precaution just to be safe. Soaking the plank for a longer amount of time also helps prevent warping.

Where to Find & Buy Planks

When I first started plank-smoking nearly 15 years ago, the only place I could get planks was the lumberyard. I'd go in, buy a great big piece of wood, and ask the guys to cut it into 10-inch-long (25cm) planks. All these years later, the lumberyard is still the best place to get planks, but you do have other options.

Many grocery stores and gourmet shops as well as many home improvement stores carry planks. However, they usually only have untreated western red cedar. While cedar is a great wood for plank-smoking, many other wonderful flavors of wood exist—as you now know! Other varieties might be harder to find, but they're worth it because of the wonderfully different flavors they bring your smoked food. I suggest speaking with your local lumberyard or searching online.

Smoking 101

Chapter

4

Learning the basics of how your smoker works is very important. Other than electric and propane smokers, most smokers use charcoal as the fuel source. Properly controlling the fire is essential to creating delicious foods because fire is what produces the heat and, therefore, the smoke, which cooks and flavors your food. Because this can be tricky, I'll give you all the inside tricks to help you nail it over time. Before you smoke any actual food, I recommend you fire up your smoker and practice controlling the temperature. It's definitely a trial-and-error kind of situation. If you practice before adding the meat, you won't waste anything.

If you're not up for all the work associated with charcoal smokers, you still have plenty of other options. You can turn your backyard grill into a smoker very easily and inexpensively. And there's plank-smoking, which is relatively simple and offers great flavor. You can even smoke in your house on your stovetop or in the oven.

No matter what your goals, you can find a type of smoking that will suit your budget and your lifestyle. To figure that out, you need to know what each type of smoking is, so let's get started!

The Basics About Charcoal Smoking

Smoking with charcoal creates an abundant amount of smoke that deeply penetrates food simply and thoroughly. Using charcoal also provides excellent value when compared with some of the other fuels used to smoke foods. Because it directly impacts your end result, I recommend you use the best-quality natural hardwood charcoal you can afford—whether lump or briquette. (Flip back to Chapter 3 for more about the different charcoal options.)

How your charcoal is arranged in the smoker plays a large role in temperature control, which, as you know, can be the biggest challenge when smoking foods. You want to minimize the number of times you need to open the smoker to refresh the charcoal.

To start, fully open the air vents on your smoker or grill and make a low pile of cold charcoal on the charcoal tray or bowl. The charcoal can be lit in a number of ways: a chimney starter, a fire starter cube, or an electric starter. Because we're aiming for a low temperature, it's important to only light a few pieces of coal in the center of the pile. Doing this will give you a longer overall burn time and better temperature control right from the start.

A tried-and-true method for checking the temperature of your charcoal is the "hand test." Hold your hand 1 or 2 inches (2.5 to 5cm) above the cooking grate and count how many seconds (Mississippi style) you can leave your hand there. If you can reach 4 or 5 seconds before it becomes too painful, the coals are ready for smoking. If the coals are so hot that you pull away before you reach 3 seconds, then they're too hot for smoking. If you can comfortably make it to 6 seconds, they're not hot enough yet. There are also visual cues to look for: The hot coals in the center of the charcoal pile should have a nice even coat of gray ash with a gentle orange glow before you put meat in the smoker.

It's best to replenish the smoker with hot coals instead of cold charcoal so the smoker can maintain its temperature. Preheat charcoal by placing it in a charcoal chimney on a fireproof/heatproof surface, lighting it, and letting it burn until the coals develop a solid coat of gray ash. Add the hot coals to the center of the charcoal tray. Start preheating additional coals—about 10 briquettes or a 1-pound (450g) lump—as soon as you notice any decline in the smoker's temperature.

Before you even light the first coal, have a plan in place for putting out the fire when you're done smoking or in case of emergency. You also need a plan for disposing of the ash and used coals. Ash and charcoal debris can seem to be totally cool, but when you remove it from the smoker, there might still be a couple live bits.

If there's no chance that children or pets will come in contact with the smoker, you can use one of these methods to put out the coals:

- Slowly snuff out the charcoal by denying it oxygen. Simply close all the doors and air vents, and within a few hours, the charcoal will extinguish itself.

- Allow the coals to burn down to ash by fully opening all vents and doors. This method has the added benefit of burning off grease and drippings inside the smoker, making cleanup easier.

- Transfer the hot coals to a metal bucket and either douse the coal with water or smother the coals with sand. Keep in mind that soaking hot coals with water will create a plume of steam and fine ash, which might not be appreciated by anyone in its path—or nearby clean windows.

Disposing of used charcoal is straightforward and simple, but you need to be careful. In a perfect world, you'd be able to leave the charcoal right where it is for 48 hours. But if you have to move them hot, like in a competition setting, start by stirring the coals to spread them out. Pour your bucket of water over the coals as you stir them. Once the coals are cool enough to safely handle, scoop the wood, ash, and debris and place them in a metal bucket. When the ash is cool enough to handle, place it on a large sheet of heavy foil and wrap it. If necessary, make two or three of these packages to dispose of them easily once the packages have cooled for several hours.

Cold hardwood charcoal ash is a natural, "green" substance and can be disposed of in the same manner as any other natural material by using proper safety precautions. The ash and small pieces of natural coal can be added to fertilizer or a compost container or wrapped in foil and disposed of in a noncombustible recycling trash can.

Smoking with Pellet Smokers

First, read the manual! Wood pellets are poured into a storage container called "the hopper." The pellets are then fed into the cooking chamber by an auger that's powered by electricity. The pellets are ignited by combustion, heating the cooking chamber. Air is then brought in through intake fans. Heat and smoke are then dispersed through the cooking chamber.

Much like an oven, pellet grills give you precise temperature control digitally or with a dial, usually ranging from 180°F to 500°F (85°C to 260°C). So you can cook "low and slow" or searing hot. Most pellet grills have a meat probe that can connect with the control board to monitor the internal temperature of the meat.

A pellet smoker is as close to "set it and forget it" as you'll reach with a smoker.

Smoking with Gas & Propane Grills

To effectively smoke on your gas grill, you need to learn how to use its lowest temperature. For single-burner models, start your fire, set the burner to low, close the lid, and wait an hour before checking the temperature. For grills with multiple burners, use an indirect heat method by using only one burner set to low. If your grill has a back burner for rotisserie cooking, don't use this burner. If after 60 minutes your grill is cruising along in a range of 200°F to 225°F (95°C to 110°C), you're looking good. If the grill has reached 250°F (120°C) or higher within an hour (too hot for most but not all smoking), you'll have to wedge the lid slightly open to lower the heat.

Wind and outdoor temperature could have a significant impact on the temperature inside your grill because most models don't have any insulation. Keep experimenting and tweaking by adjusting the heat until you can maintain a temperature in the smoking zone of 200°F to 225°F (95°C to 110°C).

Cooking over indirect heat means not having the heat source directly under the food being smoked. For gas grills with multiple burners, it's as simple as putting the food over the unlit burners. For single-burner grills, this can be more challenging depending on the configuration of the burner tube—whether it's a straight pipe or U-shaped. Solve this issue by using a metal heat shield between the grill surface and the heat source.

Smoking ribs on a gas grill with charcoal

Once you've mastered the temperature control of your grill, it's time to decide how you want to produce smoke. A tried-and-true method is to use a wood chip pouch. To make an aluminum foil smoking pouch for your grill, just fold a large rectangular piece of foil in half. Open the foil like a book and place wood pellets or presoaked wood chips in the center of one half. Fold over the other side of the foil, creating a pillow-shaped pouch, and crimp the edges together to create a tight seal. Poke several small holes on top.

Place the pouch under the cooking grate and directly over the hot burner. Metal wood chip boxes and prepackaged smoking cans (small metal cans filled with hardwood chips) are also available. It's important to have your chips in a metal bag, box, or can with only one or two very small vent holes. This will ensure the chips have enough oxygen to smolder but not so much oxygen that they ignite and add heat to the grill.

Plank-Smoking

Plank-smoking is another easy way to infuse smoke into your foods without using a conventional smoker. You can use a variety of plank woods depending on the flavor experience you're going for. (See Chapter 3.) Plank-smoking can be done on a gas grill, on a charcoal grill, or over an open fire to produce delicious, moist, and juicy smoked foods. Just make sure your unit has a tight-fitting lid to keep the smoke in. Also, make sure your plank wood is food-safe. Compared with conventional smoking, plank-smoking uses higher heat to create a very hot smoke to quickly infuse and cook the food. Some might argue that planking is grilling rather than smoking, but I disagree. You *could* use a grill as the heat source, but the fire heats the soaked plank and creates smoke, which flavors the food as it cooks.

The actual process of plank-smoking is very simple. Preheat the grill to the desired temperature. I typically recommend medium heat, about 350°F to 450°F (180°C to 230°C). Place the soaked plank on the grill and close the lid. Preheat the plank for 2 to 3 minutes or until it begins to crackle and smoke, then flip the plank. Carefully open the lid and place the meat onto the plank. Close the lid and let the cooking begin. Check every 4 to 5 minutes to ensure that the plank hasn't caught fire. Should a section of it ignite, use a spray bottle filled with water to put out the flames and reduce the heat to medium-low. Placing a foil pan that's larger than the plank under the grate to catch drippings will reduce the number of flare-ups.

Plank-smoking is a lot of fun but not if you burn the place down. Smoke is good—fire is bad. Here are a few tips to keep everyone safe:

- Keep a spray bottle filled with water handy to put out small flames.
- Keep a garden hose handy to put out large flames.
- Have a large metal container filled with water to throw the plank into if a fire breaks out.
- Have a fire extinguisher nearby—just in case.

Plank-smoked chicken thighs

- Keep a phone nearby to dial 911—better safe than sorry.
- Wear protective eyewear to protect your eyes from the smoke when opening the lid or removing the plank.
- Use a sturdy pair of long, well-made grilling tongs that can hold the weight of a plank with food on it.
- Wear thick, heat-resistant gloves to keep your hands safe. I like welding gloves.
- Always let the plank cool thoroughly before throwing it out.

There's no turning or flipping required when plank-smoking—just leave the food on the plank. The heat and the smoke will do all the work so you don't have to fuss. When the food is smoked, carefully remove the plank from the grill and transfer the hot plank to a heatproof platter, baking sheet, or unused soaked plank. This will prevent damage to tabletops or counters because the underside of the plank will be very hot. I usually use my planks a second time—in the fireplace! I've also cut planks into funky and interesting shapes to use solely for impressive table presentations.

How to Safely Smoke Indoors

If you have the right equipment and follow safety precautions, smoking food indoors is a great way to prepare healthy, flavorful food all year. It's a fantastic introduction to the world of smoking foods—with a minimal initial cost to get started. There are several different techniques available to infuse smoke into your food. Whether you're looking for an all-in-one solution to quickly smoke fish and vegetables or equipment that'll let you infuse a deep smoky flavor into a rack or two of baby back ribs, it's out there.

Stovetop smoking is normally used to achieve a quick infusion of smoke flavor into delicate, fast-cooking foods, like fish and vegetables. A properly constructed stovetop smoker will contain the smoke within the cooking chamber. Oven smoking is ideal for foods requiring a longer cooking time, and because the smoke is produced in a completely sealed environment, more of the smoke is absorbed by foods over a shorter period of time.

Stove and Oven Roasting Pan-Style Smokers

Smoking foods on the stove or in the oven can be done using purchased indoor smoking equipment or by making your own using a roasting pan with a small wire rack. Smoke is produced by using a small amount of wood chips arranged in a thin layer in the pan. The wood chips are heated to the smoldering point on the stove and the cooking can be completed on the stove or in a preheated oven.

You can buy roasting pan–style smokers that come with everything you need to get started, including wood chips and detailed instructions. The wood chips used for stovetop smoking are usually ground finer than wood chips intended for outdoor use. This is because the goal is to produce smoke quickly using a minimal amount of wood.

To smoke indoors, set a burner at medium to preheat. If you're also going to use the oven, preheat it to 250°F (120°C) and set a rack at the lowest position. Arrange a handful of wood chips in a single layer on one side of the roasting pan. Place the wire rack in the pan and top with the food to be smoked. Cover the pan tightly with aluminum foil, but leave one corner slightly open.

Place the side of the pan with the wood chips over the burner. Once the wood starts to smoke, tightly seal the open corner. If you're doing a quick smoke infusion, reduce the heat to medium-low and continue cooking for 20 to 30 minutes. If you're using the oven for a longer smoke, transfer the roasting pan to the oven. Replenish the wood chips every 30 minutes until the food is done to your liking.

Stovetop Kettle Smokers

Kettle smokers for indoor use (such as those made by Nordic Ware) are all-in-one solutions for stovetop smoking. They give you the ability to smoke larger cuts of meat for hours. Most models on the market have an internal water pan, which can be filled with other liquids (like beer, apple juice, or wine) for an additional infusion of flavor. The temperature inside the kettle is monitored with the installed lid thermometer and is adjusted by simply raising or lowering the heat on the stove burner being used.

Kettle smokers have an adjustable vent on the lid so the airflow within the cooking chamber (and around the food) can impart additional flavor compared with other stovetop smoking methods. Just remember that because the air vent also lets out smoke, don't overfill the kettle with wood chips—always follow the manufacturer's recommendations. Make sure your hood fan is turned on and working before putting the kettle smoker on your stove.

Smoking Bags

Ready-made smoking bags are great when all you want is a touch of smoke flavor and easy cleanup. Manufacturers coat one half of the inside of an aluminum pouch with a mixture of wood particles and natural syrup. A perforated ply of aluminum foil is placed over this coating. When you're ready to cook, the food goes on top of the perforated sheet and the bag is sealed up. It can then be heated in a pan or in the oven. Because there's very little air in the bag after being sealed, this method is more like steaming than smoking. It's wonderful for lightly flavoring and steaming fish or vegetables, but it's not going to get the job done if you're looking for a deep smoky flavor.

Turning Your Oven into a Smoker

Using a stovetop kettle smoker or a roasting pan–style smoker are the safest ways to smoke indoors. It's possible to use your oven's cooking chamber as a smoker by smoldering wood chips on a baking tray directly in the oven. Some people, including restaurant chefs, use wood chips in a perforated aluminum pouch or external smoke generators plumbed directly into the oven. Keep in mind that oven ventilation and fire-safety systems in restaurants are vastly superior to an average home kitchen. For this reason, I recommend you leave this method of smoking to the professional chefs.

Buying a Smoker & Accessories

By now, you should feel ready to want to start smoking some food. Maybe some ribs, a brisket, or cold-smoked cheese or salmon. Every day, smoked foods are enjoyed around the world. Every day, someone somewhere is firing up a smoker to smoke something delicious. Before you start shopping around for a smoker, you should ask yourself a few questions and set some ground rules. Because this could be a big investment, you want to make sure you know your stuff before slapping down a pile of cash for something that could end up bringing you more trouble than joy.

How Much Do You Want to Spend?

Smoking well requires a certain amount of effort. A brisket can take 12 to 16 hours to slowly smoke for competition. Are you ready to stay up all night monitoring your fire? Refreshing the wood, checking the meat, not sleeping? Are you just gonna be a weekend warrior? Think you might want to compete? There are any number of questions you should be asking yourself even before you start considering what sort of budget you want to apply to this venture. There are more than a few garages in the world with a lot of expensive equipment gathering dust and annoying a significant other. This isn't a hobby to leap into willy-nilly without some research and there's really no excuse not to do the research these days. The Internet is alive with resources.

I'm sure you don't have a money tree in your backyard—I know I don't—which means there's only so much you're willing to spend on a smoker and the accessories to go with it. (It's important you don't forget about the accessories because they help enhance your smoking experience.) I suggest allocating three-quarters of your budget on the smoker itself and the remaining one-quarter of your budget on accessories.

You can get cheap stuff, pretty good stuff, not-so-cheap stuff, and seriously pricey stuff. When creating your budget, look what you can get in the following price ranges to help you determine how much you should spend. (See Chapter 2 for details on the different kinds of smokers.)

Conservative Budget ($750 or Less)

Don't think that because you aren't spending a ton of money that you won't be able to smoke as well as the professionals. Not true. Some of the best smokers are inexpensive. Many electric smokers, water smokers, charcoal kettles, and offset barrel smokers can be purchased for under $500—including with some accessories. These types of smokers can be found on the Internet and in most big-box stores, hardware or home improvement stores, and specialty barbecue supply stores and restaurant supply stores.

Midrange Budget ($750 to $2,000)

Spending a little more offers you a greater variety of smokers, including commercial units. Kamado-style grills and heavy-duty offset barrel smokers tend to fall into this price range. Besides price, the main difference between the conservative- and midrange-priced smokers is the materials used to make them.

Typically, lower-priced smokers are made from thinner metals. The thicker the metal, the more heat is held inside the smoker. This is great for winter or cold weather smoking. For example, the thickness of metal on an offset barrel smoker priced at $300 would be quite different from one priced at $1,300. This price range will also offer a larger variety of accessories that go with the smoker to enhance your smoking experience.

Spending Some Bucks ($2,000 to $5,000)

This is for those who want to spend some serious cash on a smoker with some bells and whistles. This range usually means a large smoker with lots of stainless steel that might take up quite a bit of real estate in the backyard. You could even get a small big rig for this kind of money. (See Chapter 2.) The smokers you get at this price are definitely heavy-duty and have a huge variety of accessories to complement them, but accessories usually cost extra.

Big-Daddy Range ($5,000 and Up)

This price range is for serious heavy-duty smokers. They either come on their own trailer (for competitive barbecuing folk who want to have it all) or are for use in restaurants or catering kitchens. Smokers above the $5,000 mark aren't for the amateur.

Whether you spend $150 or $5,000, because we're still talking about your hard-earned cash, make it count. Get the best smoker you can afford that will help you achieve your goals. Don't forget to make sure it suits your lifestyle and the kind of smoking you want to do. Just avoid temptation and don't go into the red when buying a smoker because then there won't be any money left to buy the meat!

Do Your Research

We all need advice from time to time, and if there's anything I've learned, it's that people like to show off how much they know. That's especially true of barbecue enthusiasts. If you're lucky enough to have a friend with a smoker, ask them a few questions before you spend your cash. This way, you can ask anything you might be embarrassed to ask a stranger in a showroom. Sometimes, a good friend can help point you in the right direction.

The Internet is often a great place for research. You can check out specific types of smokers or look for information and reviews about a particular brand you're interested in. Also, search barbecue or smoking food forums because those are the people who do this all the time and can offer you solid advice. (You'll find a list of my favorite buddies in the Introduction.) The barbecue community is full of people who like to talk. Reach out. They're all on social media. We like to brag.

You should also talk to anyone who knows food: foodies, smoked food enthusiasts, chefs, barbecue chefs, barbecue competitors, and food bloggers. Even if they're not experts on smoking foods, they might offer tidbits of information you'll find useful—whether it's during the shopping process or the cooking stages. It never hurts to ask because it could help you find exactly what kind of smoker you're looking for.

Perhaps the most obvious way to learn what you need to know before buying a smoker is to go to the store and talk to the people who sell them. A professional smoker and barbecue retailer can answer most of your questions. I like going to the specialty stores because this is what they do best. Because the staff is trained to know what they're talking about, they can really shine some light on all the varieties out there. Plus, you get to see the merchandise in person. To me, these places are more fun than a toy store is to a kid. You can also check out Appendix B for numerous reputable books and websites that can help you.

Helpful Smoking Accessories & Tools

Anyone who's been in the barbecue section of a big-box or specialty store knows just how many accessories there are to go with a grill or smoker. It's easy to go crazy, but we all know you don't need a battery-operated grill brush. My must-have list includes these items:

- Newspaper (for the chimney bottom)
- Lighter
- Chimney (I can't live without it)
- Sharp knives
- Cutting board
- Tongs (good-quality locking chef's tongs)
- Thermometer
- Spatula (good quality and heavy-duty)
- Spray bottle
- Aluminum foil (wide, heavy-duty)
- Rags (for cleaning spills)
- Heatproof gloves (such as welding gloves—rawhide won't burn you even if wet)

These will get you through quite nicely. That said, there are many extras that aren't silly and they can really help make the smoking journey a bit easier and more enjoyable. I'll run through some examples of essential fire-starting and temperature-gauging tools. Then I'll get into a longer list of some of the must-have and optional tools and accessories you need to start smoking.

Fire Starters

A variety of products on the market can help you get your fire going, and obviously, some are better than others. Here are some of your options.

Type	Characteristics
Charcoal chimney	Most pros use this tool because it just needs a little newsprint and a lighter to give you the cleanest, longest-lasting fire for the least amount of money.
DIY fire starter recipe	Tightly pack sawdust into paper muffin cups. If you have some dryer lint, mix it into the sawdust. Melt paraffin wax or old candles in a double boiler, pour over the sawdust, and allow to cool. Slow-burning when lit, these hotcakes make great starters placed under a pile of charcoal.
Electric starters	There are many on the market these days, including coil and air-blown. Build your charcoal starter fire over the coil or blow on your piled charcoal. When you're ready to start, simply plug it in and eventually the fire is slowly revved up to white-hot coals. They're great if you don't like to handle fire and you aren't in a hurry.
Fire-starter sticks	Wood splints formed into a match-like starter, these are paraffin-soaked to start the fire easily. I don't recommend them or use them, but they aren't the worst of the bunch.
Liquid fire starters	There's nothing worse than a steak that tastes of nothing but lighter fluid and soot. It's not necessary to use an entire bottle of fluid to start a fire! In fact, don't use it—learn to light a proper fire.
Propane torch	It's exactly what it sounds like. Some people like to see sky-high flames when lighting a fire. It's not necessary, but hey, if you love flames, go for it—just use caution!
Sugarcane-based fuel gel	This is an all-natural product made from sugarcane with no flavor. If you have to use something other than a few crumpled pieces of paper, this is the starter to use.

Anyone playing with fire needs to have a hose nearby (or a bucket of water) and a fire extinguisher. Accelerants and electrical fires need different forms of extinguishers and some fires can't be put out with water because it will actually make the flames increase. If you're going to be playing with accelerants or electrical tools, make sure you have the tools recommended by the product manufacturer for putting out the fire!

Thermometers

All cooks—beginner, amateur, and pro—need to use thermometers when smoking foods. I recommend owning at least three or four different thermometers—and sometimes more than one of each. You'll need at least three different styles for smoking meat. Here are some to choose from.

Type	Characteristics
Digital internal-probe thermometer	These come in a variety of price points. Some are just like a regular probe and give you an instant digital reading. Others you can insert into the meat, leave it there, and attach the readout portion to the smoker. There are also wireless versions that can be carried with you, giving you a constant reading throughout the smoking process. I confess I have a few of these.
High-heat thermometer	This is used to test the heat of the fire in your smoker, especially with charcoal or hardwood fires. Tracking your smoking times and temperatures is important because that's information you can use to make changes or repeat successful recipes. It can also give you a more accurate cooking time for your meats.
Instant-read probe thermometer	These come with a sensitive thermometer. They're inserted into the meat at the thickest part, but ensure they don't contact bone. Use this probe to double-check your meat and make sure it's done safely and just the way you want it. I recommend having a few on hand.
Oven thermometer	This is another accurate way to take the temperature inside the smoker when the thermometer on the lid or door of the smoker isn't exact. I prefer to have one set inside at the grate level (or even on every shelf of a big rig) because temperature precision is key.
Smoker thermometer	This one stays in the smoker at all times to allow you to monitor the internal temperature of your smoker. Most smokers come with a thermometer built into the lid or door, but remember that it isn't always accurate. It will often give you the temperature in the air space above where the food is.

If you don't want to invest in all these thermometers, at the very least, you must have an instant-read thermometer for checking the doneness of your meats. Nothing ruins a party like giving your guests food poisoning. I really do recommend having at least one of each of the thermometers listed—if not a few extra thermometers on hand— in case one should stop working. You should also have backup batteries for your thermometers in case they run out of juice while you're smoking.

Toolkit for the Frequent Smoker

This might seem like an extensive list, but many of these are things you could (or should) already have in your home—you just didn't know they're part of the smoker's toolkit.

Tool	Uses
Aluminum foil	A great use for foil is to crumple it up and scrape it on your dirty grates to clean them if you don't have a brush. That's one use, but because there are too many other uses to count, make sure you always have some on hand. It's a good idea to have a regular 11-inch-wide (28cm) roll and a heavy-duty 17- or 19-inch-wide (43 × 48cm) roll.
Bamboo skewers	Look for long and thick sturdy skewers—they'll hold larger amounts of food and require less soaking than flimsy ones you buy at the supermarket.
Basting brush	I like the new silicone basting brushes because you can clean them more easily than classic pastry brushes.
Basting mop	Wherever they're selling barbecue accessories, there will likely be a little mop and bucket kit. (They really do look exactly like an old-fashioned string mop in miniature.) Sometimes, you might even find them in the cleaning aisle. This low-tech tool allows for the transfer of lots of mop liquid to the meat.
Blender/hand mixer	If you only have one electronic gadget in your kitchen, it should be one of these. A good one with a chopper attachment, a whip, and a blender attachment will give you virtually every tool you need to do multiple jobs: chop garlic, mix sauces, blend rub pastes, and—lest we forget—mix cocktails.

(continues)

Tool	Uses
Butcher paper (also known as peach or pink butcher paper)	This is a strong style of barbecue paper approved by the USDA/FDA for use in food industries. This paper doesn't tear easily. It has a "sizing" treatment that keeps it from falling apart when it gets wet, which makes it a durable paper that not only prevents leaks but also allows the meat to breathe by letting out moisture. This makes it ideal for wrapping meats for smoking because it allows the smoke flavor to be absorbed. Ultimately, it ensures the integrity of your meat by protecting it from contaminants while locking in moisture.
Butcher's twine	Because you never know when you might need to tie up a piece of meat, a big roll of butcher's twine should always be hanging close at hand.
Cookbooks and magazines	Yes, even a chef looks to other chefs for tips and inspiration—and so should you. (See Appendix B for some of my favorite cookbooks.) I also buy the summer issues of *Popular Plates*, *Bon Appétit*, *Food & Wine*, *Fine Cooking*, *Saveur*, and others that have annual barbecue editions. These offer reviews of new equipment and recipes that range from beginner to expert.
Cutting boards	Please, please, please: no goofy, cute, color-coded slicing boards. Get yourself at least one nice big board—an 18-inch (46cm) square is good. Wood or polypropylene—I don't care which, although I prefer wood. Learn to bleach it (and oil it if it's wood). Keep it clean and use it. And you should always put a damp cloth under it so it won't slide when you're using it.
Galvanized metal bucket	Keep this on hand for holding hot coals removed from your smoker.
Grill brush	You need a sturdy, long-handled wire brush with a built-in scraper. Long, drawn-out smoking means a heavy buildup of ash, which should be cleaned away to prevent fires and gas buildup.

Tool	Uses
Heatproof gloves	I already mentioned you need heat-resistant gloves. In fact, I recommend you get welding gloves. They're rawhide, which will never burn you even if they get wet. They have a nice long cuff so you can reach into a smoker without burning your arms. A good-quality pair will never wear out.
Injector	Most injectors look like large hypodermic syringes. Some have reservoirs that will hold as much as 2 cups of liquid for injecting into various meats.
Knives	You need good-quality knives—at least one of each of the following types: boning, french (or chef's), paring, fillet, slicing, and bread—as well as a cleaver. You also need a sharpening steel to keep the knives sharp. Learn to use your knives properly and take them somewhere every 6 to 12 months to get the blades ground.
Large bowls	Always use nonreactive materials (metal or glass) because of the high acid content in marinades and brines.
Large pails or bins	You need pails or bins to hold large cuts of meat during marinating and brining. Plastic storage bins are great for larger cuts, like turkeys and briskets, because they have tight-fitting lids. Make sure they'll fit in your fridge before you buy them though. Reserve these bins for food use only and always clean them well with hot, soapy water before and after each use.
Long barbecuing tongs	This is where you need to learn from a chef. Don't go out and buy one of those cute, shiny sets of tools that look best hanging from hooks. You need some long (16-inch [41cm]) stainless-steel locking tongs. There's nothing sadder than a steak on the ground because the tongs were useless.
Needle-nose pliers	Have a set reserved for cooking only and use them to pull pin bones out of fish fillets.
Nonstick cooking spray	The name speaks for itself. It's something I always like to have on hand.

(continues)

Tool	Uses
Parchment paper	We smokers use it to make packages (*en papillote*) as well as to line trays or to set directly on the grill to cook something fragile, such as seafood or other small pieces. Parchment paper is safe up to 400°F (205°C) before it will begin to smolder.
Plastic wrap (heavy-duty, heat-tolerant)	You want to use a heat-tolerant variety when you're wrapping meat—such as a brisket or sausages without casings—that's going into a smoker.
Resealable plastic bags	You'll see just how much these get used once you hit the recipe chapters. Because we smokers stick our hands in a lot of stuff, these will make sure you're keeping clean.
Rubber gloves	Rubber gloves are great for handling raw meat, but make sure you wash them as you would your actual hands: with hot, soapy water. Or buy yourself a box of disposable medical gloves. I can't begin to tell you how many of those I go through in a month.
Smoking bags	These bags aren't a must-have, but they're a great option for a smoker beginner. These bags give a light smoke flavor to foods. You just season the food as desired, place it in the bag, then heat on the oven rack, on the barbecue grate, or directly on the coals.
Spatulas	Look for ones with long, sturdy handles and a nice, big lifting surface. You might actually need two or three spatulas of different sizes and shapes to handle everything from fish to cheese.
Spoons, ladles, measuring spoons, and vegetable peeler	All these kitchen utensils are necessary to prepare and handle food easily and safely.
Spray bottles	You gotta have at least one plastic spray bottle for putting out fires and cooling down charcoal—and more for flavored spritzes.

Gadgets for the More Advanced Smoker

These aren't the tools you'll need when you start your smoking career, but they'll come in handy as you refine your craft.

Gadget	Uses
BBQ Guru	BBQ Guru is a thermometer-controlled fan that attaches to the smoker. It regulates the temperature to a chosen setting by turning the fan on and off. More oxygen equals higher heat. With the high-end versions, you can control the temperature remotely—up to 600 feet (185 meters) away. If the temperature drops in the middle of the night, it will fix itself or set off an alarm. With more complex versions, such as the DigiQ, you can even program the heat to raise or lower at scheduled times.
Bellows	They're great for stoking a fire or helping get one going. They're not easy to find, but they're a favorite tool for pros.
Cold-smoke generator	Various types of cold-smoke generators exist on the market—some are electric and others aren't. Some, such as the ProQ cold-smoke generator, stay inside the smoking chamber. Others, such as Smoke Daddy cold-smoke generators, pump the smoke into the smoking chamber through a tube. High-quality cold-smoking systems like these are designed to keep the internal temperature of the smoker below 100°F (38°C).
Diffuser plates	Typically available from manufacturers of larger rigs, these are used to provide even heat distribution under large cuts of food to be smoked, such as brisket or a big fish.
Meat grinder	If you want to make sausage, your choices for a meat grinder include old-fashioned tabletop models sold in every hardware store or high-tech electric ones that might beckon you at big-box stores these days. You can also get a grinder attachment for a stand mixer if you have one.
Meat hooks	You want something with a handle sturdy enough to haul out a whole brisket or rack of ribs from the smoker. The stainless-steel shaft needs to be long enough for reaching deep into the smoker or over hot coals so it can haul out what you need.

(continues)

Gadget	Uses
Meat-tenderizing press	This is a bunch of needles on a handle that you use to stab meat multiple times. By breaking up connective tissues, this tool allows for the deeper penetration of marinades or brines.
Rib racks	There are multiple styles of rib racks, and in this case, you definitely get what you pay for. If you're going to smoke a lot of ribs, look for a heavy-duty rack that handles easily in a hot smoker. You want one that will hold at least four full racks standing on their sides, with clear space between each.
Rotisserie	If your smoker will handle a rotisserie, the manufacturer generally has a rotisserie package designed specifically for the machine you're using.
Sausage stuffer	Generally, your grinder will include this attachment. If you're going old-school, the equipment is at the hardware store. Check out your favorite barbecue supply store or online. Resist the urge to buy an über-cheap sausage kit. Get the best you can afford.
Smoker boxes	These are designed for use with electric, charcoal, or gas smokers or grills to allow wood chips to smolder instead of burn.
Vacuum tumbler	This accessory is the best way to get a marinade into the meat. The air is removed from the drum, which helps open up the pores of the meat so marinade and water can be soaked up. Tumbling allows meat to absorb 10 to 20% more water and spice in 20 to 60 minutes than 48 hours of traditional marinating.

Although beer and whiskey aren't really tools or accessories, I consider them essential parts of a smoker's toolkit. I use a lot of whiskey (bourbon, Scotch, Tennessee, Canadian, Irish, etc.) in my smoking recipes—they really lend themselves to the smoky flavor notes I want to develop.

This is a good starter list of the most popular accessories for smokers. There are more, but because some of them are just too silly to list, use your judgment when buying accessories. Start with ones you think will make your task easier, then treat yourself to other novelty items once your basic smoking toolkit is complete. After all, if you have enough money to buy a truckload of accessories, you might want to re-evaluate and allocate some of that money to getting a more expensive, better-quality smoker. That's the piece of equipment that really matters.

Ted's 10 Commandments for Smoking Foods

There sits your smoker, poised in its suit of armor, ready to be fired up. You've spent the money, you've cursed your way through the assembly manual, and you just want to get the fire hot and start smoking something awesome. Buying a smoker is a big deal and learning how to get it going for the first time is no easy feat. Just start by taking small steps—one at a time.

When it comes to smoking foods, I have a hard-and-fast set of guidelines to help me produce the best-tasting food I possibly can. These 10 commandments will help you get things rolling the first time you fire up your smoker—and every time to follow.

Commandment #1: Be Prepared

The first thing they taught us in Boy Scouts was to always "be prepared." Proper and thorough preparation is very important to successful smoking. As you decide what to smoke, you need to ask yourself: What am I hoping to achieve by smoking this food? What's the occasion? For example, smoking something to preserve it is much different from smoking up a great dish for a backyard barbecue or tailgate party. (By the way, my favorite tailgating dishes include ribs, Texas brisket, or a pork shoulder for pulled pork.)

Once you have a plan, it's time to get things moving forward. Three main areas of preparation are needed for good smoking:

- Prepare the food.

- Prepare the fire.

- Prepare the smoker.

These steps might seem obvious, but my point is you need to plan for each of these before getting started. If you get organized for smoking properly before you start, you'll save yourself time and heartache later.

Prepare the Food

Your final result out of the smoker will only be as good as the ingredients you bought to put into it. Always buy fresh, good-quality ingredients—or the best you can afford. Keep the following in mind when shopping for foods to cook in the smoker:

- **Buying Meats:** Find a great butcher who'll help you pick the right cut for any occasion. Butchers can also trim to your specifications and guide you on fresh versus aged meats. Make a butcher your friend and you'll never go wrong. Meats with a minimum of 21 days aging are usually more tender than meat that's just been butchered. Always look for meats that are well marbled. Internal fat adds a ton of flavor and will help keep your meats moist and succulent during smoking.

- **Buying Seafood:** Because a trustworthy fishmonger is another good person to have on your side, look for a local fish and seafood market where you can buy fresh, good-quality products. Whether you're smoking salmon, tuna, mackerel, or scallops, you want your fish and seafood to be fresh, cold, and firm. Fresh will produce better results than frozen or previously frozen items.

- **Buying Produce:** Be choosy when selecting your fruits and vegetables. Look for bright colors, firm textures, and pieces that are blemish-free without any wilting. Don't be afraid to take a whiff—the produce should smell sweet and fresh. The best way to know you're getting good quality is to shop in season and locally. It's always good to support local farmers whenever possible.

Along with getting all your ingredients lined up, you need to review the recipe carefully. Many of my recipes have multiple stages, such as brining, curing, and marinating, before you even get to the smoker. Because timing is very important, make sure you allow enough time to do all the necessary steps. If you want to smoke a chicken for dinner on Saturday, you'll need a day for brining and a day for smoking, so plan to start the process on Friday. You might need to get organized a week ahead in some cases, especially if you're working on a big piece of meat. Get out the calendar and make a step-by-step plan!

Prepare the Fire

Before you bring food out to the smoker, you need to prepare the fire to create smoke. Whether you're cold- or hot-smoking, timing is key. You need to know how long your meat will take to smoke and organize your fuel sources and smoking woods accordingly.

Make sure you have enough on hand to get you through the entire smoking time, which will be different every time depending on the type of smoker being used and the weather outside. This is another reason why you need to understand your smoker and how it works. (See Chapter 2.) Be sure you soak the wood chips or chunks in advance so they're ready for you when you need them. (See Chapter 3.)

Prepare the Smoker

Lastly, fire up your smoker (per the manufacturer's instructions). If this is your first time, please be sure to **read the owner's manual—front to back**! It's not just for assembling your smoker—it also teaches you the basics of using your new smoker. The manual has enormous value: It shows the parts of your smoker and how to use it, and it often includes recipes to get you started. Keep it around so you can refer to it at a later date if you run into an issue.

If you take the time to make a plan, gather your resources, and learn about your equipment, you'll be off to the best start possible—every time!

Commandment #2: Be Patient

Every aspect of smoking food takes time—that's all there is to it! Preparing the food is the easy part. Waiting for food to cure, brine, or marinate takes time. Some items could take a week or two to cure. Waiting for foods to smoke and tending the fire to maintain a consistent temperature for even smoking take time. It also takes time for charcoal to heat to the right temperature, for wood chips to soak, and for food to actually smoke. *It takes time.* This means you need to be patient and give each step the time needed to do each of these things properly. If you have the perseverance to wait it out, you'll discover the passion of creating truly delicious foods.

Not only are you in this for the long haul, but you also need to give whatever food you're smoking a lot of attention. There's the basting or spritzing, maintaining the proper humidity, and keeping the temperature of your smoker consistent.

Believe it or not, as much as you need to tend to the smoker, because there's still a bit of downtime, here are some tips for passing the time while your food smokes:

- You don't have to sit right beside your unit. Get a digital thermometer that connects to your computer or cell phone. It will alert you to any changes in the smoker's temperature or the internal temperature of the meat, giving you more freedom to move around the backyard.

- Smoke with a friend. Companionship while you smoke is always fun!
- Let your imagination run wild: Think of all the different ways you can serve the food after it's pulled out of the smoker.

Waiting for good smoked foods can be very exciting. I think it's like the night before going on vacation—you just want to be there already. In this case, you just want to dig in already! Just don't let your excitement get the better of you. Continue to be patient. Remember: Good things come to those who wait—and, oh boy, it's gonna be good!

Commandment #3: Don't Peek!

Believe me, I know this is easier said than done. I know how hard it is to not peek. It was one of the things I found most difficult in the beginning too. You think to yourself: It's harmless—just a quick look to see how things are coming along. But every time you open any part of the smoker (firebox door, lid, or door to the main smoking chamber), you lose valuable sweet smoke as well as heat (if you're hot-smoking). So the more you peek, the longer it takes to smoke. For every 30 seconds the lid is off your smoker or the door is open, add about 20 minutes to the smoking time. Does it still seem harmless?

Once you have a steady smoke and a steady temperature going—keep the smoker closed! Adjust vents to maintain a constant temperature and just let the food hang out to smoke. Get dual-probe thermometers (one for the meat and one for the internal temperature of the smoker) to keep you informed about what's happening inside the smoker and prevent the need for a look-see. Every time you feel the urge to peek, take a sip of beer or your favorite beverage instead. Try setting up a "peeking jar" you have to put money into every time you peek. At least if you break the rules, you can treat yourself to some cold beer or new accessories for your smoker. Or use the time your food is in the smoker wisely by preparing your other side dishes or basting sauces. Keep yourself busy. Remember, the less you peek, the sooner you eat!

Commandment #4: Keep 'Er Steady

Keeping your smoker running smoothly at a constant temperature isn't as easy as it sounds. It's a little easier if you're using an electric or propane smoker—you can set the temperature digitally. But a charcoal or hardwood smoker is much more challenging.

When you work with a charcoal or hardwood smoker, it's important to monitor the burn time of the charcoal or wood. It might take you a while to understand what works best in your smoker. Keep track of the type of charcoal you use (such as lump or briquette, mesquite or hickory, blended or pure charcoal). These all burn at different temperatures and you might find that a particular charcoal works better in your smoker. You need to experiment. Once you figure out which coal works best, you can more easily manage the temperature in your smoker going forward. The same applies to your wood choice.

Most smokers have some kind of air vent. The vents are the throttles of the natural smoker. Kettle smokers usually have three vents on the bottom of the fire bowl and one on the lid. Offset barrel smokers have a door vent to the firebox and a chimney. By opening or closing the bottom and top vents, you can control the temperature. Open them wide to increase the temperature. Or close them up to varying degrees to either maintain or lower the temperature.

Before you set up your smoker, be sure to monitor the wind direction and position the smoker to prevent the vents and firebox from pointing directly into the wind. Excessive wind could make it harder to maintain proper low smoking temperatures or it could blow out your fire if you're using a propane smoker.

When reloading charcoal into the smoker, remember that a little goes a long way. Add small amounts of hot charcoal to your smoker—a little at a time—to keep the temperature even. Adding too many hot coals might cause your smoker to spike in temperature. Some folks like to add cold charcoal to the perimeter of the hot coals, allowing the charcoal to heat slowly. This method works well to maintain the temperature, but I'm not a fan of the flavor it produces. Charcoal needs to be burned until it's white-hot and beginning to form a thin layer of white ash to give off its sweetest smoke flavor. I always say that until it reaches white, it's still raw smoke. Pure smoke should be clear or with just a hint of white. The darker the smoke, the dirtier the smoke—and you don't want that.

The easiest way to maintain the temperature is to use a digital thermometer with a blower fan. Many different varieties of this tool are on the market, but the principle is pretty much the same for each. The fan portion of the accessory attaches to the main vent-control panel on your firebox and a thermometer probe is mounted inside the smoker. Should the temperature drop, the fan starts up and pushes a little even flow of air onto the cooling coals to help boost the internal temperature. On kamado-style grills, these mount on the front of the smoker at the bottom. On box smokers, they attach to the firebox on the side.

Commandment #5: Keep It Moist—Unless ...

It's important to keep the food in the smoker moist. This is especially true when smoking at a hotter temperature to ensure the meat doesn't dry out. The food just needs a mist or spritz to keep it moist and delicious. So go ahead, share your beer with the food in the smoker—it'll make you both happy. Or try injecting meats with water or other liquids—my favorite is butter. Either way, it'll add moisture and succulence to whatever you're smoking.

Humidity is an important factor in smoking foods. I like to keep my humidity levels high in the smokehouse when I hot-smoke. Water smokers create humidity relatively easily from a water pan that sits above the fuel and creates steam. That steam blends with the smoke to add flavor and keep meats moist. With other smokers, humidity is created naturally through the design of the smoker. Food will release moisture and create its own humidity. Because a tightly sealed smoker will keep the heat and humidity in, avoid venting if you're trying to maintain that humidity.

Not every food you smoke requires a high humidity level. When cold-smoking cheeses, you need a dry smoking environment to keep the cheese from sweating. If it does sweat, it means the smoker is too warm. Because humidity can promote mold, if you're smoking to preserve meats, the less moisture the better. Remove excess moisture by air-drying your meats for 6 to 24 hours before smoking, thus reducing the moisture.

Always pat meats dry with paper towels to remove excess moisture from marinades. Keep meats cold and unwrapped to allow them to dry. Air-drying chicken and turkey before smoking will also produce a crispier skin, which is especially good when eating wings or drumsticks.

Commandment #6: Keep It Safe and Clean

This is a big one: You always need to make safety a priority when smoking foods. The smoker itself can be dangerous, but you also need to take precautions when handling foods going into the smoker. There are a lot of rules in each of these areas and I'm going to do my best to teach you everything you need to know.

Smoker Safety

Once you've purchased a smoker, you need to decide where you're going to put it. Because the majority of smokers for home use are designed for outdoor use, that's where you should put it! Place it at least 2 to 3 feet (60 to 90 meters) away from the house and away from windows in a well-lit and well-ventilated area. Avoid setting it up near trees, shrubs, or flowers. Because it's never safe to move a hot smoker, make sure it's where you want it before you fire it up. You should have nothing obstructing the path to the smoker, ensuring you don't trip and fall into it. Always keep children and pets away from the smoker, especially the firebox. Refer to the manufacturer's instructions for more details on safe smoker placement.

Use caution when working with smokers and be sure to have fire-safety equipment on standby just in case. A fire extinguisher, a water hose, and a bucket of water are all good things to have on hand. You never know when or why a fire might get out of control. To protect yourself, you should always tie long hair back and avoid wearing long, flowing clothes. The temperature inside a smoker might not be that hot, but rest assured, the firebox gets red hot! Always wear gloves and use utensils when handling foods or the smoker itself. It's not a bad idea to have a well-stocked first-aid kit nearby to take care of minor burns and cuts.

I always recommend you never leave your smoker unattended once you fire it up. It's always best to be close in case something happens so you can react quickly and fix the problem. If you're not around, you risk losing control of your smoker and could end up with overcooked food, spoiled food, or even a roaring fire. It does happen—and always when you least expect it. So get comfy and stay put. I like to smoke with friends. That way, someone is always watching the smoker. If you must watch the big game while your food smokes, then do what I did: I made a man cave off my smoking deck. It's fully loaded with the comforts of any garage: beer fridge, draft fridge, liquor cabinet, flat-screen TV, couch, table, chairs, and heat. Everything I need to get me through the long haul. Just make sure you enjoy your adult beverages responsibly and don't drink so much that you can't maintain a completely safe smoking environment.

Practicing Proper Food Safety

Random cases of food poisoning are rare, but it's almost always caused by poor food-handling practices. Although you can't guarantee you'll never get sick, you can reduce your chances by taking necessary precautions.

Bacteria that cause foodborne illness are tiny organisms that require such conditions as moderate temperature, moisture, oxygen, and a food source to survive and breed. With most microorganisms, if you eliminate one of these things, you limit their growth. Cooking foods to the proper temperature will ensure you eliminate the risk of most foodborne illnesses. Once you hit 140°F (60°C), you're out of the danger zone. When you reach 165°F (75°C), bacteria can no longer survive. Generally speaking, one of the best things about smoking is that by slow-cooking foods over a long period of time, it's likely the food will not only reach a safe temperature but will also exceed it. A brisket is a good example: It's cooked to 185°F (85°C) for slicing or 205°F (95°C) for shredding. And if that weren't reassuring enough, you take it 20 to 40 degrees Fahrenheit (10 to 25 degrees Celsius) higher because you need it to be super tender. Done properly, smoking is a very safe way to cook.

Because food safety starts at the grocery store, here are some tips when shopping for meat, poultry, and fish:

- Always visit the meat and fish departments after you've done all your other shopping so food spends the least amount of time out of refrigeration.

- Meat and poultry products should feel cold to the touch. If they don't feel cold, don't buy them.

- Grab extra bags in the produce department to store meat packages in to prevent juices from leaking onto other products in your shopping cart.

- Choose packages that are tightly wrapped and have no tears or punctures.

- Choose packages that are dry. Liquid is an indication of temperature abuse.

- Check the sell-by date and make sure there's enough time to marinate, brine, or cure the product before it expires.

When buying directly from a butcher, your food won't be in packages, but the same guidelines apply. Ask to confirm the sell-by dates if necessary. The meat should be cold, dry, and without a strong odor. Strong smells indicate age or improper storage.

Once you get the meat home, get it into the fridge or freezer as quickly as possible. Keeping foods cold will inhibit bacterial growth. It's also important you maintain a safe temperature in your refrigerator and freezer. Your refrigerator temperature should be set below 40°F (5°C) to keep foods out of the danger zone. The danger zone, which promotes the growth of foodborne bacteria, is between 40°F and 140°F (5°C and 60°C). Remember the chef's motto: Keep hot food hot and cold food cold!

Food Safety Temperatures Chart

Temperature	Status of Bacterial Growth
165°F (75°C) and higher	Most bacteria die within seconds.
141°F to 164°F (61°C to 74°C)	This temperature is perfect for holding hot foods and sauces. Existing bacteria aren't necessarily killed but don't multiply either—and, with rare exception, pose no danger.
DANGER ZONE 40°F to 140°F (5°C to 60°C) **DANGER ZONE**	Bacteria thrive and multiply. Limit the exposure of perishable foods to less than 1 hour.
33°F to 39°F (1°C to 4°C)	Refrigerated food storage. Bacteria don't die. They still multiply—but relatively slowly. Food is safe here for a limited time.
32°F (0°C) and lower	Frozen food storage. Existing bacteria don't die but are held stable.

I recommend removing meats from the foam trays they're sold in before storing the meats in the fridge. Rinse the meat under cold water (except for ground meats), pat dry with paper towels, and then wrap loosely with wax paper. This allows the surface to dry, making it less likely that bacteria will grow. Place meat on a plate or tray to catch drippings before putting it in the coldest part of the fridge. The bottom shelf is ideal because if there's a spill, it won't contaminate other foods items below it.

The following table gives some information on refrigerator storage. The recommended storage times are based on a refrigerated temperature of 37°F (3°C).

Recommended Meat, Poultry, and Fish Storage Guidelines

Food Item	Storage Time
Beef, lamb, pork, veal, game (most cuts)	3 to 5 days
Ground meats	2 to 4 days
Chicken, turkey, duck, game birds	2 days
Ground poultry	1 to 2 days
Fish (steaks and fillets)	1 to 2 days
Shellfish	1 to 2 days
Variety meats (liver, heart, etc.)	1 day

The times specified are guidelines, but always use your best judgment and common sense, even if it contradicts the table. If you doubt the safety of a piece of meat, discard it. I know it's painful to throw away an expensive cut of meat, especially if you're unsure, but it's not nearly as painful as knowing you've given someone food poisoning.

Remove fresh meat and poultry from their original packaging and rewrap them tightly using freezer paper or resealable plastic freezer bags before placing in the freezer. Try to remove as much air as possible to prevent condensation, which causes freezer burn. Always thaw frozen meats in the refrigerator, not at room temperature.

One of the biggest causes of food poisoning is cross-contamination. Follow these tips to prevent that:

- Always wash your hands, cooking utensils, work surfaces, and cutting boards with hot, soapy water before and after handling raw meat, poultry, and seafood.

- Never place cooked foods on a cutting board or surface that previously held raw meat. (You can use the same cutting board—just make sure it's been thoroughly cleaned before placing cooked food on it.) The safest practice is to have several cutting boards that are assigned to specific jobs. Use one for raw meats, poultry, and fish; one for cooked foods; one for vegetables; and one for fruits and other sweet ingredients.

• Cook all meat and poultry products to safe internal temperatures to eliminate any harmful bacteria. (See the following table.) Using a thermometer is the only way to be certain your meat and poultry are cooked to the proper temperature. Color and clear juices aren't safe indicators of doneness.

The US Department of Agriculture (USDA) says the following temperatures will produce safely cooked but still flavorful meats.

Internal Temperatures of Safely Cooked Meats

Meat	Internal Temperature
Ground beef, veal, lamb, pork	160°F (71°C)
Beef, veal, and lamb—roasts, steaks, chops (medium-rare)	145°F (63°C)
Beef, veal, and lamb—roasts, steaks, chops (medium)	160°F (71°C)
Beef, veal, and lamb—roasts, steaks, chops (well-done)	170°F (75°C)
Pork—roasts, steaks, chops (medium)	160°F (71°C)
Pork—roasts, steaks, chops (well-done)	170°F (75°C)
Ham—raw, cooked before eating	160°F (71°C)
Ham—fully cooked, to reheat	140°F (60°C)
Ground chicken or turkey	165°F (74°C)
Whole chicken or turkey	185°F (85°C)
Chicken or turkey—breasts, roasts	165°F (74°C)

Get all leftovers into the fridge as soon as possible, and once they're chilled through, wrap them tightly. You can speed up the chilling process by dividing large quantities into smaller portions or spreading food out into a thin layer. Generally, meat and poultry leftovers can be stored in the refrigerator for up to 3 days and in the freezer for up to 1 month. And always remember the golden rule: When in doubt, throw it out!

Commandment #7: Practice, Practice, Practice

The more you practice your smoking techniques, the easier they become and the better your results will taste. Take it from me! I practice a lot. In fact, every time I fire up a smoker, I consider it another practice session. Every time you smoke, it's a chance to improve on what you did last time and create new flavors that will make you and your guests deliciously happy.

There are a few things to practice to get really comfortable and confident with your smoker. First is learning to start the fire. Practice starting fires for charcoal or hardwood smokers in a variety of different ways. You'll eventually figure out which works best for you. Some starters are designed to not only light the fuel but to also do it quickly. Time how long it takes for lump charcoal to reach the perfect white-hot temperature and compare it with the timing for briquette charcoal. After the fire has started, because learning to control it will make smoking food much easier, practice adding fuel and working the vents. Remember, with charcoal, less is often more. You don't need a lot of charcoal to generate a lot of heat.

You can also experiment with different woods to create different smoke flavors and find out which sweet smoke flavor you like best. Practice with soaked and unsoaked wood chips, and compare chips with chunks or logs. (See Chapter 3 for details on all the options.) There's also bark and no bark to play around with. All these factors contribute to the essence of the smoke that will flavor your foods. Try a few different combinations until you find your favorite blends.

Also try out various temperatures. The lower the temperature, the longer it takes to smoke, and the hotter the temperature, the faster it'll smoke. Both can have great results, but through practice, you'll find a balance that best suits your tastes. Practice your recipes by adjusting and tweaking them as you move along to create your own versions of smoked perfection.

Should you run into issues during your practice sessions that you're unsure how to fix, just turn to the experts. Your smoker manufacturer's website should have a lot of information and associates to assist you. The Internet is full of wonderful information and people who can help troubleshoot. There are many great smoking and barbecue professionals online who are willing to share what they know. I know I am, so check me out at www.tedreader.com and hopefully I can help you. Get out there and practice smoking something delicious!

Commandment #8: Take Notes

I have a fantastic memory, but as I get older, I'm finding it's not as good as it once was, so taking notes and keeping a journal of what I've done is important. It allows me to accurately recall what I did so I know what adjustments to make for next time or how to exactly duplicate it. Keeping track of what you've done will only help make you a better smoker. Here's an example of one of my entries:

Category	Notes
Recipe name	Smoked Boston Butt
Weight	1 bone-in butt (13.5 pounds [6kg])
Brine	Basic Brine
Brine time	24 hours
Rub	Ted Reader's Bone Dust BBQ Seasoning Rub, 12 hours
Wood smoke	Blend of hickory, apple, and maple chunks (equal parts)
Soaked or unsoaked	Soaked
Smoker	Offset barrel smoker
Charcoal	Sugar maple lump charcoal, 15 to 20 pounds (7 to 9kg)
Starter	Charcoal chimney
Spritz	Apple juice and whiskey
Injection	None
Barbecue accessory	Spray bottle
Smoker temperature	200°F (95°C)
Vent	Variable
Outside temperature	65°F (18°C)
Weather	Raining with a slight wind from the northeast

Smoking Environment and Activity

	Hour 1	Hour 2	Hour 3	Hour 4	Hours 5 to 6	Hours 7 to 8	Hours 9 to 10	Hours 11 to 12	Hours 13 to 15
Smoker temperature (°F)	220	200	235	220	200	200	200	185	225
Meat temperature (°F)	56	75	88	113	122	145	160	185	205
Spritz	x	x	x	x	x	x	x	x	x
Added charcoal			x		x		x		
Added wood	x	x	x	x	x	x	x		
Beer	x	x	x		x	x		x	x
Vents	open	½	open	½	¼	¼	¼	¼	¼

Always leave yourself some space on the sheet where you can jot notes and record ideas for next time as they come to you. Make notes on how it looked, how it tasted, and what you might do differently. Also, take pictures of the food throughout the entire process. This will give you a more accurate account of how the meat looked during the different stages of cooking.

Commandment #9: Make It Tasty

It's easy to get lost in all the planning and variables when smoking foods, but let's not forget what our main objective is here: making tasty food! Here are some clues on how you'll know if your smoked foods are tasty:

* Bones twist easily from the meat on a smoked pork shoulder—it's ready for pulling.

* You come in the house and your spouse says you smell … of smoke.

* There's nothing left but empty plates and full bellies.

* A hot-smoked scallop melts in your mouth like milk chocolate.

* A smoked brisket oozes juicy goodness, leaving a puddle on your plate that needs to be sopped up with some fresh bread.

* After eating your smoked feast, you need a shower instead of a napkin.

* Your neighbors are drooling to come over for a nibble.

* The local firefighters show up because they saw smoke.

* Your family's eyes are rolling into the back of their heads while they tell you the food was delicious.

Because the addition of aromatics makes for some tasty smoking, scatter fresh herb sprigs (rosemary, thyme, or lavender) onto the hot coals in your smoker to add a flavor boost to the food you're smoking.

My barbecue rig parked in a lake. Why in a lake? Because I could.
It was one very hot day and this was the easiest way to keep cool.

Commandment #10: Have Fun!

You're in this to create delicious food, but you should be having fun while you're doing it. I love food and I truly enjoy the work that goes into preparing it. Whether I'm grilling something over hot coals or smoking something low and slow, I'm always having a good time. So relax and don't get stressed out. Sometimes, you'll fail. Even I fail sometimes. Well … not very often anymore. But do what I do: Open a beer, make some notes, and order a pizza. You had fun, you screwed up, and you learned something. Carry on.

Smoking food in your backyard is meant to be enjoyable. The sweet smell of smoke, tending the fire, and smoking food to delicious perfection—that's what it's all about. It's a rewarding hobby and your whole family can savor the results. So enjoy yourself: Grab a buddy, have a refreshing beverage, and get smoking. Cheers!

Me chillin' in my backyard while my meat smokes

Layering the Flavor

Because smoking dries food, we need to take steps to combat this, such as brining, marinating, and curing. Adding flavor to your food at the beginning is going to make a huge difference at the end. We slather spice rubs and pastes all over the food—and also inject flavor into the food—to add the next layer of flavor. Finally comes sauces, bastes, and spritzes—and because they're added last, these flavors are the most detectable. That's why you want to use something that complements the other flavors you've already used in previous steps.

The marinades, cures, rubs, spritzes, and more in these chapters are good starting points for each of these techniques and you can use them for years to come. But don't be afraid to add your own personal touches or make adjustments according to your likes and dislikes. This is your rodeo and you call the shots.

Brines, Marinades & Cures

Slowly smoking meat—whether beef or poultry—is a slamming way to enhance the natural flavors of your beast of choice and it's natural to want to build on those flavors. Brines, marinades, and cures help do that.

Layering and building flavors are skills that needs constant practice. You'll never know all the possible flavor combinations out there, but don't worry—you'll have a good time experimenting. I've provided you with several recipes for layering flavors with suggested pairings at the end of this chapter, but ultimately, because you know your likes and dislikes better than anyone, go with what sounds good to you. Just don't get too carried away because the goal is to enhance the meat's flavor, not mask it with seasonings.

Take your time with the flavoring steps and think them through. Make sure the next step complements the last step. If you're really into layering flavors, keep a smoking journal. (See Chapter 6 for an example.) Write down what you do each time to remember what worked so you can build on it. Be sure to also jot down what didn't work so you don't do that again! The day you were inspired to add Dr Pepper to a marinade is as important as the day you oversalted the chicken. Each note will make you a better flavor specialist.

Brine Recipes

Brines are salty solutions that help lean meats hold their moisture as well as stay juicy and tender during cooking. They often have other components, such as beer, sugar, herbs, and spices, but they don't add much flavor to the end result. Salt is what penetrates and softens the protein strands, making the meat moist and tender. Lean meats without much marbling, notably poultry and pork, will hold their moisture and be more tender if brined before cooking—even if they're overcooked. Because chicken and turkey are so lean, I almost always recommend brining them. Otherwise, the length of time needed for smoking could severely dry them out.

Salt in a brine draws out the water content in the meat. It will then dissolve in the natural water content of the meat while softening its proteins. A change occurs in the cells of the meat as it absorbs salt through brining. Because it will first expel and then draw and hold more water than it originally contained, the meat stays moist during a long smoke.

Always use a container large enough to keep the meat submerged in the brine. You need to weigh down the meat so it's constantly submerged because any exposed meat will breed bacteria. Position a heavy plate right side up over the meat or top with a heavy, moisture-proof object—such as a clean, foil-lined brick or a large can of tomatoes—to weigh down your meats in the brine.

Most brine times range from 12 to 24 hours. This is relative to how long it takes the brine to penetrate into and break down the meat tissues. Here's a trick you can use to save time and refrigerator space: By injecting the brine into several different areas in the meat, you can cut hours off the brine time. The time varies depending on the cut and the size of the meat, but a brine-injected chicken needs about 20 minutes and a pork shoulder will need about 4 hours—but that's much faster than submerging for 24 hours. (See Chapter 8 to learn more about injecting meat.)

Timing your brine depends on the type of protein. Fish should be brined no longer than 30 to 90 minutes because it will become too salty. Most meats in the 6- to 10-pound (2.7 to 4.5kg) range will do fine with an overnight brining of 12 to 18 hours. Large cuts of meat, such as turkeys, brisket, and shoulders, need a combination of injection and submersion, and they can be held for 18 to 24 hours (but no longer!). Brining for too long will result in the opposite of what you're going for. Eventually, the salt will draw out all the water from the meat cells and you'll end up with a very dry, overly salty dinner. Refer to the following table for how long to brine different meats.

The standard ratio of a brine shouldn't exceed ½ cup of salt to 4 cups of liquid. Always rinse meat under cold running water to wash off excess salt and dry with paper towels before proceeding with the next flavoring step.

Timing Guidelines for Brining

Type of Protein	Cut	Weight	Time
Beef			
	Back ribs	1.5 to 2.5lb (680g to 1.2kg)	none
	Short ribs	1 to 2lb (450g to 1kg)	none
	Tenderloin (whole)	2lb (1kg)	none
	Tri-tip roast	2 to 3lb (1 to 1.4kg)	none
	Top sirloin roast	10lb (4.5kg)	none
	Prime rib roast	4 to 6lb (1.8 to 2.7kg)	none
	Brisket (whole)	8 to 12lb (3.6 to 5.4kg)	24 to 48 hours
	Brisket (half)	4 to 6lb (1.8 to 2.7kg)	24 hours
	Flank steak	2lb (1kg)	48 hours
	Steak (2 inches [5cm] thick)	12 to 16oz (340 to 450g)	none
Veal			
	Chop	8 to 12oz (225 to 340g)	none
Pork			
	Loin	3 to 5lb (1.4 to 2.3kg)	24 to 36 hours
	Shoulder	6 to 8lb (2.7 to 3.6kg)	24 to 48 hours
	Ribs	1.5 to 3.5lb (680g to 1.6kg)	12 hours
	Tenderloin	0.5 to 2lb (225g to 1kg)	12 hours
	Belly	10 to 12lb (4.5 to 5.4kg)	24 to 48 hours
Lamb			
	Rack	1 to 2lb (450g to 1kg)	none
	Leg (boneless)	4 to 9lb (1.8 to 4.1kg)	none
	Shoulder	1 to 2lb (450g to 1kg)	none

(continues)

Timing Guidelines for Brining *(continued)*

Type of Protein	Cut	Weight	Time
Chicken			
	Whole	4 to 6lb (1.8 to 2.7kg)	24 hours
	Half	2 to 3lb (1 to 1.4kg)	24 hours
	Breasts (boneless)	4 to 8oz (110 to 225g)	12 hours
	Breasts (bone-in)	6 to 12oz (170 to 340g)	12 hours
	Thighs	5 to 8oz (140 to 225g)	12 hours
	Legs	4 to 8oz (110 to 225g)	12 hours
	Wings (about 12)	1 to 2lb (450g to 1kg)	12 hours
Turkey			
	Whole	14 to 18lb (6.4 to 8.2kg)	24 to 48 hours
	Breast (boneless)	5 to 7lb (2.3 to 3.2kg)	12 to 24 hours
	Leg/thigh	2 to 4lb (1 to 1.8kg)	12 to 24 hours
Duck			
	Whole	4 to 6lb (1.8 to 2.7kg)	24 hours
	Breast (boneless)	5 to 7oz (140 to 200g)	12 hours
Other Poultry			
	Cornish hen	1 to 2lb (450g to 1kg)	12 hours
	Quail	6 to 10oz (170 to 285g)	6 to 8 hours
Fish & Seafood			
	Fish (fillet or steak)	8 to 16oz (225 to 450g)	30 minutes
	Shellfish	1 to 2lb (450g to 1kg)	30 minutes
	Salmon (whole)	5 to 8lb (2.3 to 3.2kg)	12 hours
	Salmon (side)	2 to 5lb (1 to 2.3kg)	12 hours
	Salmon (fillet)	6 to 12oz (170 to 340g)	30 minutes

Basic Brine

A standard brine consists of two main ingredients: water and salt. I prefer kosher salt over iodized salt because I find it gives the brine a cleaner, less salty finish. A good rule of thumb is for every 4 cups of water, add ¼ cup of kosher salt, but be careful when scaling up this recipe because it can easily become too salty.

Prep Time	Cook Time	Yield
5 minutes	30 minutes	8 cups

8 cups cold water
½ cup kosher salt
¼ cup granulated sugar

1. In a large stockpot on the stovetop over high heat, add the water. Cover the pot and bring the water to a rolling boil.

2. Stir in the salt and sugar until dissolved. Return to a boil, then remove the pot from the heat.

3. Allow the brine to cool to room temperature. Cover and refrigerate until chilled through. Use this brine with pork or poultry.

Apple & Honey Brine

Salt and water sometimes just aren't enough! I find that apple and honey add a little sweetness to pork or poultry. Plus, some fresh herbs make all the difference.

Prep Time	Cook Time	Yield
20 minutes	40 minutes	12 cups

8 cups cold water

6 cups apple juice

¾ cup kosher salt

½ cup honey

¼ cup freshly cracked black peppercorns

¼ cup chopped fresh parsley leaves

8 garlic cloves, chopped

1 medium sweet onion, chopped

1 cinnamon stick (3 inches [7.5cm] long)

3 sprigs of fresh sage or 3 tbsp dried sage leaves

2 sprigs of fresh thyme or 2 tbsp dried thyme leaves

1 tbsp crushed red pepper flakes

1 tsp cumin seeds

1. In a large stockpot on the stovetop over high heat, combine the water and apple juice. Cover the pot and bring the mixture to a rolling boil.

2. Stir in the salt, honey, peppercorns, parsley, garlic, onion, cinnamon stick, sage, thyme, red pepper flakes, and cumin seeds. Return to a boil, then remove the pot from the heat.

3. Allow the brine to cool to room temperature. Cover and refrigerate until chilled through. Use this brine with pork or poultry.

Mango & Citrus Brine

This brine is chock-full of fresh fruit, making it pretty intense. All those bright and fresh flavors marry beautifully with the smoke to make a memorable meal. Enjoy!

Prep Time	Cook Time	Yield
45 minutes	40 minutes	16 cups

8 cups cold water

4 cups ginger ale (about two 12oz [350ml] cans)

2 cups mango juice or purée

3 medium oranges, quartered

3 medium lemons, quartered

3 medium limes, quartered

3 green onions, chopped

3 to 5 red Thai or bird's-eye chili peppers, chopped

¾ cup kosher salt or table salt

½ cup firmly packed light brown sugar

¼ bunch of fresh thyme

¼ bunch of fresh cilantro

2 tbsp freshly ground black pepper

2 pieces of fresh ginger (3 inches [7.5cm] long each), sliced

1. In a large stockpot on the stovetop over high heat, combine the water, ginger ale, and mango juice. Cover the pot and bring the mixture to a rolling boil.

2. Stir in the oranges, lemons, limes, green onions, chili peppers, salt, brown sugar, thyme, cilantro, black pepper, and ginger. Return to a boil, then remove pot from the heat.

3. Allow the brine to cool to room temperature. Cover and refrigerate until chilled through. Use this brine with pork, poultry, and seafood.

Maple & Whiskey Brine

The flavors of maple and whiskey work wonderfully together. Use a whiskey that's a little sweeter, such as bourbon or a Tennessee whiskey.

Prep Time	Cook Time	Yield
10 minutes	30 minutes	12 cups

12 cups cold water

4 cups Tennessee whiskey

2 cups maple syrup

½ cup firmly packed light brown sugar

2 tbsp mustard seeds

2 tbsp freshly ground black pepper

1 tbsp cracked coriander seeds

4 garlic cloves, minced

¾ cup kosher salt

1. In a large stockpot saucepan on the stovetop over high heat, combine the water, Tennessee whiskey, maple syrup, brown sugar, mustard seeds, pepper, coriander seeds, and garlic. Cover the pot and bring the mixture to a rolling boil.

2. Stir in the salt until dissolved. Return to a boil, then remove the pot from the heat.

3. Allow the brine to cool to room temperature. Cover and refrigerate until chilled through. Use this brine with beef, game, poultry, and pork, especially brisket, tri-tip steak, and pork loin.

Recipe Note: Boiling whiskey in the brine cooks off the alcohol, which produces a less boozy flavor. If the kick of alcohol is what you're looking for, add the whiskey after the salt and then immediately remove the pot from the heat.

Marinade Recipes

Marinades will tenderize meats, but they only really penetrate about ⅛ inch (3mm) into the flesh. That's why tough cuts get a little longer marinating time—it's the best way to ensure you get a tender result. Keeping meat in a marinade longer isn't going to help— it's actually going to make it worse. After a certain point, the marinade will work against the meat by drawing out all the moisture, creating a tough and grainy texture. Refer to the following table for how long to keep meats in marinades.

A good marinade can add some good, strong flavor though. These flavors will develop in the refrigerator, but they also continue to develop during the smoking process. Fish and poultry will absorb more flavor from a marinade than denser cuts, such as beef, pork, or lamb.

Marinades always include salt and some type of acid. The acidic component can be as simple as lemon juice or it can be wine, vinegar, other citrus juices, alcohols, or even some dairy products, such as yogurt or buttermilk. Sugar and honey or other sweet ingredients aid in balancing out the acidic ingredients and also help produce a flavorful crust on the surface of the smoked meat. Of course, you also need other aromatic flavors, such as oils, herbs, spices, garlic, and/or any other flavoring agents that strike your fancy.

You can (and should!) bring out your best friend the injector to add flavor deep into the meat. (See Chapter 8 for more on injectors.) You can even periodically inject during a long smoke to help keep the meat moist. For food safety, never inject marinade into the meat during the last half hour of the smoke or baste with it during the last 10 minutes to avoid any possibility of bacterial contamination.

Timing Guidelines for Marinating

Type of Protein	Cut	Weight	Time
Beef			
	Back ribs	1.5 to 2.5lb (680g to 1.2kg)	24 hours
	Short ribs	1 to 2lb (450g to 1kg)	24 hours
	Tenderloin (whole)	2lb (1kg)	24 hours
	Tri-tip roast	2 to 3lb (1 to 1.4kg)	24 hours
	Top sirloin roast	10lb (4.5kg)	24 to 48 hours
	Prime rib roast	4 to 6lb (1.8 to 2.7kg)	24 to 48 hours
	Brisket (whole)	8 to 12lb (3.6 to 5.4kg)	24 hours
	Brisket (half)	4 to 6lb (1.8 to 2.7kg)	24 hours
	Flank steak	2lb (1kg)	48 hours
	Steak (2 inches [5cm] thick)	12 to 16oz (340 to 450g)	8 hours
Veal			
	Chop	8 to 12oz (225 to 340g)	4 to 6 hours
Pork			
	Loin	3 to 5lb (1.4 to 2.3kg)	24 hours
	Shoulder	6 to 8lb (2.7 to 3.6kg)	24 hours
	Ribs	1.5 to 3.5lb (680g to 1.6kg)	12 hours
	Tenderloin	0.5 to 2lb (225g to 1kg)	12 hours
	Belly	10 to 12lb (4.5 to 5.4kg)	24 hours
Lamb			
	Rack	1 to 2lb (450g to 1kg)	6 to 8 hours
	Leg (boneless)	4 to 9lb (1.8 to 4.1kg)	24 hours
	Shoulder	1 to 2lb (450g to 1kg)	24 hours

Type of Protein	Cut	Weight	Time
Chicken			
	Whole	4 to 6lb (1.8 to 2.7kg)	24 hours
	Half	2 to 3lb (1 to 1.4kg)	24 hours
	Breasts (boneless)	4 to 8oz (110 to 225g)	6 to 8 hours
	Breasts (bone-in)	6 to 12oz (170 to 340g)	6 to 8 hours
	Thighs	5 to 8oz (140 to 225g)	6 to 8 hours
	Legs	4 to 8oz (110 to 225g)	6 to 8 hours
	Wings (about 12)	1 to 2lb (450g to 1kg)	6 to 8 hours
Turkey			
	Whole	14 to 18lb (6.4 to 8.2kg)	24 hours
	Breast (boneless)	5 to 7lb (2.3 to 3.2kg)	12 hours
	Leg/thigh	2 to 4lb (1 to 1.8kg)	12 to 24 hours
Duck			
	Whole	4 to 6lb (1.8 to 2.7kg)	24 hours
	Breast (boneless)	5 to 7oz (140 to 200g)	12 hours
Other Poultry			
	Cornish hen	1 to 2lb (450g to 1kg)	6 to 8 hours
	Quail	6 to 10oz (170 to 285g)	4 hours
Fish & Seafood			
	Fish (fillet or steak)	8 to 16oz (225 to 450g)	15 minutes
	Shellfish	1 to 2lb (450g to 1kg)	15 minutes
	Salmon (whole)	5 to 8lb (2.3 to 3.2kg)	2 to 3 hours
	Salmon (side)	2 to 5lb (1 to 2.3kg)	30 minutes
	Salmon (fillet)	6 to 12oz (170 to 340g)	15 minutes

Stout & Coffee Marinade

Dark ales with a smooth drinking flavor are the best choice for this marinade. The more bitter ales will overpower the meat you're smoking and the goal is to enhance the meat's flavor, not take over.

Prep Time	Cook Time	Yield
15 minutes	none	5 cups

2 (12oz [350ml]) bottles of stout beer

2 cups strong brewed coffee

12 garlic cloves, minced

1 large yellow onion, minced

½ cup Worcestershire sauce

2 tbsp fresh coarsely ground black pepper

2 tbsp dried onion flakes

¼ cup chopped fresh rosemary leaves

2 tbsp molasses

2 tbsp vegetable oil

1 tbsp kosher salt

1 tbsp grainy Dijon mustard

1. In a large bowl, combine the beer, coffee, garlic, onion, Worcestershire sauce, pepper, onion flakes, rosemary, molasses, vegetable oil, salt, and Dijon mustard. Mix until well combined and the salt has dissolved.

2. Tightly cover the bowl and store in the fridge for up to 1 week. Use this marinade with red meats, especially tri-tip steak, picanha sirloin cap, and dinosaur ribs.

Cuban Mojo Marinade

Seville oranges give this marinade a true Cuban flavor. The robust flavors of the cumin and red pepper flakes make a great combination for a marinade, but it's the addition of citrus that turns this into a real tropical experience.

Prep Time	Cook Time	Yield
20 minutes	none	2 cups

1 cup freshly squeezed Seville orange juice

¼ cup freshly squeezed lemon juice

¼ cup olive oil

1 head of fresh garlic, finely minced

½ cup chopped fresh oregano leaves

2 tsp granulated sugar

2 tsp freshly ground black pepper

1 tsp ground cumin

1 tsp kosher salt

1 tsp crushed red pepper flakes

1. In a large bowl, combine the orange juice, lemon juice, olive oil, garlic, oregano, sugar, pepper, cumin, salt, and red pepper flakes. Mix until well combined.

2. Tightly cover the bowl and store in the fridge for up to 1 week. Use this marinade with chicken and seafood.

Variation: Also known as a bitter orange or a sour orange, a Seville orange works best for this recipe. If you can't find a Seville orange, replace it with ¾ cup of freshly squeezed orange juice and ¼ cup of freshly squeezed lime juice.

Korean Bulgogi Marinade

The combination of hot chilis and soy sauce with the sweetness of hoisin sauce and mirin makes this marinade very spicy, but you can control the level of heat by adjusting the amounts of spicy ingredients. For a tame marinade, reduce the amount of fresh chilis, chili sauce, and/or hot sauce. If you like it crazy-spicy, just add more of all those ingredients—but be careful not to pop your top!

Prep Time	Cook Time	Yield
15 minutes	none	8 cups

½ cup naturally brewed soy sauce

1 cup hoisin sauce

2 green onions, finely chopped

2 to 3 red Thai or bird's-eye chili peppers, minced

¼ cup minced fresh garlic

¼ cup minced fresh ginger

¼ cup mirin (rice wine)

3 tbsp light brown sugar

1 tbsp fresh coarsely ground black pepper

2 tbsp sambal oelek (red chili sauce)

1 tsp sesame oil

1 tsp sesame seeds

1. In a large bowl, combine the soy sauce, hoisin sauce, green onions, chili peppers, garlic, ginger, mirin, brown sugar, black pepper, sambal oelek, sesame oil, and sesame seeds. Mix until well combined.

2. Tightly cover the bowl and store in the fridge for up to 2 weeks. Use this marinade with beef, pork, and chicken.

Smoked Garlic Marinade

Forget adding liquid smoke to your marinades—this is the real deal! Smoking the garlic adds an intense, smoky dimension to the marinade and therefore to whatever you're marinating. Fresh herbs balance everything by adding a touch of sweetness.

Prep Time	Cook Time	Yield
15 minutes	none	2 cups

1 cup vegetable juice cocktail (such as V8, Mott's Garden Cocktail, or Heinz Vegetable Cocktail)

½ cup balsamic vinegar

¼ cup chopped fresh basil leaves

¼ cup chopped fresh oregano leaves

¼ cup chopped fresh parsley leaves

¼ cup chopped fresh thyme leaves

24 smoked garlic cloves, puréed

2 tbsp olive oil

2 tbsp honey

1 tsp crushed red pepper flakes

1 tsp kosher salt

1 tsp freshly ground black pepper

1. In a large bowl, combine the vegetable juice cocktail, balsamic vinegar, basil, oregano, parsley, thyme, garlic, olive oil, honey, red pepper flakes, salt, and pepper. Mix until well combined.

2. Tightly cover the bowl and store in the fridge for up to 1 week. Use this marinade with ribs, pork chops, chicken, and turkey.

Recipe Note: To make smoked garlic, preheat the smoker to 220°F (105°C) and use oak, mesquite, pecan, hickory, or apple wood. Place the 24 garlic cloves on a smoker rack. Place the rack in the smoker and smoke the garlic for 3 hours.

Gin & Tonic Marinade

With its refreshingly sweet, fruity flavor, this marinade is so yummy, you might be tempted to drink it! It also doubles as a great dressing for grilled vegetables and fresh green salads.

Prep Time	Cook Time	Yield
15 minutes	none	3 cups

1 cup herbaceous gin

2 cups tonic water

½ cup chopped fresh herbs (such as mint, parsley, thyme, and cilantro leaves)

¼ cup freshly squeezed lemon juice

¼ cup olive oil

¼ cup honey

4 garlic cloves, minced

1 stalk of lemongrass, smashed and finely chopped

1 green onion, chopped

1 red chili pepper, minced

1 tsp minced ginger

1 tsp kosher salt

1 tsp freshly ground black pepper

1. In a large bowl, combine the gin, tonic, mixed herbs, lemon juice, olive oil, honey, garlic, lemongrass, green onion, red chili pepper, ginger, salt, and pepper. Mix until well combined.

2. Tightly cover the bowl and store in the fridge for up to 1 week. Use this marinade with fish, poultry, and pork.

Whiskey & Cola Marinade

One of my favorite beverages is a whiskey on the rocks with a splash of cola. In this marinade, the cola quickly breaks down the fibers of the meat to tenderize it and the whiskey imparts a rich smoky flavor.

Prep Time	Cook Time	Yield
15 minutes	none	2 cups

2 (12oz [350ml]) cans of cola

1 cup Tennessee whiskey

¼ cup chopped fresh parsley leaves

3 tbsp Worcestershire sauce

2 tbsp vegetable oil

2 tbsp chopped fresh rosemary leaves

1 tsp freshly ground black pepper

6 garlic cloves, minced

dash of hot sauce

pinch of ground cinnamon

1. In a large bowl, combine the cola, Tennessee whiskey, parsley, Worcestershire sauce, vegetable oil, rosemary, pepper, garlic, hot sauce, and cinnamon. Mix until well combined.

2. Tightly cover the bowl and store in the fridge for up to 2 weeks. Use this marinade with tough cuts, such as beef ribs, short ribs, brisket, and skirt and flank steaks.

Variation: Many soft drinks make great marinade bases. Try ginger ale, orange soda, lemon-lime soda, or even root beer!

Cure Recipes

Curing is a term basically used for saving or preserving meat. It covers such processes as drying, salting, and smoking. Applying a dry cure to meats is a way to control moisture and flavor. When applied to homemade meat products, the term often refers to preserving with salt and nitrite. I don't like using nitrites nor do I care for some of the other commercial preservatives, such as ascorbate and erythorbate. Meat cured only with salt has a better flavor and will have a slightly darker color than commercially cured products, but at least it's chemical free. The curing compound penetrates through meat and draws out moisture. This reduces the weight of the end product, which concentrates the flavor and results in a darker color.

There are quite a few factors to consider when determining a cure's formulation and the amount of time to let a meat stand in the cure. A higher salt content in the cure mixture will speed up the process, but the larger the piece of meat, the longer it will take to cure. A fattier cut of meat will also increase the amount of time it needs to sit in the cure. And, of course, the moisture content of the specific type and cut of meat will impact the amount of time it takes to cure sufficiently. The more moisture a meat has to begin with, the longer it will take. Acid or alkaline levels in the meat will also affect the amount of time it needs to stay in the cure—a lower pH level will result in a faster cure—but we don't need to go quite that deep. The following table gives guidelines for how long to cure different meats.

The longer you want to keep the meat, the longer it will need to stay in the cure. Meat cured strictly for preservation can be hung to dry for as long as a year. The result is a piece of meat that will be safe at room temperature for lengthy periods of time, such as Italian prosciutto. However, the cures in this book are basically just another form of flavoring. When it comes down to it, we're using a mixture that includes the seasonings of a rub and the salt of a brine. We aren't going to leave the meat in a cure anywhere near as long as we would if we needed to preserve it for a year. Our purpose is to reduce the moisture in the meat and create a concentrated flavor that complements a smoky flavor. I encourage you to give it a try. Once you've mastered a couple recipes, you might be inspired to try your own!

Timing Guidelines for Curing

Type of Protein	Cut	Weight	Time
Beef			
	Back ribs	1.5 to 2.5lb (680g to 1.2kg)	none
	Short ribs	1 to 2lb (450g to 1kg)	none
	Tenderloin, whole	2lb (1kg)	none
	Tri-tip roast	2 to 3lb (1 to 1.4kg)	none
	Top sirloin roast	10lb (4.5kg)	none
	Prime rib roast	4 to 6lb (1.8 to 2.7kg)	none
	Brisket (whole)	8 to 12lb (3.6 to 5.4kg)	8 to 12 days
	Brisket (half)	4 to 6lb (1.8 to 2.7kg)	6 to 8 days
	Flank steak	2lb (1kg)	none
	Steak (2 inches [5cm] thick)	12 to 16oz (340 to 450g)	none
Veal			
	Chop	8 to 12oz (225 to 340g)	none
Pork			
	Loin	3 to 5lb (1.4 to 2.3kg)	none
	Shoulder	6 to 8lb (2.7 to 3.6kg)	none
	Ribs	1.5 to 3.5lb (680g to 1.6kg)	none
	Tenderloin	0.5 to 2lb (225g to 1kg)	3 to 6 days
	Belly	10 to 12lb (4.5 to 5.4kg)	5 to 10 days
Lamb			
	Rack	1 to 2lb (450g to 1kg)	none
	Leg (boneless)	4 to 9lb (1.8 to 4.1kg)	none
	Shoulder	1 to 2lb (450g to 1kg)	none

(continues)

Timing Guidelines for Curing *(continued)*

Type of Protein	Cut	Weight	Time
Chicken			
	Whole	4 to 6lb (1.8 to 2.7kg)	none
	Half	2 to 3lb (1 to 1.4kg)	none
	Breasts (boneless)	4 to 8oz (110 to 225g)	none
	Breasts (bone-in)	6 to 12oz (170 to 340g)	none
	Thighs	5 to 8oz (140 to 225g)	none
	Legs	4 to 8oz (110 to 225g)	none
	Wings (about 12)	1 to 2lb (450g to 1kg)	none
Turkey			
	Whole	14 to 18lb (6.4 to 8.2kg)	none
	Breast (boneless)	5 to 7lb (2.3 to 3.2kg)	6 to 8 days
	Leg/thigh	2 to 4lb (1 to 1.8kg)	none
Duck			
	Whole	4 to 6lb (1.8 to 2.7kg)	none
	Breast (boneless)	5 to 7oz (140 to 200g)	4 to 6 days
Other Poultry			
	Cornish hen	1 to 2lb (450g to 1kg)	none
	Quail	6 to 10oz (170 to 285g)	none
Fish & Seafood			
	Fish (fillet or steak)	8 to 16oz (225 to 450g)	2 to 4 days
	Shellfish	1 to 2lb (450g to 1kg)	2 to 4 days
	Salmon (whole)	5 to 8lb (2.3 to 3.2kg)	6 to 10 days
	Salmon (side)	2 to 5lb (1 to 2.3kg)	3 to 4 days
	Salmon (fillet)	6 to 12oz (170 to 340g)	2 days

Basic Cure

Try using flavored salts in your cure recipe to change the flavor of your meat. Smoked salt, lemon salt, and chili-infused salts are just three of the many varieties of flavored salts available.

Prep Time	Cook Time	Yield
5 minutes	none	1½ cups

1 cup kosher salt

½ cup granulated sugar

2 tsp freshly ground white pepper

2 tsp celery salt

1. In a small bowl, combine the salt, sugar, white pepper, and celery salt. Mix until well combined.

2. Store the cure in an airtight container in a cool, dry, and dark place for up to 4 months. Use this cure with fish, chicken, pork chops, pork belly, and duck.

Fish Cure

Sweet and salty flavors are blended with the heat of black pepper and the smokiness of alcohol. This cure works well with salmon and other fish or shellfish. If you'd like to omit the alcohol from this recipe, replace the same amount with a juice that isn't too acidic, such as apple juice.

Prep Time	Cook Time	Yield
15 minutes	none	5 cups

3 cups kosher salt

4 cups chopped fresh dill

1 cup granulated sugar

¼ cup fresh coarsely ground black pepper

3 tbsp grated lemon zest

½ cup cognac, brandy, Armagnac, rum, or whiskey

1. In a medium bowl, combine the salt, dill, sugar, pepper, and lemon zest. Mix until well combined.

2. Generously rub the cure over the surface of 4 pounds (1.8kg) of fish and drizzle the cognac over the top. Cover the bowl and refrigerate for 2 days for every 1 inch (2.5cm) of thickness. Use this cure with salmon, tuna, trout, mackerel, and halibut.

Variation: For **Margarita Cure**, use lime zest for the lemon zest, fresh cilantro for the fresh dill, and *reposado* tequila for the cognac. Or for **Harvey Wallbanger Cure**, use orange zest for the lemon zest, use equal parts thyme and parsley for the dill, and an orange-flavored vodka for drizzling.

Aromatic Cure

Pairing allspice and thyme truly enhances the flavor of mild proteins. There's just something about warm spices with a smoky flavor that warms my heart—and belly!

Prep Time	Cook Time	Yield
15 minutes	none	2½ cups

2 cups kosher salt

¾ cup granulated sugar

1 tbsp freshly ground black pepper

1 tbsp freshly ground white pepper

1 tbsp onion powder

1 tbsp garlic powder

1 tbsp celery salt

1 tbsp ground allspice

1 tsp dried thyme leaves

1 tsp ground ginger

1 tsp ground cinnamon

½ tsp ground nutmeg

1. In a medium bowl, combine the salt, sugar, black pepper, white pepper, onion powder, garlic powder, celery salt, allspice, thyme, ginger, cinnamon, and nutmeg. Mix until well combined.

2. Store the cure in an airtight container in a cool, dry, and dark place for up to 4 months. Use this cure with poultry, halibut, and pork belly.

Rubs, Pastes & Injections

Although you can buy rubs, pastes, and injections, as you'll see in this chapter, making your own is simple—and fun!

Rub Recipes

A rub is a dry mixture of spices, dried herbs, sugar, and salt that gets massaged into meats before smoking to add flavor. Its purpose is to enhance the flavor of meat without overwhelming or masking its natural flavor. Rubs tend to have salt and sugar as their base and commercial rubs in particular are very high in salt—up to 50%. I've kept the sugar and salt low in these rub recipes so they have more versatility. Too much salt will just dry out the meat, and if used on a brined piece of meat, that rub could make the food entirely too salty. Besides, salt's not that good for us. Sugar is used to balance the flavors of the other ingredients, but I don't like to use too much because it can cause the outside of the meat to char. I like to keep the dry herb content low for the same reason.

You should apply a rub to meat in abundance and massage it with a bit of vigor. Take care not to have uneven areas of heavily rubbed flesh and bare spots. Cover the meat evenly and completely—even the back side of ribs where it's all bone. Gently push your fingers under the skin of poultry to rub directly onto the flesh because the seasoning won't go through the skin to flavor the meat itself. But also rub the skin for a crispy flavored exterior to protect the flavored flesh beneath. Set aside rubbed meats for anywhere from 30 minutes to overnight to allow the spices to permeate the meat.

The following table lists some of the common ingredients I always keep in my kitchen. It's meant to be a starting point and inspiration for your own spice mixtures, but as I say over and over, your only limitation is your own imagination. Some of the best flavors I found by accident. For example, I learned that mayonnaise slathered all over a salmon fillet before putting it in the smoker or peanut butter used as the base for a pork loin paste will create flavors that will blow you away! Experimenting also taught me that maraschino cherry juice also makes a great addition to a pork paste.

Smoker's Basic Spice Rack

Dry Ingredients	Wet Ingredients
allspice (ground or whole)	anchovies
anise seed (ground or whole)	apple cider vinegar or other vinegars
black pepper (ground or whole)	assorted sodas and colas
cayenne (ground)	beer
celery salt	bourbon or other whiskeys
chili powder	chipotle peppers in adobo sauce
cinnamon (ground and sticks)	hoisin sauce
coriander (ground or whole)	honey
cumin (ground or whole)	horseradish
curry powder	lemon juice
dried ancho pepper	lime juice
dried chipotle powder	maple syrup
dried lemon zest	mixed fresh herbs
dried oregano leaves	mustards (Dijon, yellow, spicy)
dried sage leaves	oil (vegetable and olive)
dried thyme leaves	orange juice
mustard powder	oyster sauce
garlic powder or granulate	puréed garlic
ginger (ground)	puréed jalapeño
lemon pepper	puréed onion
nutmeg (ground or whole)	soy sauce
onion powder or granulate	wine (red and white)
salt (kosher and sea)	Worcestershire sauce
sugar (granulated and brown)	

You can even go so far as to toast and grind your own spices. Toasting whole spices before grinding is always a good idea—it releases all the natural oils in the spices and allows their true flavors to come through. Purchase raw spices at a reputable store where you can be sure they're fresh. Low and slow also applies here. Keep the temperature of your oven no higher than 325°F (160°C), but I prefer 275°F (135°C). Spread the spices in a thin, even layer on a baking sheet, ensuring to not overload the tray. Roast them just until you begin to smell the fragrance of the spices. Don't burn them! Because there's no salvation for burnt spices, if you take them too far in the oven, just throw them away and start again. Let them cool to room temperature and grind them. You can use a mortar and pestle, but a good coffee grinder is also handy for this purpose. Just make sure you have one dedicated to spices and one dedicated to coffee—unless you like cumin-flavored coffee!

Dried spices can be stored in an airtight container for up to 9 months in a cool, dark place. Because spices will lose their intensity over time, you might want to consider grinding them as you need them. Dried herbs should be stored for no more than 3 to 4 months.

There are a few things to remember when you decide to create your own dry rub recipes: Start simply because balance is key. You don't want one flavor to take over the whole mixture—you want a nice combination of ingredients to make a new flavor. A dry rub must never contain anything fresh, such as chopped herbs or minced garlic. Fresh ingredients will decrease the longevity of the mixture and the flavors will continue to develop and become too strong. So now let's get into the rub recipes.

Beginner's Rub

Use this recipe as an outline for creating your own rub or you can merely modify this recipe to suit your preferences. Stick to the proportions, but try adding creative variety to the specified ingredients, such as using hickory or smoked salt, cane or demerara sugar, different herbs and spices, more or less heat, and so on. Be brave, but remember our mantra: Less is more. Store rubs in an airtight container for 3 to 6 months in a cool, dark place. You don't want them hanging around any longer than that because the flavors in spices tend to diminish over time.

Prep Time	Cook Time	Yield
15 minutes	none	n/a

1 tsp kosher salt

1 tsp granulated sugar

2 tbsp sweet paprika

1 tbsp mustard powder

1 tsp freshly ground black pepper

1 tsp ground cayenne

1 tsp garlic powder

1 tsp onion powder

2 tsp dry herb or spice #1

2 tsp dry herb or spice #2

2 tsp dry herb or spice #3

Basic Barbecue Rub

Nothing beats a good dry rub. This is a recipe that's a good place to start for making your first barbecue rub. It goes great on pork ribs and chops as well as on chicken, turkey, shrimp, scallops, and even popcorn.

Prep Time	Cook Time	Yield
15 minutes	none	2½ cups

½ cup paprika

¼ cup chili powder

3 tbsp kosher salt

2 tbsp ground coriander

2 tbsp garlic powder

2 tbsp light brown sugar

2 tbsp celery salt

2 tbsp mustard powder

1 tbsp freshly ground black pepper

1 tbsp dried thyme leaves

1 tbsp dried oregano leaves

1 tbsp ground cumin

1 tbsp ground cayenne

1. In a large bowl, combine the paprika, chili powder, salt, coriander, garlic powder, brown sugar, celery salt, mustard powder, blank pepper, thyme, oregano, cumin, and cayenne. Mix until well combined.

2. Store the rub in an airtight container in a cool, dry, and dark place for up to 4 months. Use this rub with ribs, pork, chicken, and turkey.

Cajun Rub

Louisiana isn't shy about its culinary delights and Cajun dishes especially burst with great flavors. This rub will give food a smoky twist straight from the land of bayous before it even hits the smoker and the cayenne will add a solid kick of heat.

Prep Time	Cook Time	Yield
15 minutes	none	1½ cups

3 tbsp ground cayenne

2 tbsp kosher salt

2 tbsp sweet paprika

1 tbsp smoked paprika

1 tbsp granulated sugar

1 tbsp hot mustard powder

1 tbsp freshly ground black pepper

1 tbsp freshly ground white pepper

1 tbsp garlic powder

1 tbsp onion powder

2 tsp ground cumin

1 tsp dried oregano leaves

1 tsp dried thyme leaves

1 tsp ground coriander

½ tsp dried sage leaves

1. In a large bowl, combine the cayenne, salt, sweet paprika, smoked paprika, sugar, mustard powder, black pepper, white pepper, garlic powder, onion powder, cumin, oregano, thyme, coriander, and sage. Mix until well combined.

2. Store the rub in an airtight container in a cool, dry, and dark place for up to 4 months. Use this rub with veal, pork, chicken, fish, beef, and lamb.

Garlic & Herb Rub

Because most rubs are dry, they have a long shelf life. This rub won't last nearly as long, but the flavors are great, adding brightness that dry rubs don't, so give it a shot. It rocks!

Prep Time	Cook Time	Yield
15 minutes	none	¾ cup

½ cup coarsely ground sea salt

2 tbsp chopped fresh chives

2 tbsp chopped fresh oregano leaves

2 tbsp chopped fresh parsley leaves

2 tbsp chopped fresh thyme leaves

1 tbsp freshly ground black pepper

1 tbsp freshly ground white pepper

1 tbsp granulated sugar

8 garlic cloves, minced

1. In a large bowl, combine the salt, chives, oregano, parsley, thyme, black pepper, white pepper, sugar, and garlic. Mix and toss until well combined.

2. Store the rub in an airtight container in the refrigerator for up to 5 days. Use this rub with beef, veal, lamb, and chicken.

Variation: Change up the types or quantities of the fresh herbs to create new flavor combos. For example, try cilantro, mint, basil, sage, thyme, and oregano. Be creative!

Jamaican Jerk Rub

If you've been to Jamaica and had a real taste of jerk-seasoned food, you know what the flavor is all about. The heat from Scotch bonnet peppers, green onion, thyme, and Jamaican allspice is what makes jerk food.

Prep Time	Cook Time	Yield
15 minutes	none	1 cup

2 tbsp ground Jamaican allspice (pimento pepper) or another ground allspice

2 tbsp ground cayenne

2 tbsp habañero pepper powder or Scotch bonnet pepper powder

1 tbsp kosher salt

1 tbsp freshly ground black pepper

1 tbsp granulated sugar

1 tbsp granulated onion

1 tbsp garlic salt

1 tbsp dried thyme leaves

1 tsp mustard powder

½ tsp ground nutmeg

¼ tsp ground cinnamon

1. In a large bowl, combine the allspice, cayenne, habañero pepper powder, kosher salt, black pepper, sugar, granulated onion, garlic salt, thyme, mustard powder, nutmeg, and cinnamon. Mix until well combined.

2. Store the rub in an airtight container in a cool, dry, and dark place for up to 4 months. Use this rub with pork, chicken, and fish.

Memphis Rib Rub

In Memphis, Tennessee, ribs are traditionally served dry. That's right—without sauce. Just a great rub and sweet smoke are all you need to create some of the finest-tasting ribs in the country. Many people like saucy ribs, but a true rib lover will always be down for a tasty dry rack. Sauce is for dipping!

Prep Time	Cook Time	Yield
15 minutes	none	2 cups

½ cup paprika

3 tbsp kosher salt

2 tbsp firmly packed light brown sugar

2 tbsp onion powder

1 tbsp freshly ground black pepper

1 tbsp celery salt

2 tsp ground cayenne

2 tsp garlic powder

1 tsp dried oregano leaves

1 tsp dried thyme leaves

1 tsp ground cumin

1 tsp ground coriander

½ tsp ground allspice

1. In a large bowl, combine the paprika, kosher salt, brown sugar, onion powder, pepper, celery salt, cayenne, garlic powder, oregano, thyme, cumin, coriander, and allspice. Mix until well combined.

2. Store the rub in an airtight container in a cool, dry, and dark place for up to 4 months. Use this rub with ribs, pork butt, and chicken.

Tandoori Rub

Tandoori is an Indian dish that's traditionally grilled quickly, but I like to think that using a smoker is a great way to combine old flavors with new techniques. Make sure you rub the meat 24 hours prior to smoking to ensure you get that rich red color that's synonymous with tandoori.

Prep Time	Cook Time	Yield
15 minutes	none	2 cups

½ cup paprika

3 tbsp ground cumin

2 tbsp ground cayenne

2 tbsp ground coriander

1 tbsp kosher salt

1 tbsp granulated sugar

1 tbsp ground cardamom

1 tbsp ground cinnamon

1 tbsp freshly ground black pepper

1 tsp ground cloves

1. In a large bowl, combine the paprika, cumin, cayenne, coriander, salt, sugar, cardamom, cinnamon, pepper, and cloves. Mix until well combined.

2. Store the rub in an airtight container in a cool, dry, and dark place for up to 4 months. Use this rub with pork ribs and chicken.

Recipe Note: Combine ¼ cup of Tandoori Rub and 1 cup of plain yogurt as a marinade for chicken, pork ribs, and lamb.

Mediterranean Rub

This rub is loaded with flavorful ingredients: garlic (lots of it), red pepper, sun-dried tomatoes, onion, herbs, and fennel. The big seasoning boost comes from chicken stock powder, which really amps up the meatiness of the chicken. Because this rub is tasty and versatile, make a big batch because you're going to use it all up!

Prep Time	Cook Time	Yield
10 minutes	none	2 cups

- ½ cup granulated garlic
- ¼ cup kosher salt
- ¼ cup firmly packed light brown sugar
- 2 tbsp crushes red pepper flakes
- 2 tbsp finely chopped sun-dried tomatoes (about 3 tomatoes)
- 2 tbsp MSG-free chicken soup base powder
- 2 tbsp fresh medium-ground black pepper

- 2 tbsp granulated onion
- 1 tbsp dried parsley flakes
- 1 tbsp dried basil leaves
- 1 tbsp dried oregano leaves
- 1 tbsp coarsely ground fennel seeds
- 2 tsp dried thyme leaves
- 2 tsp ground cayenne

1. In a large bowl, combine the garlic, salt, brown sugar, red pepper flakes, sun-dried tomatoes, chicken soup powder, black pepper, onion, parsley, basil, oregano, fennel seeds, thyme, and cayenne. Mix until well combined.

2. Store the rub in an airtight container in a cool, dry, and dark place for up to 4 months. Use this rub with ribs, pork, chicken, veal, beef, fish, and seafood.

Recipe Note: Combine this rub with some olive oil and use as a paste on a rack of lamb before smoking. You can also combine this rub with olive oil and vinegar for a dressing.

Chipotle & Cinnamon Rub

Cinnamon adds a sweet and nutty flavor to your meats that's really delightful. Try this rubbed on scallops—it'll bring a whole new meaning to the word "delicious."

Prep Time	Cook Time	Yield
15 minutes	none	1 cup

½ cup ground chipotle powder

¼ cup ground cinnamon

2 tbsp sweet paprika

2 tbsp granulated sugar

2 tbsp firmly packed light brown sugar

2 tbsp ground cumin

2 tbsp ground allspice

1 tbsp ground cloves

1 tbsp ground ginger

1 tbsp garlic powder

1 tbsp kosher salt

1. In a large bowl, combine the chipotle powder, cinnamon, sweet paprika, granulated sugar, brown sugar, cumin, allspice, cloves, ginger, garlic powder, and kosher salt. Mix until well combined.

2. Store the rub in an airtight container in a cool, dry, and dark place for up to 4 months. Use this rub with chicken, ribs, pork, and seafood.

Recipe Note: Because grinding your own cinnamon sticks gives a much sweeter perfume to the rub, avoid store-bought cinnamon and go for the more natural flavor.

Cold-Smoked Sea Salt

Smoking sea salt gives it a sweet and slightly nutty flavor. This is robust and an easy way to naturally add smoke to your favorite recipes instead of using liquid smoke.

Prep Time	Smoker Temp	Smoke Time	Yield
15 minutes	125°F (50°C)	4 to 6 hours	4 cups

4 cups coarse sea salt

1. Preheat the smoker to 125°F (50°C) for cold-smoking. Spread the sea salt in an even layer on a smoker rack lined with aluminum foil.

2. Place the rack in the smoker and smoke until the salt is smoky brown and has a distinct smoke flavor, about 4 to 6 hours, gently stirring every hour. Remove the rack from the smoker and allow the salt to cool.

3. Store the salt in an airtight container in a cool, dry, and dark place for up to 4 months. Use this salt with prime rib roast, leg of lamb, steaks, chops, chicken, and turkey.

Recipe Note: Using an electric box smoker is an easy way to smoke salt. You can also smoke salt in a heavy-bottomed cast-iron pan over an open fire. Just make sure you set aside a good amount of time because it takes a while and you need to stir it frequently.

Paste Recipes

A paste is created when oil or another liquid ingredient is added to a rub. You can also specifically create a wet seasoning mixture, which is sometimes called a "wet rub" or a "slather." Pastes adhere to the meat a little better than dry rubs, but they tend to deliver a milder flavor. Pastes are commonly used on lean cuts to add moisture and flavor.

A paste is applied like a rub: thoroughly massaged into the meat with a nice, even coating. Once it's applied, place the meat in a resealable plastic bag and refrigerate for anywhere from 20 minutes (for seafood) to 24 hours (for large cuts of meat). The best paste consistency is thick enough to stay on the meat while it sits but thin enough to slather on with your hands or a mop.

Pastes should always be stored tightly covered in the refrigerator. A general rule of thumb is that pastes that contain oil should last a good 3 weeks in the fridge. Pastes without oil are usually only good for 5 to 7 days.

Hot & Spicy Barbecue Paste

Sometimes, you just want to kick it up a notch—and this paste will sure do the trick. For the best flavor and to really give your food that spicy kick, allow the meat to marinate for at least 24 hours prior to smoking. Want an extra heated boost? Try ghost, scorpion or Carolina Reaper chili peppers. But be very careful with the really seriously, really hot peppers.

Prep Time	Cook Time	Yield
30 minutes	none	1 cup

¼ cup **Memphis Rib Rub** (page 119)

4 garlic cloves, minced

3 chipotle chilies in adobo sauce, minced

2 fresh red jalapeños or red chili peppers

1 green onion, minced

2 tbsp chopped fresh parsley leaves

3 tbsp olive oil

1. In a food processor, combine the rib rub, garlic, chipotle chilies and adobo sauce, jalapeños, green onion, parsley, and olive oil. Pulse until very smooth. Add water 1 tablespoon at a time as needed.

2. Store the paste in an airtight container in the fridge for up to 1 week. Rub this paste on pork ribs, chops, and shoulders as well as on poultry.

Margarita Paste

Nothing's more refreshing than a margarita on a hot summer's day when working over a hot smoker. So while you have all the ingredients out, mix up a pitcher to enjoy with family and friends while the smoker does its thing. In this paste, the sweet, smoky flavor of tequila contrasts well with the tang of fresh lime.

Prep Time	Cook Time	Yield
30 minutes	none	1½ cups

½ cup chopped fresh cilantro leaves

¼ cup freshly squeezed lime juice

2oz (60ml) Reposado or Añejo tequila

2 to 3 jalapeños, minced

2 large garlic cloves, minced

2 tbsp kosher salt

2 tbsp olive oil

2 tbsp honey

1 tbsp firmly packed light brown sugar

1 tbsp freshly ground black pepper

1 tsp grated lime zest

1 tsp Dijon mustard

1. In a large bowl, combine the cilantro, lime juice, tequila, jalapeños, garlic, salt, olive oil, honey, brown sugar, pepper, lime zest, and mustard. Mix until well combined.

2. Store the paste in an airtight container in the refrigerator for up to 1 week. Rub this paste on chicken, pork, and seafood.

Espresso Paste

Coffee isn't just for your morning pick-me-up or to drink with cakes and pastries. The sweet and savory flavor combination of this rub is a bit out there (would you expect anything less from me?), but it's awesome—trust me!

Prep Time	Cook Time	Yield
20 minutes	none	2 cups

½ cup mocha-flavored coffee beans

¼ cup French vanilla-flavored coffee beans

6 garlic cloves, minced

½ cup chopped fresh herbs (such as parsley, sage, rosemary, and thyme leaves)

¼ cup freshly ground black pepper

¼ cup olive oil

2 tbsp molasses

2 tbsp balsamic vinegar

1 tbsp firmly packed light brown sugar

kosher salt, to taste

1. In a resealable plastic bag, combine the mocha and French vanilla coffee beans. Use a heavy-bottomed saucepan to crush the beans into small granules, but don't crush them too finely.

2. In a large bowl, combine the coffee beans, garlic, mixed herbs, pepper, olive oil, molasses, balsamic vinegar, brown sugar, and salt. Mix until well combined.

3. Tightly cover the bowl and store the paste in the fridge for up to 2 weeks. Use this paste on steaks, chops, prime rib, and rack of lamb.

Recipe Note: I find it best to make this rub at least a day ahead to allow the coffee beans to soften and release more flavor.

Injection Recipes

Injectors are sometimes called a smoker's best friend. The injector isn't just for brining and adding moisture—it also aids in the efforts to layer and enhance flavors. You can fill an injector with many different liquids. You can use the same mixture the meat was brined or marinated in to reinforce the flavor profile. Or you can use an entirely different recipe for the injection that will complement the brine, marinade, rub, and paste already used. It's all about the layers and what you like! In a barbecue competition, you'll often see the old pros injecting their championship meats during the long, slow smoke. It's because they know this is what will help bring home that title!

Chive & Butter Injection

This combination of sweet, fresh chives and rich, creamy butter will make anything more delicious. I first used this injection on slow-smoked chicken breasts and they were awesome. The key to this recipe is to let the chives steep in the melted butter. This extracts the wonderful green chlorophyll, which makes this butter bright green!

Prep Time	Cook Time	Yield
30 minutes	1 hour	1 cup

1 cup chopped fresh chives

½ tsp kosher salt

½ tsp freshly squeezed lemon juice

1 cup (2 sticks) unsalted butter

1. In a large bowl, combine the chives, salt, and lemon juice. Allow to rest until the chives soften, about 30 minutes.

2. In a medium saucepan on the stovetop over medium-low heat, melt the butter. Add the chive mixture and reduce the heat to low. Cook until the chives are very soft and fragrant, about 1 hour, stirring often.

3. Use a hand mixer to blend the mixture until smooth. Strain through a fine-mesh sieve, pushing as much of the pulp through as possible. Discard the solids.

4. Fill an injector with the mixture and plunge the needle into the meat. Press the plunger to release the mixture. Use this injection with poultry, fish, and seafood.

Variation: Replace the chives with any fresh herbs: Dill, parsley, sage, rosemary, cilantro, basil, or oregano will give your smoked foods a buttery herb boost. A simple herbed butter mixture like this one is great when injected into the breast of your holiday turkey. The increase in internal fat of the bird will make the meat moist and juicy.

Rum & Maple Injection

I love the combination of spiced rum and maple syrup. Although you're using it as an injection, you can also drizzle this mixture as a finishing touch on so many things. What enriches this injection is butter, which makes just about everything much tastier.

Prep Time	Cook Time	Yield
10 minutes	10 minutes	1 cup

1 cup maple syrup

4oz (120ml) spiced rum

2oz (60ml) freshly squeezed orange juice

½ tsp kosher salt

½ tsp fresh finely ground black pepper

1 cup (2 sticks) unsalted butter, cubed

1. In a medium saucepan on the stovetop over medium heat, combine the maple syrup, spiced rum, orange juice, salt, and pepper. Cook until steaming but not boiling. (You don't want to boil off the alcohol in the rum.)

2. Remove the pan from the heat. Whisk in the butter a couple cubes at a time until well combined.

3. Fill an injector with the mixture and plunge the needle into the meat. Press the plunger to release the mixture. Use this injection with beef, pork, and poultry.

Recipe Note: Buy real maple syrup—it's worth the coin because the flavor makes all the difference in this recipe. Stay away from the artificial table syrups—they just won't cut it.

Basting, Sauces & Spritzes

You've brined, marinated, injected, and/or rubbed your meat. Now it's time for the next step in flavor layering: basting, saucing, and spritzing. These are added at the smoker, and if done properly, they're the *pièce de résistance*.

Then again, this is also the place where a beautifully prepared piece of meat can be ruined by an improperly applied baste or sauce or even by adding anything at all— they're not always necessary. One of the places I often find I'm arguing about this is when smoking ribs. If all the other steps are done well, ribs don't always need sauce. Putting sauce on almost seems like a disguise to the meat. Sometimes, serving the sauce on the side as a dunk is the better option.

Basting with Caution

In the smoking world, a baste is usually referred to as a "mop." Every committed smoker has a few of these miniature cotton string doohickeys. The cotton strings absorb lots of liquid and gently apply the sauce to the meat's surface. You don't want to baste too often because every time the smoker's door is opened, almost 50% of the heat and smoke escapes. This causes a fluctuation in the cook time and ultimately can affect the quality of the end result. Basting or mopping isn't always necessary when you have a fatty meat with lots of marbling or a nice fat cap—unless, of course, your mop is part of your plan to build flavor. Lean meats and poultry should definitely be basted to create a nice, crisp skin.

Many of the recipes in this chapter include a basting mixture developed specifically for that particular flavor profile. However, you can baste with a variety of mixtures. Use your favorite barbecue sauce—homemade or prepared—and just thin it out with some water, beer, wine, or liquor. You want a mixture you can apply in thin, even layers. You can even use a marinade (if it hasn't come in contact with raw meat) that isn't too acidic.

It's a good idea to keep the baste mixture hot while smoking—just set it over low heat on the back burner on your stovetop. This can decrease the possibility of any foodborne illnesses. It's also a good practice to leave the mop submerged in the simmering baste for at least 90 seconds after using it on partially cooked meats. Likewise, it's also best to wait until halfway through the smoking time to start basting. Leave the lid closed until then—no matter what! You don't want to lose any heat while that smoke is first being laid down on your meat. For long-smoked meat, I'd then give it a good juicy mop every 45 minutes until the last 30 minutes. That's when I'd lay on whatever sauce I wanted to glaze it with.

This might begin to seem redundant to mention, but it can't be said enough: Refrigerate your bastes and sauces until you're ready to use them. Never dip your brush or mop directly into the sauce container. Pour the sauce you intend to use into a bowl and work from there. If there's any left in the bowl when you're done, discard it.

Sauce Recipes

Barbecue sauces come after basting, and when smoking, you should apply the sauce—and leave it to take on a glaze—about 30 minutes before the meat is ready to come off the smoker. Whatever their origin or style, barbecue sauces tend to have a high sugar content. It's nothing more than a seasoned sweet-and-sour liquid. In Kansas City, it's tomato-based with sweet and smoky notes. In Memphis, it's tomato-based with some zing and heat. They're both the thickness of ketchup. In the Carolinas, the sauce is thin and yellow from a vinegar and mustard base. And in the Deep South, they use mayonnaise-based sauces.

Whatever the style, they all break down similarly. It starts with a base, such as ketchup, mustard, mayonnaise, or vinegar. Next, there's something to sweeten it, such as granulated sugar, molasses, or even cola. Then the sweetness needs to be balanced out with an acid, such as lemon juice or vinegar, or an alcohol, such as beer or wine. Next, you want to bulk it up and make it pourable with something like orange juice, apple juice, or even Dr Pepper. Lastly, season it with dry and liquid ingredients, such as Worcestershire sauce, garlic powder, or even a bit of your favorite rub or paste. The sauce should be smooth, but don't let this limit your creativity. Throw in chopped fruits and vegetables. Sauces can be puréed with a hand or regular blender or a food processor. After you try a few of the recipes in this chapter, you'll get a feel for the formula and hopefully have the confidence to venture farther afield.

Large cuts—such as a pork shoulder destined to become luscious pulled pork—don't necessarily require glazing. While I recommend adding a light coating of sauce to ribs and chicken wings or thighs, I also like to just put a couple big bowls of sauce on the table because sometimes there's nothing better than a good self-serve dunk.

Sauces are meant to be finishing touches. They should never be slapdash. You want them to provide the final complement to what you've spent as much as 24 hours preparing. Remember, you need to keep this part of the process to the last 30 minutes or less—just enough time to heat it and make it sticky and visually appetizing to one and all. If you overdo it, you'll just end up with your head in your hands—and with a sticky, burnt mess.

Kansas City Barbecue Sauce

Kansas City is considered the sauce capital of the United States. Its barbecue sauce has four main characteristics: It's thick, rich with tomato flavor, a little sweet, and has a bit of a spicy kick. This is my version—and I think it's pretty darn good!

Prep Time	Cook Time	Yield
15 minutes	65 minutes	8 cups

¼ cup bacon fat (pan drippings) or butter

1 cup diced sweet onions (such as Vidalia or Maui)

4 large garlic cloves, minced

4 cups ketchup

1 cup tomato paste

1 cup water

1 cup firmly packed light brown sugar

½ cup molasses

⅓ cup Worcestershire sauce

¼ cup apple cider vinegar

2 tbsp **Basic Barbecue Rub** (page 115)

1 tsp kosher salt

1 tsp freshly ground black pepper

1 tsp ground cayenne

1 to 3 drops of hickory-flavored liquid smoke

hot sauce, to taste

1. In a large saucepan on the stovetop over medium heat, melt the bacon fat. Add the onions and garlic. Sauté until the onions have softened but not browned, about 3 to 5 minutes.

2. Add the ketchup, tomato paste, water, brown sugar, molasses, Worcestershire sauce, apple cider vinegar, barbecue rub, salt, pepper, cayenne, liquid smoke, and hot sauce. Bring to a simmer until thick, about 1 hour, stirring occasionally.

3. Remove the pan from the heat. Use a hand mixer to purée the mixture until smooth. Strain the mixture through a fine-mesh sieve. Discard the solids.

4. Store the sauce in an airtight container in the fridge for up to 2 weeks. Use this sauce on pork ribs, pulled pork, brisket, chicken, and turkey.

Recipe Note: This is a great base to use when experimenting and creating your own custom barbecue sauce or as the barbecue sauce in other recipes later in this book.

Wasabi, Bourbon & Teriyaki Sauce

This is a bit of a weird combination, but it's delicious! The bourbon, soy, and wasabi blend with the added sweetness of brown sugar to create quite a tangy sensation when basted on smoked food. This sauce is also great on grilled steaks.

Prep Time	Cook Time	Yield
15 minutes	30 minutes	3 cups

1 tbsp vegetable oil

½ cup finely diced yellow onions

8 garlic cloves, minced

1 tbsp minced fresh ginger

1 cup firmly packed light brown sugar

⅓ cup dark soy sauce

¼ cup sweet rice vinegar

2 tbsp molasses

1 tbsp hot horseradish

1 tsp Worcestershire sauce

½ tsp freshly ground black pepper

½ cup ginger ale

3 tsp cornstarch

1½ tsp wasabi powder

2oz (60ml) bourbon whiskey

1. In a medium saucepan on the stovetop, heat the vegetable oil over medium heat. Add the onions, garlic, and ginger. Sauté until the onions have softened but not browned, about 3 to 4 minutes, stirring often.

2. Add the brown sugar and stir until smooth. Stir in the soy sauce, rice vinegar, molasses, horseradish, Worcestershire sauce, and pepper. Bring to a boil, then reduce the heat to low. Simmer for 15 to 20 minutes, stirring occasionally.

3. In a medium bowl, whisk together the ginger ale, cornstarch, and wasabi powder until smooth. Add to the saucepan, stirring rapidly until well combined.

4. Raise the heat to medium. Return the mixture to a boil, then reduce the heat to low. Simmer until thickened, about 1 minute. Remove the pan from the heat. Stir in the bourbon. Allow the sauce to cool completely.

5. Store the sauce in an airtight container in the fridge for up to 2 weeks. Use this sauce on beef ribs, short ribs, prime rib, lamb, chicken, and jerky.

Cherry Cola Basting Sauce

This is a fun recipe that's put together with five store-bought products. I call it Cherryaki because of the cherry pie filling, soy sauce, and cola. You can baste this sauce on beef brisket, short ribs, pork shoulder, and ribs. Give it a go!

Prep Time	Cook Time	Yield
20 minutes	15 minutes	4 cups

2 cups cherry pie filling

½ cup light brown sugar

¼ cup low-sodium soy sauce

2 tbsp chipotle hot sauce

1½ cups flat cola, room temperature

1. In a medium saucepan on the stovetop over medium heat, combine the cherry pie filling, brown sugar, soy sauce, chipotle hot sauce, and flat cola. Stir occasionally until the sauce boils. Reduce the heat and simmer for 15 minutes. Remove the pan from the heat.

2. Store the sauce in an airtight container in the fridge for up to 2 weeks. Use this sauce with beef brisket or short ribs, pork butt, ribs, and even chicken thighs.

Memphis-Style Barbecue Sauce

The best way to describe this Memphis-style barbecue sauce is it's a little spicy, a little sweet, and loaded with flavor. It has a bit of a kick that comes from the cayenne, but it's not too hot. The sauce also balances itself with a nice tang from vinegar and mustard. You're gonna love it!

Prep Time	Cook Time	Yield
30 minutes	10 minutes	5 cups

2 tbsp butter

½ cup diced yellow onions

3 large garlic cloves, minced

1½ cups tomato paste

½ cup yellow mustard

¾ cup white vinegar

¼ cup apple cider vinegar

⅓ cup firmly packed light brown sugar

¼ cup Worcestershire sauce

1 tsp kosher salt

2 tsp freshly ground black pepper

1 tsp ground cayenne

1 tsp celery salt

1 tsp mustard powder

1. In a medium saucepan on the stovetop over medium heat, melt the butter. Add the onions and garlic. Sauté until the onions have softened but not browned, about 3 to 5 minutes.

2. Stir in the tomato paste, mustard, white vinegar, and apple cider vinegar. Add the brown sugar, Worcestershire sauce, kosher salt, pepper, cayenne, celery salt, and mustard powder. Simmer until thickened, about 5 minutes, stirring frequently. Remove the pan from the heat.

4. Use a hand mixer to purée the mixture until smooth. Strain the mixture through a fine-mesh sieve. Discard the solids.

5. Store the sauce in an airtight container in the fridge for up to 2 weeks. Use this sauce with ribs and chicken or drizzle it on shredded pulled pork before serving.

Recipe Note: Use an injector to inject this sauce into chicken, turkey, and pork!

Carolina Sweet Mustard Sauce

The smell of smoke coming from a barbecue joint in the Carolinas always makes me crave their sweet mustard sauce. It's bright yellow from mustard and turmeric, and the sweetness of apple offsets the kick of mustard. Slop it on just about anything—it's sure to brighten up your day.

Prep Time	Cook Time	Yield
20 minutes	30 minutes	3 cups

2 tbsp butter

2 medium yellow bell peppers, seeded and diced

2 hot yellow banana peppers, chopped

1 small yellow onion, finely chopped

4 garlic cloves, minced

½ cup yellow mustard

½ cup honey

¼ cup granulated sugar

¼ cup apple cider vinegar

¼ cup apple juice

1 tsp ground turmeric

1 tsp freshly ground black pepper

½ tsp ground cumin

½ tsp ground cayenne

kosher salt, to taste

1. In a medium saucepan on the stovetop over medium-high heat, melt the butter. Add the yellow bell peppers, yellow banana peppers, onion, and garlic. Sauté until the peppers and onion are softened but not browned, about 3 to 5 minutes.

2. Reduce the heat to medium. Stir in the mustard, honey, sugar, apple cider vinegar, apple juice, turmeric, black pepper, cumin, and cayenne. Bring to a boil, then reduce the heat to low. Simmer until reduced by one-third, about 20 to 30 minutes, stirring occasionally. Season with the salt. Remove the pan from the heat.

3. Use a hand mixer to purée the mixture until smooth. Strain the mixture through a fine-mesh sieve. Discard the solids. Allow the sauce to cool completely.

4. Store the sauce in an airtight container in the fridge for up to 2 weeks. Use this sauce on chicken, pulled pork, and ribs.

Variation: For a seriously spicy sauce, omit the banana peppers and replace them with yellow or orange Scotch bonnet or habañero peppers.

Alabama White Sauce

Big Bob Gibson's Bar-B-Q restaurant in Decatur, Alabama, made this white barbecue sauce famous. The best way to describe is it's like ranch dressing—only way tastier. This goes best splashed on smoked chicken. #itbetasty!

Prep Time	Cook Time	Yield
30 minutes	10 minutes	3 cups

1½ cups mayonnaise

½ cup ranch dressing

¼ cup apple cider vinegar

¼ cup apple juice

2 tbsp hot horseradish

2 tbsp freshly squeezed lemon juice

1 tsp Worcestershire sauce

1 tsp hot sauce

1 tsp kosher salt

1 tbsp freshly ground black pepper

1 tsp garlic powder

1 tsp mustard powder

½ tsp ground cayenne

1. In a medium saucepan on the stovetop over medium heat, combine the mayonnaise, ranch dressing, apple cider vinegar, apple juice, hot horseradish, lemon juice, Worcestershire sauce, hot sauce, salt, pepper, garlic powder, mustard powder, and cayenne. Bring the mixture to a low boil, stirring constantly. Adjust the seasonings as desired.

2. Lower the heat to low and keep the sauce warm until ready to use.

Apple Butter Barbecue Glaze

The combination of sweet apple and maple with tangy ketchup and spicy jalapeños makes this sauce really flavorful and a hit with just about everybody.

Prep Time	Cook Time	Yield
30 minutes	30 minutes	5 cups

3 tbsp butter

½ cup minced yellow onions

2 red jalapeños or red chili peppers, chopped

2 garlic cloves, crushed

2 cups unsweetened applesauce

2 cups ketchup

½ cup apple juice

½ cup apple butter

¼ cup maple syrup

3 tbsp apple cider vinegar

½ tsp kosher salt

½ tsp freshly ground black pepper

1. In a medium saucepan on the stovetop over medium heat, melt the butter. Add the onions, peppers, and garlic. Sauté until the vegetables have softened, about 3 to 5 minutes, stirring occasionally.

2. Stir in the applesauce, ketchup, apple juice, apple butter, maple syrup, apple cider vinegar, salt, and pepper. Reduce the heat to low and simmer until thickened, about 20 minutes, stirring occasionally. Remove the pan from the heat.

3. Use a hand mixer to purée the mixture until the texture resembles applesauce. Strain the mixture through a fine-mesh sieve. Discard the solids.

4. Store the glaze in an airtight container in the fridge for up to 2 weeks. Use this glaze on ribs or with barbecue pulled pork, chicken, and turkey.

Spritz Recipes

If you've ever watched a barbecue documentary or a televised barbecue competition, then you've probably noticed the pros spraying their meats with a mysterious mixture. The old pros in Memphis can be seen opening the smoker really quickly to spray the meat with something, then closing the doors just as quickly. Some of them are spraying apple juice, which is commonly used on a whole hog or ribs.

Spritzing has become very popular because you can do it fast, which limits the amount of heat lost. It's also another way to load up the flavor. You can do something as simple as apple juice or orange juice, but you can use all sorts of ingredients. Some use reserved marinade (as long as it didn't come in contact with raw meat) or you can create a special spritz designed to complement all your other flavoring steps. Check out these recipes for inspiration on what to fill your squeeze bottle with.

When spritzing food, I like to set the spray nozzle to mist to give foods just a fine spray. Spritz about 6 to 8 inches (15.25 to 20cm) away from the food in an even layer. Be careful of the stream setting on the bottle because it can puncture your foods, especially delicate fish or seafood.

Lemon & Ginger Wine Spritz

The sweet buttery flavor of Riesling wine is so fresh-tasting when blended with ginger ale and freshly squeezed lemon juice!

Prep Time	Cook Time	Yield
5 minutes	none	4 cups

2 cups Riesling wine

1 cup flat ginger ale, room temperature

1 cup lemonade

1. Use a funnel to fill a spray bottle with the Riesling, ginger ale, and lemonade. Shake to mix well.

2. Store the spritz in the fridge for up to 1 week. Use this spritz on poultry, fish, seafood, and pork.

Spiced Rum & Apple Spritz

This blend of spices with the rum and apple juice gives you a tasty complex flavor and a rich, smooth sweetness. This is glorious on pork, but try it on beer can chicken or a turkey breast. It be tasty!

Prep Time	Cook Time	Yield
5 minutes	none	4 cups

2 cinnamon sticks (2 inches [5cm] long each)

1 tbsp whole black peppercorns

1 whole star anise

3 cardamom pods

2-inch (5cm) piece of fresh ginger, sliced

2 cups apple juice

1 cup dark spiced rum

1 cup cold water

1. Stuff the cinnamon sticks, peppercorns, star anise, cardamom pods, and ginger into a spray bottle. Use a funnel to add the apple juice, rum, and water. Shake to mix well.

2. Store the spritz in the fridge for up to 2 weeks. Use this spritz on lamb or beef. Add some sage and it's wonderful on poultry.

Honey & Herb Spritz

For this spritz, I like to add fresh sprigs of rosemary—or just about any herb I have on hand—to the spray bottle to infuse that flavor into the orange juice and honey. The longer you let the spritz stand, the more herb flavor will come through.

Prep Time	Cook Time	Yield
5 minutes	none	4 cups

1 to 2 sprigs of fresh rosemary, thyme, oregano, basil, mint, or sage

2 cups warm water

1 cup freshly squeezed orange juice

1 cup liquid honey

1. Stuff the rosemary sprigs into a spray bottle, keeping as many leaves on the stems as possible.

2. Use a funnel to add the water, orange juice, and liquid honey. Shake to mix well. Allow the spritz to rest for at least 4 hours or up to overnight.

3. Store the spritz in the fridge for up to 2 weeks. Use this spritz on pork, chicken, and game meats.

Meat, Meat & More Meat ... & Fish

The word "meat" doesn't just refer to beef. It's used as a blanket term for any protein that comes from an animal: veal, pork, lamb, game, poultry, fish, and seafood. I'm drooling just thinking about all the wonderful meats I've bought from my butcher and put in my smoker!

There are many cuts of meat out there, but in these chapters, I explain most of them so you'll understand what you're asking for when you head to the butcher shop or grocery store. Start simple—maybe with a pork butt—and work your way up to the more advanced cuts, such as brisket or ribs. Don't worry: It won't be long before you know exactly what you're doing. The recipes in these chapters are sure to inspire you to get out there and smoke something delicious!

Beef Recipes

10

If there's one thing you gotta know about me, it's that I'm a meat guy. I love meat. There's nothing more satisfying than setting a perfectly smoked, juicy, crusted piece of beef before your family and friends. It's that first cut through the dark, fragrant crust into a juicy pink interior, bringing forth a geyser of rich, natural juices that draws stares of awe from everyone at the table. All the work you've done—brining, marinating, rubbing, stoking the coals, basting, glazing, and spritzing—is suddenly so worth it. Amid the oohs and ahhs, your chest puffs out a little and you sit back to enjoy the sounds of people enjoying something you created. That's what smoking meat means to me.

Some of my greatest relationships are with butchers. I grew up in a small town outside Toronto and going to the butcher shop as a kid was definitely a highlight of my youth. Staring through the glass at all the glistening cuts of meat and listening to my mother or father discussing the relative merits of a rib eye steak versus a strip loin steak was like music to me. My dad was definitely a barbecue guy; I guess that's where I got it from. He even built his own first grill. When my dad started stoking up the grill I was right there watching and getting the lowdown from him. Some of these conversations were great bonding moments for us. When it became obvious that the culinary world was where I was going, I don't think he was surprised.

None of this is possible, though, if you don't get the right cut of meat. If you can, find a good old-fashioned butcher—one who doesn't just present you with plastic-wrapped bundles. They're still out there—it just takes a little research on your part. Find someone you can talk to face-to-face and build a relationship with. Once you do, hang on to them! You want someone who understands exactly what you're looking for when you tell them you want a brisket flat, totally trimmed, and cleaned for the smoker but with some of the fat left intact. But before you find a butcher, you need to have a good understanding of meat on your own.

Breaking Down the Different Cuts of Beef

Beef is separated into four basic major (primal) cuts: chuck, loin, rib, and round. Generally, cuts from the chuck and round are less tender and require moist heat or long, slow cooking—like smoking! Because the loin and rib are more tender, you can cook them with dry heat methods, such as broiling or grilling. The less tender cuts are typically the ones that end up in the smoker most often, but that's not to say a smoked steak isn't worth the time. It's obviously going to take longer than grilling it, but a smoked prime rib or 2-inch-thick (5cm) rib eye steak can transport you to heaven for a short while.

The main thing that affects the tenderness, marbling (the delicate veins of fat running through the meat), and flavor of meat (all meats) is where it comes from on the animal. An area that gets worked hard in the day-to-day activities of an animal's life is going to be tougher with less marbling, but it also has more flavor. The tenderloin doesn't really do much. That's why you, as the cook, don't have to do much to it because it's going to melt in your mouth no matter what—unless you overcook it! However, because the round, shank, and chuck work hard to move the cow around and keep its head up, they become tough but loaded with beefy flavor. The following figure and tables detail the cuts of beef and the features of those cuts.

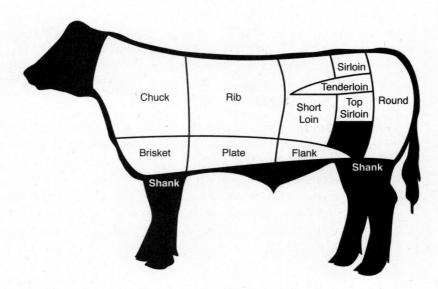

Cuts of beef

Forequarter Cuts

Cut	Characteristics
Chuck	This includes bone-in chuck steaks, arm and blade roasts (the blade is also known as a "flat-iron steak"), boneless clod steaks and roasts, and chest short ribs. These are very tough pieces of meat and well suited for the art of smoking.
Ribs	These include short ribs, prime rib, and rib eye steak.
Brisket	This is a very coarse-textured muscle. The heavy layer of fat and sternum or breastbone are removed before selling. It's often sold in a flat-cut half and point-cut half, and it's used for stewing meat, barbecue, corned beef, and pastrami.
Shank	This is the toughest cut and is most often used for stews and soups.
Plate	This is where the rest of the short ribs come from as well as pot roast and outside skirt steak. The remaining meat is usually ground because it's cheap, tough, and fatty.

Hindquarter Cuts

Cut	Characteristics
Short loin	T-bone and porterhouse steaks are cut from the short loin if bone-in; the New York strip is cut from the short loin if boneless.
Sirloin	This produces top sirloin and bottom sirloin, including tri-tip roast.
Tenderloin	As a separate subprimal, this can be cut into filet mignon, tournedos, and tenderloin steaks. It can also be left whole as a roast. When it's cut with the bone in, it becomes part of T-bone and porterhouse steaks.
Round	This provides top, bottom, and eye of round steaks and roasts.
Flank	This is basically used for flank steak or inside skirt steak.

The most important thing to remember when selecting a cut and recipe is that it's going to affect the time needed to smoke. A tender cut won't take nearly as long as a tough cut, but you're going to be nursing the smoker for a while to check the meat so it doesn't overcook.

Beef-Buying Basics

The names for various cuts vary regionally and nationally. This can become confusing when using a cookbook. I'm from Canada, where a boneless top loin steak is called a strip loin steak. In the United States, this same steak might be called a Kansas City steak, a New York strip steak, a hotel-cut strip steak, an ambassador steak, or a club sirloin steak—just to name a few.

When buying beef, read the label. It should list the primal cut somewhere, so even if the name of the cut is different from what I've called for, you'll know if it's from the tender or tough region of the cow. Smoking was initially practiced as a way of making cheap or even discarded cuts edible. Over time, they've became more than just edible—they've become the glorious institution of American barbecue!

Now just because a cut is tough doesn't mean it's not good quality. All beef is graded and there are three main grades: USDA Prime, USDA Choice, and USDA Select. Very little Prime makes it to retail sale because less than 2% of all graded beef achieves the Prime status and the majority of it goes to the restaurant industry. I always recommend you buy the best you can afford and there's absolutely no shame in choosing the less tender pieces or the Choice or Select grades. The cooking method is what will raise them to another level. Select is the easiest grade to find and it's about 5 to 7 cents a pound cheaper than Choice. Because it has the least amount of marbling, it will benefit the most from the brine and/or marinade techniques discussed in Chapter 7.

Another thing to look for when shopping for beef is color. The meat should be bright cherry red without any gray spots. If it's vacuum-packed, the meat won't be bright red, but if it's fresh, it'll turn bright red about 5 to 10 minutes after opening the package. Good beef should be firm to the touch, not mushy. The packaging should be fairly dry because excess moisture in the tray usually indicates temperature abuse. Loin and rib cuts should have marbling running through the flesh and there shouldn't be a lot of big clumps of fat.

Be sure to match your selected cuts with the right cooking method and flavor combinations. For example, tender cuts need shorter smoking times and more delicate flavors, while tougher cuts need longer smoking times and can take on more robust flavors. The following recipes will give you some ideas about how to smoke and add great flavor to a good variety of beef cuts.

An Introduction to Brisket

When it comes to smoking beef, the big daddy of all the cuts is a brisket. It's one of the hardest things to learn how to smoke—and it's also an expensive cut. A whole 15-pound (6.8kg) brisket could cost anywhere from $50 all the way up to $150 depending on the grade, age, and quality. If you want a tasty, tender, juicy brisket, you need to buy the best you can afford. I like certified Angus beef or prime whole briskets. Because brisket is the hero of this recipe, invest in the quality.

Beef brisket is a relatively tough cut of meat. It's from the breast/lower chest area of beef cattle (and veal, bison, and water buffalo all also have a tasty plump brisket). When a brisket is cooked perfectly, the meat should jiggle with delight and ooze juicy goodness. You know what I mean: when it melts in your mouth and it makes you moan or squeal with delight.

How do you create a brisket that good? Here are some basics to get you started. First, your raw material is the most important. As noted before, get the best brisket you can afford. It's traditionally sold three ways: whole, flat cut, or point cut. The flat is leaner and is a much tougher part of the brisket, whereas the point is well marbled. The flat is also smaller than a whole brisket and less expensive, which makes it attractive when wanting to smoke brisket. But most people who start cooking with the flat versus a whole brisket are usually disappointed with the results, which often include the brisket being dry, tough, and stringy. Your best bet is to either choose a well-marbled point or a whole brisket. You can get smaller sizes that range from 8 to 12 pounds (3.6 to 5.4kg) or 12 pounds (5.4kg) and up.

Look for these qualities when shopping for a whole brisket:

- It should be relatively uniform in thickness from one end to the other. This will help with a more even smoke.

- It should have uniform fat coverage of at least ¼ inch (0.5cm) across the entire cap and the fat should be white, not yellow.

- The meat should be nicely marbled with fat.

- It's best if it's been aged at least 28 days, which helps with the tenderness.

Talk to your butcher—they'll be your best guide on what to choose.

Beef Brisket

A Texas pit boss once told me that true Texas brisket needs no seasoning: no salt, no pepper, no nothing—just sweet oak smoke and patience. I like to use 2 parts kosher salt and 1 part fresh coarsely ground black pepper, but you can season your brisket how you like.

Prep Time	Smoker Temp	Smoke Time
20 minutes	180°F to 220°F (80°C to 105°C)	12 to 16 hours

wood suggestions: cherry, oak, hickory, maple, or whiskey barrel

1 whole brisket (about 12 to 15lb [5.4 to 6.8kg]), aged and well marbled

½ cup kosher salt

¼ cup fresh coarsely ground black pepper

1. Pat dry the brisket with paper towels. Place the brisket on a smoker rack and refrigerate for 24 hours.

2. Preheat the smoker to 180°F to 220°F (80°C to 105°C). Use cherry, oak, hickory, maple, or whiskey barrel wood.

3. Rub the salt and pepper into the meat, ensuring the brisket has an even coating. Insert a thermometer probe into the thickest part of the brisket.

4. Place the rack in the smoker and smoke the brisket until the internal temperature reaches 170°F (75°C), about 6 to 8 hours. Make sure to maintain a 200°F (95°C) smoker temperature for the best results. After the first 2 hours, spritz the brisket with some beer or water if desired.

5. Remove the rack from the smoker and remove the probe from the brisket. Tightly wrap the brisket in three layers of butcher paper. Reinsert the probe into the brisket. Place the brisket back on the rack and return the rack to the smoker. Continue to smoke until the internal temperature reaches 200°F to 205°F (95°C to 100°C). If you want your brisket a little firmer, smoke until the internal temperature reaches 195°F (90°C).

6. Remove the rack from the smoker place and place the wrapped brisket in a large cooler. Place kitchen towels atop the brisket. Close the cooler lid and allow the brisket to rest for 1 hour.

7. Unwrap the brisket and slice the meat across the grain before serving.

Variation: Some folks like to inject brisket to increase the moisture and assist in keeping the brisket moist and juicy throughout the smoke. Try using beef broth, and if you want to live on the edge, inject the brisket with some melted butter.

Recipe Notes: You can trim the brisket to leave about ¼ to ½ inch (0.5 to 1.25cm) of fat coverage, but trimming the fat might mean you lose some juiciness. My philosophy is to trim a little and cook it all. You paid for it, don't waste it, and fat is flavor. It helps keep your brisket moist. The oyster of the beef brisket—called the "decal"—is the most prized piece of meat. This piece of beef is surrounded on all sides by fat and sits on top of the thickest part of the brisket point. When the brisket is perfectly cooked, this decal is moist, juicy, and succulent.

Reverse-Seared Tomahawk Steak

I've cooked steaks in a whole host of manners: cast-iron pans, gas grills, charcoal grills, open firepits, and smokers. I've cooked steaks on salt blocks and hot stones, wrapped and smoked in hay, and even directly on coals. But of all the methods of cooking a steak, my favorite is the reverse sear.

This cooking method involves two styles of outdoor cooking: smoking and grilling. You first smoke the steak low and slow to give the meat the opportunity to relax and take in some smoky flavors—to warm up slowly, not to be thrown directly onto the hot grill to tighten up. It's like a sweet, smoky sauna for your steak. Once the smoking is done and your desired internal temperature is met, you then sear the steak at about 625°F (330°C)—hot and fast to caramelize and char the outside. It's a sublime cooking method—one that does require time and patience—but by following the reverse-sear method of cooking a steak, you'll enjoy the best steak ever!

Prep Time	Smoker Temp	Smoke Time
10 minutes	215°F to 225°F (105°C to 110°C)	1 to 2 hours

wood suggestions: oak, cherry, hickory, or maple

2 bone-in tomahawk steaks (about 2 to 3 inches [5 to 7.5cm] thick and 2½ to 3lb [1.2 to 1.4kg] each)

½ cup butter

1 tbsp chopped fresh dill

2 tbsp kosher salt

1 tbsp fresh coarsely ground black pepper

1 tsp granulated garlic

1. Remove the steaks from the fridge about 30 minutes to 1 hour prior to smoking.

2. Preheat the smoker to 215°F to 225°F (105°C to 110°C). Use oak, cherry, hickory, or maple wood.

3. In a small bowl, combine the butter and dill. Brush the steaks with this mixture. Reserve some of the mixture for basting when the steaks come out of smoker.

4. In a separate small bowl, combine the salt, pepper, and granulated garlic. Sprinkle this mixture all over the steaks, rubbing the seasonings into the meat. Insert a thermometer probe into the side of a steak without touching bone, pushing the probe into the meat about 1½ inches (3.75cm).

5. Place the steak in the smoker—using the indirect heat method—and smoke until the internal temperature reaches 110°F to 115°F (45°C to 50°C). (This is below rare doneness.) Because this might happen quickly, don't leave your steaks alone—keep an eye on their progress.

6. Preheat the grill to 625°F (330°C).

7. Once the steaks reach the aforementioned internal temperature, you have to work quickly to perform the reverse sear. Remove the steaks from the smoker and brush them with the reserved butter and dill baste. Place the steaks on the grill and sear them for 2 to 3 minutes per side maximum.

8. Remove the steaks from grill and allow them to rest for 2 to 3 minutes. Slice the steaks against the grain before serving.

Variation: You can use this method of cooking steaks for a variety of cuts. New York strip and thick-cut beef fillets are especially outstanding when prepared this way. Don't forget to try this method with a tri-tip sirloin roast. It's definitely #tdf (to die for).

Recipe Note: Leftover smoked steaks make great sandwiches. Thinly slice the meat before serving on toasted baguettes or rolls.

Picanha with Root Beer Marinade

Picanha is a well-known cut of beef popularized in Brazil that's usually called "top sirloin" in the United States. Although I'm a big fan of root beer, I never thought to marinate meat in it. My buddy told me about what he does for his smoked sirloin roasts, but I took it a step further and added a paste to enhance that root beer note.

Prep Time	Smoker Temp	Smoke Time
30 minutes	225°F (110°C)	3 to 4 hours

wood suggestions: maple, oak, or cherry (or a blend of all three)

1 top sirloin beef roast (about 6 to 8lb [2.7 to 3.6kg])

3 (12oz [350ml]) cans plus ½ cup of root beer, divided

½ cup hoisin sauce

½ cup firmly packed light brown sugar

3 garlic cloves, minced

2 tbsp minced ginger

2 green onions, minced

1 tbsp freshly ground black pepper

1 tbsp sesame seeds

2 tbsp soy sauce

2 tbsp kosher salt

1. In a large resealable plastic bag, combine the beef roast and 3 cans of root beer. Refrigerate for 8 hours.

2. In a medium bowl, combine the hoisin sauce, brown sugar, the remaining ½ cup of root beer, garlic, ginger, green onions, pepper, sesame seeds, and soy sauce. Mix until well combined. (Store in an airtight container in the fridge for up to 2 weeks.)

3. Preheat the smoker to 225°F (110°C). Use maple, oak, or cherry wood or a blend of all three.

4. Pay dry the roast with paper towels. Rub the salt into the meat, then rub the hoisin paste all over the roast. Insert a thermometer probe into the center of the roast.

5. Place the roast in the smoker and smoke until the internal temperature reaches 135°F (60°C) for medium-rare to medium doneness, about 3 to 4 hours. (Because this is a relatively lean cut of beef, you don't want to take it past medium.)

6. Remove the roast from the smoker and tent with aluminum foil. Allow to rest for 15 minutes. Use a sharp knife to thinly slice the roast. Serve on toasted buns.

Prime Rib

Nothing beats a good old-fashioned prime rib roast, but let me tell you: It's that much better when it's smoked! Smoking gives prime rib all the respect and love it deserves. Ask your butcher for a roast that's been dry-aged for at least 21 days.

Prep Time	Smoker Temp	Smoke Time
30 minutes	235°F (115°C)	3 to 4 hours

wood suggestion: oak whiskey barrel (chunks or chips), soaked in water

½ cup plus 1 tsp Tennessee whiskey, divided

¼ cup Worcestershire sauce

½ cup minced garlic

2 tbsp plus ½ tsp freshly ground black pepper

2 tbsp kosher salt, plus more

3 tbsp olive oil

1 prime rib roast with 6 bones (10 to 12lb [4.5 to 5.4kg])

¼ cup hot Dijon mustard

1 tbsp extra-hot horseradish

1. Preheat the smoker to 235°F (115°C). Use oak whiskey barrel chunks or chips. Use a funnel to fill a spray bottle with ½ cup of whiskey and the Worcestershire sauce. Shake to mix well.

2. In a medium bowl, combine the garlic, 2 tablespoons of pepper, and salt. Add the olive oil and mix until a paste forms. Rub the paste all over the roast, pressing firmly into the meat. Place the roast on a smoker rack and insert a thermometer probe into the center of the roast.

3. Place the rack in the smoker and smoke until the internal temperature reaches 130°F to 145°F (55°C to 65°C) for rare to medium-rare doneness, about 3 to 4 hours. Spritz the roast with the whiskey mixture every 30 minutes.

4. Remove the rack from the smoker. Loosely tent the roast with aluminum foil and allow to rest for 10 to 15 minutes.

5. In a medium bowl, combine the Dijon mustard, horseradish, the remaining ½ teaspoon of pepper, and the remaining 1 teaspoon of whiskey. Mix well to combine. Season with salt to taste.

6. Carve the prime rib and serve with the mustard sauce.

Four-Pepper Beef Tenderloin with Cognac & Butter Injection

In this recipe, Szechuan peppercorns have a unique aroma and a slightly lemon flavor. They're really not as spicy as other peppercorns, but they do create a bit of a tingle on your tongue. You can find Szechuan peppercorns at Asian markets, specialty food stores, and well-stocked grocers.

Prep Time	Smoker Temp	Smoke Time
30 minutes	250°F (120°C)	1½ to 2 hours

wood suggestions: oak and mesquite, soaked in water

3oz (90ml) cognac or brandy, divided

1 tbsp olive oil

8 garlic cloves, minced

2 tsp Dijon mustard

2 tsp honey

¼ cup chopped fresh herbs (such as parsley and rosemary leaves)

2 tbsp cracked black peppercorns

2 tbsp cracked pink peppercorns

2 tbsp cracked white peppercorns

2 tbsp cracked Szechuan peppercorns

1 tbsp kosher salt

½ cup butter (1 stick)

1 trussed center-cut beef tenderloin roast (1½ to 2lb [680g to 1kg])

1. Preheat the smoker to 250°F (120°C). Use a blend of oak and mesquite woods.

2. In a medium bowl, combine 2 ounces (60 milliliters) of cognac, olive oil, garlic, Dijon mustard, honey, and mixed herbs. Mix until well combined. Set aside.

3. In a small bowl, combine the black peppercorns, pink peppercorns, white peppercorns, Szechuan peppercorns, and salt. Toss well and set aside.

4. In a small saucepan on the stovetop over medium-low heat, melt the butter. Stir in the remaining 1 ounce (30 milliliters) of cognac. Keep warm until ready to use.

5. Baste the tenderloin with most of the cognac mixture and firmly press the peppercorn mixture into the meat. Inject most of the butter mixture into the tenderloin. Insert a thermometer probe into the center of the roast. Brush the tenderloin with the remaining cognac mixture.

6. Place the tenderloin in the smoker and smoke until the internal temperature reaches 130°F (55°C) for medium-rare or 145°F (65°C) for medium doneness, about 1½ to 2 hours. Inject the roast with any remaining butter mixture. During the smoking process, this will keep the tenderloin moist and succulently delicious.

7. Remove the roast from the smoker and allow to rest for 5 to 10 minutes. Slice the roast into ¼- to ½-inch (0.5 to 1.25cm) slices before serving.

Recipe Note: Beef tenderloin is considered the best cut of beef because it's tender and very lean. Because the lack of fat makes it susceptible to becoming tough and dry if overcooked, it's best served rare to medium-rare to medium at the absolute most. I like it rare (125°F [55°C]).

Cherry & Whiskey Eye of Round

Eye of round is one of the lesser-known smoked meats, which is truly a shame. Here's the lowdown on this cut: It's tough, lean, and best when served thinly sliced or shaved. To best enjoy this steak, make sure you always use a brine or a marinade, never cook past medium, and always use a razor-sharp knife to slice the steak as thinly as possible.

Prep Time	Smoker Temp	Smoke Time
30 minutes	200°F to 225°F (95°C to 110°C)	2 to 3 hours

wood suggestions: cherry or oak

1 eye of round beef roast (4lb [1.8kg])

½ cup **Garlic & Herb Rub** (page 117), divided

1 cup cherry juice

1 cup cola

1½ cups cherry whiskey or brandy, divided

1 cup water

1. Preheat the smoker to 200°F to 225°F (95°C to 110°C). Use cherry or oak wood soaked in water.

2. Rub the roast with ¼ cup of the rub. In a large resealable plastic bag, combine the roast, cherry juice, cola, and ½ cup cherry whiskey. Seal the bag, removing as much air as possible. Refrigerate for 24 hours, turning the bag every 4 to 6 hours.

3. Remove the roast from the marinade and discard the liquids. Rub the roast with the remaining ¼ cup of the rub. Place the roast on a smoking rack and insert a thermometer probe into the center of the roast.

4. Use a funnel to fill a spray bottle with the water and the remaining 1 cup of cherry whiskey. Shake to mix well.

5. Place the rack in the smoker and smoke until the internal temperature reaches 140°F to 145°F (60°C to 65°C) for medium doneness, about 2 to 3 hours. Spritz the meat occasionally with the cherry whiskey mixture.

6. Remove the rack from the smoker. Loosely tent the roast with aluminum foil and allow to rest for 10 minutes.

7. Thinly slice or shave the roast using a sharp knife. Serve immediately on toasted rolls with desired garnishes.

Recipe Note: Keep your knives honed with a sharp edge by giving them a few passes on a sharpening steel before each use. Knives are the most important tool in the kitchen and a sharp blade will always make kitchen prep and slicing easier.

Beef Ribs with Chocolate Stout

The flavor of chocolate and the boldness of a strong stout make these beef ribs sing with deliciousness. Ask your butcher for really meaty beef ribs. Special-order them if you have to—the extra cost will be worth it. Try to get racks with 8 bones so all your efforts can feed a crowd. Nothing beats watching your family gnaw on sweet, smoky bones, trying to get every last bit of the tender meat.

Prep Time	Smoker Temp	Smoke Time
30 minutes	225°F (110°C)	6 to 8 hours

wood suggestions: cherry, oak, maple, hickory, or whiskey barrel

3 racks of meaty beef back ribs (about 3 to 4lb [1.4 to 1.8kg] each)

6 (12oz [350ml]) bottles of chocolate-infused stout or porter, divided, plus more

½ cup kosher salt

¼ cup fresh coarsely ground black pepper

¼ cup granulated garlic

½ cup unsalted butter (1 stick)

½ cup Worcestershire sauce

3 tbsp beef stock concentrate

2 tbsp firmly packed light brown sugar

1 tbsp hot horseradish

4 garlic cloves, minced

1 tsp chopped fresh rosemary leaves

1. In a large container, combine the ribs and 5½ bottles of stout, making sure the ribs are submerged. (It might be necessary to weight the ribs so they stay submerged. I use a small cast-iron pan. A couple heavy cans would also work.) Add more stout as needed to ensure the ribs are completely covered. Cover the container and refrigerate the ribs for 24 hours.

2. Preheat the smoker to 225°F (110°C) with a good amount of humidity. Use cherry, oak, maple, hickory, or whiskey barrel wood.

3. In a small bowl, combine the salt, pepper, and granulated garlic. Remove the ribs from the container and pat dry with paper towels. Sprinkle the seasoning mixture over the ribs on all sides. Insert a thermometer probe into the meatiest part of the ribs without touching bone.

4. In a small saucepan on the stovetop over medium-low heat, combine the butter, Worcestershire sauce, beef stock, brown sugar, horseradish, garlic, rosemary, and the remaining ½ bottle of stout. Cook until the butter has melted and the mixture is well combined, stirring constantly.

5. Place the ribs in the smoker and smoke until the internal temperature reaches 170°F (80°C), about 6 to 8 hours, basting frequently with the butter sauce.

6. Remove the ribs from the smoker and brush the ribs with more of the butter sauce. Tightly double-wrap the ribs in butcher paper and return the ribs to the smoker. Continue to smoke until the internal temperature reaches 205°F (100°C) and the bones move freely.

7. Remove the ribs from the smoker. Unwrap the butcher paper and baste the ribs with any remaining butter sauce before serving.

Prime Rib Burgers with Horseradish Cream

One of the most comforting foods is a hamburger—and I do love my burgers. This recipe results in a mighty beast of a burger—one that's so moist and juicy that it ruins a T-shirt, and when you're finished eating, all that's left is a puddle beneath your feet. To enjoy that kind of experience, ask your butcher to freshly grind you some prime rib. You want to have your burger grind contain about 25% fat—because fat is flavor!

Prep Time	Smoker Temp	Smoke Time
30 minutes	235°F (115°C)	1½ to 2 hours

wood suggestions: oak, hickory, cherry, mesquite, maple, or pecan

4lb (1.8kg) ground prime rib, chilled

2 tbsp beef stock concentrate

1 tbsp Worcestershire sauce

1 tbsp balsamic glaze

1 tbsp chopped fresh rosemary

4 tbsp melted butter

12 sprigs of fresh rosemary leaves, chopped

kosher salt, to taste

freshly ground black pepper, to taste

8 brioche burger buns, toasted

for the cream

½ cup whipped cream cheese

¼ cup sour cream

¼ cup mayonnaise

1 tbsp extra-hot horseradish

1 tsp chopped fresh chives

kosher salt, to taste

freshly ground black pepper, to taste

1. Form the prime rib into 8 equal-sized balls, pressing firmly but gently to ensure the meat sticks together. Flatten each ball into a 4-inch-wide by 1½-inch-thick (10cm by 3.75cm) patty. Place the patties on a large baking pan. Cover and refrigerate for 2 hours.

2. Preheat the smoker to 235°F (115°C). Use oak, hickory, cherry, mesquite, maple, or pecan wood.

3. In a small bowl, combine the beef stock, Worcestershire sauce, balsamic glaze, rosemary, and butter. Mix until well combined.

4. Line a smoker rack in the smoker with the rosemary sprigs. Evenly space the patties on top of the rosemary. Season with salt and pepper. Insert a thermometer probe into one of the burgers.

5. Smoke the burgers until the internal temperature reaches 160°F (70°C) for fully cooked, about 1½ to 2 hours. If you want to see a little red, aim for 145°F (65°C) for medium doneness.

6. In a medium bowl, making the horseradish cream by combining the cream cheese, sour cream, mayonnaise, horseradish, and chives. Season with salt and pepper. Transfer to a small serving dish and chill until ready to serve or for up to 3 days.

7. Remove the burgers from the smoker. Spread the cream on each bottom bun and add your favorite toppings before adding the top bun. Serve immediately.

Recipe Note: Freshly ground prime rib is always the best. If you don't have a grinder at home, ask the butcher to do it for you before you leave the shop. Don't let them give you a hard time about it either: Because you're paying top dollar for this cut, they should make sure you're satisfied!

Santa Maria Tri-Tip with Cabernet Wine Mop

A tri-tip roast comes from the bottom sirloin and gets its name from its triangular shape. Look for a roast that's well marbled and has a good amount of external fat. This fat will help keep the roast moist as well as flavor the meat. And keep a close eye on the temperature so you don't overcook this delicate piece of meat.

Prep Time	Smoker Temp	Smoke Time
30 minutes	200°F (95°C)	3 to 4 hours

wood suggestions: red wine barrel, oak, maple, cherry, or grapevine

2 cups cabernet sauvignon wine

¼ cup plus 2 tbsp good-quality red wine vinegar, divided

2 tbsp minced roasted garlic (about 12 cloves)

1 tbsp soy sauce

2 tbsp chopped fresh parsley leaves

2 tsp crushed red pepper flakes

¼ cup plus 2 tbsp olive oil, divided

kosher salt, to taste

3 tbsp fresh coarsely ground black pepper, plus more

1 beef tri-tip roast (2 to 5lb [1 to 2.3kg])

15 sprigs of fresh rosemary, tied to form a brush

1 large sweet onion, peeled and quartered

2 ripe avocados, peeled, pitted, and diced (with pits reserved)

3 green onions, chopped

ground cayenne, to taste

1. Preheat the smoker to 200°F (95°C). Use red wine barrel, oak, maple, cherry, or grapevine wood.

2. In a large bowl, combine the cabernet sauvignon, ¼ cup of red wine vinegar, garlic, soy sauce, parsley, and red pepper flakes. Mix until well combined. Add ¼ cup of olive oil in a slow, steady stream while whisking until fully incorporated. Season with salt and set aside.

3. Firmly press the black pepper into the roast. Place the roast on a smoking rack and insert a thermometer probe into the center of the roast.

4. Place the rack in the smoker and smoke until the internal temperature reaches 130°F to 145°C (55°C to 65°C) for medium-rare to medium doneness, about 3 to 4 hours. Every 20 to 30 minutes, use the rosemary brush to baste the roast with the wine mixture.

5. Preheat a grill to 400°F to 500°F (205°C to 260°C). Grill the onion quarters until tender and lightly charred, about 10 to 15 minutes, turning occasionally. Remove the onion quarters from the grill. Allow them to cool before thinly slicing.

6. In a large bowl, combine the onion slices, avocado, the remaining 2 tablespoons of red wine vinegar, and the remaining 2 tablespoons of olive oil. Add the green onions. Season with salt, pepper, and cayenne. Place the avocado pits in the mixture to prevent oxidization. Cover the bowl with plastic wrap, ensuring the plastic touches the surface of the mixture, and refrigerate until ready to serve.

7. Remove the rack from the smoker. Loosely tent the roast with aluminum foil and allow to rest for 10 minutes. Carve the roast across the grain into thin slices. Serve with the avocado mixture.

Recipe Note: If you're lucky enough to live near a vineyard, you should visit early in the spring to find out when they'll trim their grapevines. These cuttings can bring great flavor to your smoked meats. They're also great as skewers for grilling meats. I'm lucky I live in an Italian neighborhood because in the spring, there are plenty of vine cuttings lining the streets for easy picking.

Beef Jerky

Beef jerky is a tasty treat and a good snack for those counting their carbs. I gotta say, I love using my Bradley electric smoker to make my beef jerky. This smoker makes the process easier and always gives me an even smoke. Oh yeah—and their jerky racks are a huge help.

Prep Time	Smoker Temp	Smoke Time
1 hour	140°F (60°C)	8 to 12 hours

wood suggestions: oak, hickory, or maple

1 beef eye of round roast (2 to 3lb [1 to 1.4kg])

½ cup soy sauce

½ cup hoisin sauce

¼ cup maple syrup

1 tbsp beef stock concentrate

1 tbsp sambal oelek (red chili sauce) or sriracha hot sauce

2 tbsp freshly ground black pepper

1 tsp granulated garlic

hefty pinch of ground cayenne

1. Use a sharp knife to trim all visible fat and sinew from the outside of the roast. Place the roast in the freezer until slightly frozen but still soft enough to slice, about 2 hours. Use a meat slicer or a very sharp carving knife to cut the roast across the grain into ¼-inch (0.5cm) slices.

2. Place a 12-inch (30.5cm) square of plastic wrap on a flat work surface. Place 2 slices of beef on the plastic and top with a second 12-inch (20.5cm) square of plastic wrap. Use a meat mallet to gently pound the slices until they're an even thickness and a little thinner than when you started. Repeat this step with the remaining beef. Remember: The thicker the slices, the longer it takes to dry them out.

3. In a medium bowl, combine the soy sauce, hoisin sauce, maple syrup, beef stock, sambal oelek, pepper, garlic, and cayenne. Mix until well combined.

4. Place the roast slices on a large baking sheet. Pour the soy sauce mixture over the slices, gently turning them to evenly coat. Cover the sheet and refrigerate for 3 days, turning once daily.

5. Preheat the smoker to 140°F (60°C). Use oak, hickory, or maple wood. Keep the humidity level to a minimum: Don't fill the water pan in the smoker.

6. Remove the beef from the marinade and discard the liquids. Pat dry with paper towels. Make sure to keep the beef dry because the smoke won't penetrate if there's any moisture. Evenly space the slices in a single layer on a smoker rack.

7. Place the rack in the smoker and smoke until the beef is dry and has reduced in size by about 60%, about 8 to 12 hours.

8. Remove the rack from the smoker and allow the jerky to cool completely. Serve immediately or store in an airtight container in the fridge for up to 6 weeks.

Recipe Note: You can make jerky from almost any type of meat that can be thinly sliced and air-cured. Most of us are familiar with beef jerky, but historically, it was made from buffalo, deer, elk, and antelope. Now it's become trendy to dry turkey, salmon, ostrich, or even moose.

Meatloaf

Meatloaf is one of my favorite family meals. Nothing's more satisfying than a plate of creamy mashed potatoes topped with slow-smoked meatloaf and covered in gravy. Let's get tasty! First step, head to your butcher for some freshly ground beef. At my restaurant, The Joint, our smoked meatloaf is made from a 50/50 blend of ground brisket and chuck. You want your meat to have about 25% fat in it and freshly ground is always best over store-bought, tray-packed beef.

Prep Time	Smoker Temp	Smoke Time
30 minutes	235°F (115°C)	2 hours

wood suggestions: maple, hickory, oak, pecan, or cherry

2 tbsp butter

1½ cups finely chopped white onions

8 garlic cloves, minced

3lb (1.4kg) freshly ground beef

3 tbsp cornstarch or potato starch

¼ cup chopped fresh parsley leaves

1 cup crushed hickory sticks

Worcestershire sauce, to taste

kosher salt, to taste

freshly ground black pepper, to taste

¾ cup hickory-smoked barbecue sauce

¼ cup light brown sugar

splash of dark beer or stout

2 tsp cold butter

1. In a small skillet on the stovetop over medium-high heat, melt the butter. Add the onions and garlic. Sauté until tender, about 2 to 3 minutes. Remove the skillet from the heat and allow the onions and garlic to cool completely.

2. In a large bowl, combine the ground beef, onions, garlic, cornstarch, parsley, and hickory sticks. Season with the Worcestershire sauce, salt, and pepper. Mix until well combined.

3. Form the mixture into a log about 12 to 15 inches (30.5 to 38cm) long and about 4 to 5 inches (10 to 12.5cm) wide and tall. Place the log on an oven-safe pan or on a soaked food-safe plank. Brush the log with butter and refrigerate for 2 hours.

4. In a microwave-safe dish, combine the barbecue sauce, brown sugar, and beer. Microwave on high for 1½ minutes. Stir in the cold butter and set aside.

5. Preheat the smoker to 235°F (115°C). Use maple, hickory, oak, pecan, or cherry wood.

6. Place the pan in the smoker and smoke the meatloaf until the internal temperature reaches 160°F (70°C), about 2 hours. Occasionally baste with the barbecue sauce.

7. Remove the pan from the smoker and allow the meatloaf to rest for 10 minutes. Slice before serving.

Short Ribs

This is a fun and tasty way to impress your friends. Ask your butcher for a 3- to 4-bone section of beef short rib plate. It should be well marbled and have about 2 to 3 inches (5 to 7.5cm) of meat on top of the bone. This is a premium cut, and when smoked just right, it's mighty fine!

Prep Time	Smoker Temp	Smoke Time
30 minutes	235°F (115°C)	4 to 5 hours

wood suggestion: cherry wood

1 beef short rib plate (3 to 4 bones) (3 to 4lb [1.4 to 1.8kg])

2 tbsp olive oil

kosher salt, to taste

freshly ground black pepper, to taste

1 cup coffee beans, plus more

4 sprigs of fresh rosemary

1. Rub the short ribs with olive oil and season with salt and pepper. Push the seasonings into the meat and fat to ensure penetration.

2. Preheat the smoker to 235°F (115°C). Use cherry wood and the coffee beans. Add more coffee beans as desired to ensure you give a hint of coffee smoke to the beef. Insert a thermometer probe into the meatiest part of the ribs without touching bone.

3. Place the ribs in the smoker and smoke until the internal temperature reaches 170°F (80°C), about 3 hours. Remove the ribs from the smoker and tightly wrap them in butcher paper. Return the ribs to the smoker and continue to smoke until the internal temperature reaches 205°F (100°C).

4. Remove the ribs from the smoker and allow them to rest for 30 minutes. Unwrap, slide the meat off the bones, and serve immediately.

Pork Recipes

Does anything offer the smoker more versatility than the humble pig? Every cut from a pig is smoker-friendly—right down to the tail, although that's an acquired taste. To me, there's just nothing better than pulled pork shredded from the butt as soon as it's removed from the smoker. Glistening with juicy fat, a fragrant pile of moist, meaty morsels is like an aphrodisiac. Who can resist? It's that ratio of fat to meat and the adaptable mild flavor of the meat that make pork perfect for smoking. You can spice it sweet or savory—or hot as hell. Pork can take it all!

I could rhapsodize for endless pages on how I love pork or we can just agree right now that pork is the perfect choice for the smoker. Let's dissect—figuratively, of course—this glorious animal to learn about all its beautiful cuts—tough and tender alike.

Assorted Pork Cuts

Like with beef, tender cuts of pork come from the ribs and loin. The best cuts are from higher up on the animal—thus the old saying "high on the hog"—while the shank and shoulder muscles have the toughest cuts. The following table details how the different cuts break down.

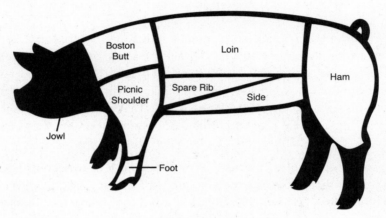

Cuts of pork

Cut	Characteristics
Boston butt	Also called "pork butt," this cut comes from the upper shoulder, which consists of parts from the neck, shoulder blade, and upper arm. It's moderately tough, with a good deal of connective tissue, but after 12 or 16 hours in the smoker, it turns into some pretty tasty pulled pork. It can also be cut into steaks or ground for sausages.
Pork shoulder	Also called "picnic shoulder," this cut is pretty tough and is usually cured and/or smoked. It's also used for making ground pork or sausage meat. It's not ideal, but you can also roast the pork shoulder.

Cut	Characteristics
Pork loin	Because hogs are bred to have extra-long loins, they can have up to 17 ribs—unlike beef and lamb, which only have 13 ribs. The entire pork loin can be smoked—bone-in or boneless. It can also be cut into individual chops or cutlets. The tenderloin is taken from the rear of the pork loin and baby back ribs come from the upper rib cage area of the loin.
Ham	The back legs of the hog are where we get fresh, smoked, or cured hams.
Ham hock	This is taken from the joint at the shank end of the ham, where it joins the foot. It's used extensively in southern US cuisine. A smoked ham hock is a fabulous addition to all kinds of comfort foods. Keep a ready supply to stir into a pot of baked beans, split pea soup, rice and beans, chili, or succotash.
Pork belly or side	The pork belly or side is where we get pancetta and bacon!
Pork spare ribs	These are taken from the belly side of the ribs, where they join the breastbone. Tougher than back ribs, spare ribs are best prepared by smoking very slowly over a low temperature.
Pork jowl	This is mostly used to make sausages, although it can also be cured and made into bacon. In Italian cooking, cured pork jowl is referred to as *guanciale*.
Feet	Pork feet can be cured, smoked, and even pickled. Pig feet are a key ingredient in the traditional Mexican soup called *menudo*.

What You Need to Know About Sausage

Let's talk sausage! But first, let me ask you a question: What *is* a sausage? Do you really know? A sausage is chopped or ground meat with added fat and seasoning, ground seafood with fat and seasoning, or even ground vegetables with fat and seasoning. That's it. No real mystery and no secret ingredients with weird names, although you can definitely find those sorts of sausages in a retail setting. If you can make a meatloaf, you can make a sausage. You just need to add the stuffing step. You might be surprised to find out it's actually kinda fun!

You'll only need one piece of equipment beyond what you probably already have in your kitchen. You could go out and buy an expensive sausage stuffer at a good kitchen or restaurant supply store. But if you have a stand mixer, then you're in luck! A good-quality, high-powered stand mixer almost always has a grinder/sausage attachment available. If not—and if the pocketbook still protests—you can get an affordable, hand-crank meat grinder at a hardware store. You know, like the kind your grandmother would attach to a table to grind beef. Whatever you end up with, just make sure it has coarse- and fine-grinding plates so you can experiment with different textures.

Grinding your own meat isn't absolutely necessary, but it's very satisfying, especially if you want to get fancy and combine various meats with exotic seasonings. When making sausages, it's okay to let your imagination take over. You might even come up with really creative flavor and texture combinations. Read my recipe for a basic Polish sausage later in this chapter and you'll get a sense of how straightforward the process can be.

Whether you grind the meat yourself, have your butcher do it, or buy the packaged stuff from the supermarket, you need to remember a few things to ensure success. First, last, and always, stick to this rule: Keep it cold! Everything—from the meat and the tools to all the additional ingredients—must always be kept cold. I even chill the grinder attachment. If you're grinding or stuffing a lot, break the meat up into separate packages so you never have too much out of the fridge at a time. Besides the safety issue, which is always paramount, the chilled components will ensure the meat emerging from the grinder will be firm and compact, falling out in tight little nuggets or tubes.

To produce tender sausage in your smoker, aim for a meat-to-fat ratio of 80/20 or even up to 70/30. Because a lot of that fat melts away during smoking, your sausage won't be greasy. I like to add about ½ cup of cold water with a bit of crushed ice to every 5 pounds (2.3kg) of meat filling when I mix it. This ensures the filling maintains a good chill that will help it through the stuffer. Handle the meat very gently and wear latex gloves so you don't warm the mixture with your hands.

Once you've perfected my recipe, you can venture farther afield. There are many classic sausage recipes to inspire you: bratwurst, hot and sweet Italian, even breakfast sausages. Or take a page from us chefs, who have opened up this one wide. You'll see such creative combos as chicken and apple, lamb and mango chutney, rabbit with pistachio, and so on. I love to put cheese in my sausages. As I always say, your only limitation is your imagination.

Once you have your cold meat mixture and your grinder is set up for stuffing, you need casing. You can choose from two basic kinds: natural and collagen. Natural casings are made from the intestines of hogs, sheep, and cattle. These are by far the most popular. Because they're packed in dry salt or brine, you need to flush them with water and soak them before using. They come in different sizes, so select whatever makes sense for what you're making. Beef casings are the biggest and used for such things as bologna or mortadella. These are tough casings and can be handled fairly roughly.

Collagen casings are an edible by-product of animal hide—usually cattle—and come in a variety of sizes and colors. When you stuff this casing, the meat adheres to it very tightly, making it difficult to peel away. Because collagen is quite delicate, once you stuff these casings, try not to handle them too much. A normal collagen casing isn't the ideal casing for a smoked sausage because it doesn't always support the weight of sausage when hung in a smoker. You can purchase extra-thick collagen casings that will stand up to the smoker and they're much easier to use without a lot of preparation. There are pros and cons for both types of casings. It comes down to personal preference in the end.

Let's Talk Bacon

Okay, I admit I'm not the most modest guy. But in this case, ask my friends: I make awesome bacon! Without fail, it's the one thing my friends will ask for when they come mooching. So now I'm a meat guy, a sausage guy, *and* a bacon guy.

Bacon is easily one of the most heavily processed products in the modern marketplace. It's made in huge plants where speed to market is the goal above all others. The curing solutions for mass-produced bacon contain synthetic nitrates in excess despite the wealth of health concerns connected to this additive. Nitrates are used to help ensure food safety by preventing botulism, which is one of the deadliest foodborne illnesses. And all those synthetic nitrates give you that bright pink, slimy product we've all come to know as bacon. But it doesn't have to be that way. Once you've made your own bacon and tasted the true luscious smoky notes, you'll never be able to eat the prepackaged stuff again.

Follow my recipe for maple-smoked bacon later in this chapter. Once you have a feel for making bacon, you can experiment and put a bit of yourself in it by adding your own personal touches to the cure. I promise you, once you've bitten into my smoked bacon, you'll find yourself on the hunt for more bacon recipes. Anyone who knows my cookbooks knows I have a huge crush on bacon.

When I make bacon, I'll usually make at least a whole pork belly's worth. After it comes out of the smoker, I portion it out and wrap it well in plastic wrap to freeze. It will last in the freezer for up to 3 months. (Any longer and it will start to taste a bit rancid—but my batches never last longer than 3 months anyway!). In the fridge, it's good for about 2 weeks, which isn't as long as the store-bought stuff. But I ask you: Who has bacon in the fridge for more than 2 weeks? If I know it's there, I'm thinking of ways to use it!

When you first read the recipe, you're going to think I'm crazy because on paper, it looks like way too much work. Although it takes 7 days, in terms of actual effort, it's less than 30 minutes' worth of work. Patience is the word! While it's curing, you don't have to do anything but wait. Then it's only going to be in the smoker for something like 3 hours and then voilà—homemade bacon!

Rockin' Ribs

Ribs are one of the things I'm best known for. In my other life, I'm a corporate development chef for one of the largest rib producers in North America. You might have eaten some of my work in a restaurant chain or retail store we sell to. There's nothing—and I mean nothing—as good as a rack of baby back ribs pulled from the smoker after about 4 or 5 hours of serious slow-smoking tender love and care. The aroma, the taste, and the texture as you bite into a rib and feel the meat pull away from the bone with just the tiniest bit of effort are unparalleled. If the bone can be pulled out of a rack with no resistance at all, it's overcooked. After that first bite, take a long look at the gorgeous pinky-red ring the smoke leaves and try not to suck on the bone—but, of course, you will.

When you decide to succeed at perfect ribs, that's when you really need a butcher you can trust. Making friends with your butcher is the best way to guarantee success on the smoker. A good butcher will open a case of ribs and let you choose the best three or four slabs. A good butcher will also help by preparing special cuts and ordering exotic meats. Be kind to your butcher and they'll be kind to you!

Preparation is 99% of success when smoking. A huge part of that preparation is choosing the right ribs, but first, you need to know what you're looking for. The following table breaks down all the kinds of pork ribs out there.

Kind	Characteristics
Baby back ribs	These ribs are from the strip of rib bones the butcher gets when boning a whole loin. The button bones are the tailpiece of the rack and should be removed. Back ribs are a chef's favorite pick because they're so versatile. They cost more because they have a higher meat-to-bone ratio and they contain some of the tenderloin and loin meat. They're the most tender cut and they can do very well on the grill. In the smoker, you have to be very careful not to overcook back ribs. They can be so tender that the bones just fall out when you go to lift the smoker rack.
Country-style ribs	These ribs are very meaty but tough, making them another rib born for the smoker. They come from the rib end and they usually have only a few bones attached.
Spare ribs	These ribs are cut from the side—where they attach to the breastbone—and there's usually soft bone brisket attached. This soft bone brisket should be removed. Spare ribs with large clumps of fat should be avoided. The flap of meat that runs down to the last three ribs can be left or trimmed and cooked separately. Butchers used to discard this cut because it's very tough and no one thought the average consumer could do anything with it—but we know better, don't we? These ribs were made for the smoker. They have the perfect ratio of fat to meat that's ideal for the smoker but too fatty and tough for the grill. After 4 hours in the smoker, the fat will melt into the meat, making it rich and tender.
St. Louis and Kansas City ribs	St. Louis ribs are spare ribs trimmed to remove the sternum bone, cartilage, and rib tips. Kansas City ribs are an even more closely trimmed spare rib because the hard bone is removed.

There are various other cuts in the pork rib category, such as rib tips, riblets, and button ribs. These ribs are basically a way to sell every last morsel of the rib section of an animal, but they're not necessarily smoker-friendly. I don't cover them in this book, but you're welcome to investigate on your own. You might find something you really like. Me, I'm a baby back ribs guy.

Also, I know we're in the pork chapter, but because we're already talking about ribs, let's go over the other types of ribs out there.

Kind	Characteristics
Beef ribs	These are huge ribs cut from the loin. They can be very meaty, but they can also be very fatty and full of tough cartilage. Long, slow cooking in the smoker turns them into something to behold. When you eat a really good plate of these huge ribs, there's no way you won't be dripping with juices and have such a dirty face you'll need a shower—but you'll have no regrets! My recipes for Beef Ribs with Chocolate Stout (page 162) and Prime Rib Burgers with Horseradish Cream (page 164) could change your life.
Bison and venison ribs	These ribs are also from the loin. They can be absolutely delicious, but as with all game, they require a little extra TLC. Because game tends to be extremely lean, you'll see that my game rib recipes involve adding a lot of moisture. Game takes a longer time in the smoker and tolerates stronger flavors than more domesticated meats. Game ribs aren't always easy to find at the local grocery store. But your friend the butcher will know where to get these.
Lamb ribs	These are cut from the forequarter (front) of the lamb. The rack is oblong in shape, with layers of fat and lean meat. Lamb ribs are sweet and rich with flavor.

I know we got a bit off topic because this chapter is an ode to the pig—my favorite of all the animals. Shhhh, don't tell the others though!

Back to buying ribs: No matter what kind they are, ribs should show a healthy layer of meat all over the slab. There shouldn't be any bones showing on the slab. These are called "shiners." You only want to see the bones peeking out at the ends. Check carefully for shiners with back ribs because they're produced if poorly butchered. With spare ribs, there will be cartilage and the split breastbone attached. There will also be heavy fat over the last three bones. Remove the cartilage and trim the heavy fat—but only the excess on those last three bones. You'll need the rest for the smoker.

You'll find lots of how-to information you need to prepare ribs in my rib recipes in this chapter and in Chapter 10. But there's one thing that needs a special mention to guarantee success: Remove the membrane! Please! The thick membrane that covers the back of your rack of ribs—no matter what kind—must go. The seasoning and smoke can't penetrate it. This step makes or breaks your ribs. Some people score it in a diamond shape. That's cheating and it just produces a lot of very chewy bits because it's tough and inedible. It's not hard to remove. Just slide the back of a dinner knife under the silver skin anywhere along the rack. If it resists in one spot, try another. Lift and loosen this skin until you can grab it with your fingers and a paper towel. (It's very slippery.) Pull it firmly but gently off the ribs. It should peel away in one large sheet, but if it breaks, use the knife to restart at another section. Once you've done two or three, you'll wonder what all the fuss was about.

Now that you practically know all there is to know about pigs, let's get to the recipes!

Pork Tenderloin

This is a pretty easy recipe and a great place for you to start when it comes to smoking foods, especially because pork tenderloin is an inexpensive tender cut of pork. Tackling a large cut of meat can be daunting and expensive, but pork tenderloin is a quick and easy cook that gives you a chance to learn the basics of smoking foods and barbecue.

Prep Time	Smoker Temp	Smoke Time
10 minutes	235°F (115°C)	1 to 1½ hours

wood suggestions: apple, pecan, hickory, or maple

2 whole pork tenderloins (about 1 to 1½lb [450 to 680g] each), silver skin trimmed

2 tbsp vegetable oil or olive oil

4 tbsp barbecue seasoning rub

2 tbsp melted butter

4 tbsp pure maple syrup

1. Preheat the smoker to 235°F (115°C). Use apple, pecan, hickory, or maple wood.

2. Rub the tenderloins all over with the vegetable oil. Firmly press the barbecue rub into the meat. Insert a thermometer probe into the thickest part of a tenderloin.

3. Place the tenderloins in the smoker and smoke until the internal temperature reaches 135°F (60°C), about 1 to 1½ hours.

4. In a small bowl, combine the butter and maple syrup.

5. Remove the tenderloins from the smoker and brush with the butter and syrup mixture. Allow the tenderloins to rest for 5 minutes. Slice before serving.

Recipe Note: You can use any barbecue seasoning rub you like: Use one from this book or from the Internet; use a prepackaged rub from a host of barbecue aficionados; or create your own—and have some tasty fun experimenting.

Pork Belly Burnt Ends

My buddy Big Dog made me a batch of pork belly burnt ends that made me moan. His were smoked in a stick burner he built himself—a mighty tasty DIY project that puts smiles on everyone's faces. This is my version of his tasty recipe.

Prep Time	Smoker Temp	Smoke Time
15 minutes	275°F (135°C)	4 hours

wood suggestions: apple, pecan, hickory, or maple

5lb (2.3kg) raw pork belly, rind removed

½ cup **Cajun Rub** (page 116)

2oz (60ml) bourbon whiskey

8 tbsp dark brown sugar

1 cup barbecue sauce

½ cup maple syrup

¼ cup Louisiana-style hot sauce

4 tbsp butter

1. Preheat the smoker to 275°F (135°C). Use apple, pecan, hickory, or maple wood.

2. Cut the pork belly into 1½-inch (3.75cm) squares. In a large bowl, combine the pork belly and rub. Toss to evenly coat. Evenly space the pork belly on a smoker rack. Insert a temperature probe into the thickest part of the pork belly.

3. Place the rack in the smoker and smoke until the internal temperature reaches 170°F (80°C), about 2 to 2½ hours.

4. Remove the rack from the smoker and place the pork belly in a large bowl. Add the bourbon whiskey, brown sugar, barbecue sauce, maple syrup, hot sauce, and butter. Toss to evenly coat. Transfer everything to a roasting pan and cover tightly with aluminum foil.

5. Place the pan in the smoker and continue to smoke until the internal temperature reaches 200°F to 205°F (90°C to 95°C) and the sauce is reduced and sticky.

6. Remove the pan from the smoker and allow the pork to rest for 15 minutes before slicing and serving.

Recipe Note: I think this is a great meat snack but also quite tasty stacked on a toasted buttered bun with some slaw and extra sauce for dunking.

Pulled Pork

When most folks get started smoking foods, one of the first items they want to make is pulled pork. There are a lot of different ways to make smoked pulled pork, but when you're starting out for the first time, you want it easy—and this recipe offers that. Ask your butcher for a pork picnic roast—bone-in and rind on. This is an inexpensive cut of pork and weighs about 3 to 5 pounds (1.4 to 2.3kg), making your first pulled pork smoke a little less daunting. Once you've mastered this smaller shoulder cut, move on to the whole Boston butt, which weighs 12 to 15 pounds (5.4 to 6.8kg). These take a lot longer to smoke, but the principles are the same.

Prep Time	Smoker Temp	Smoke Time
10 minutes	200°F (95°C)	4 to 5 hours

wood suggestion: hickory

1 bone-in, rind-on pork picnic roast
   (about 3lb [1.4kg])

2 tbsp vegetable oil

4 tbsp barbecue seasoning rub

apple juice

2 to 3 tbsp apple cider vinegar

hot sauce (optional)

crushed red pepper flakes, to taste

kosher salt, to taste

freshly ground black pepper, to taste

1. Preheat the smoker to 200°F (95°C). Use hickory wood.

2. Rub the roast all over with the vegetable oil. Firmly press the barbecue rub into the pork, ensuring to get the seasoning into all the crevices. Insert a thermometer probe into the center of the roast. Fill a spritz bottle with apple juice.

3. Place the roast in the smoker and smoke until the internal temperature reaches 165°F to 170°F (75°C to 80°C), about 2 hours. Occasionally spritz with the juice.

4. Remove the roast from the smoker and wrap tightly in a double layer of aluminum foil. Return the roast to the smoker and continue to smoke until the internal temperature reaches 200°F (95°C), about 2 to 5 hours more.

5. Remove the roast from the smoker and allow to rest for 15 minutes.

6. Remove the aluminum foil and reserve the juices. Twist the center bone—it should pull cleanly from the meat. Discard this bone. Remove the outer rind from the meat and scrap any excess meat and fats from inside the rind. Place all the meat and fats in a large bowl. (Discard the rind or pop it back into the smoker to crisp up for some tasty crackling.)

7. Use your hands to gently pull the pork shoulder into large chunks. Season with apple cider vinegar, a dash or two of hot sauce (if using), red pepper flakes, salt, and pepper.

8. Serve immediately on toasted buns with your favorite barbecue sauce on the side.

Pork T-Bones with Smoked Strawberry & Rhubarb Compote

Big, thick, meaty T-bone pork chops are ideal for serving to your family and friends. Paired with a compote made from smoked strawberries and rhubarb, this dish is unique and delicious.

Prep Time	Smoker Temp	Smoke Time
30 minutes	250°F (125°C)	2 to 3 hours

wood suggestions: cherry, pecan, hickory, apple, or oak

4 T-bone pork chops (about 2 inches [5cm] thick each), tenderloin intact

¼ cup honey

½ cup **Basic Barbecue Rub** (page 115)

1 pint (340g) fresh strawberries, hulled

2 large fresh rhubarb stalks, peeled and coarsely chopped

⅓ cup granulated sugar

⅓ cup firmly packed light brown sugar

½ cup apple juice

1 tbsp freshly squeezed lemon juice

½ tsp finely grated lemon zest

2 tbsp gourmet-style barbecue sauce

1 tsp cold unsalted butter

kosher salt, to taste

freshly ground black pepper, to taste

1. Preheat the smoker to 250°F (125°C). Use cherry, pecan, hickory, apple, or oak wood.

2. Working on one side at a time, brush the pork with honey and press the barbecue rub into the meat. Insert a thermometer probe into the thickest part of one chop—close to the bone but not touching the bone. Place the chops on a smoker rack.

3. Place the rack in the smoker and smoke until the internal temperature reaches 145°F to 150°F (65°C to 70°C), about 2 to 3 hours. (You can do less if you wish. I like the chops at 140°F [60°C].)

4. Place the strawberries on a smoker rack and place the rack in the smoker. Smoke until dull in color, about 30 minutes. Remove the rack from the smoker and allow the strawberries to cool slightly.

5. In a medium saucepan on the stovetop over medium heat, combine the rhubarb, granulated sugar, brown sugar, and apple juice. Cook until the rhubarb has softened, about 10 to 12 minutes, stirring occasionally. Stir in the lemon juice and zest, barbecue sauce, and strawberries.

6. Reduce the heat to medium-low. Cook until the strawberries have softened and the compote has thickened, about 10 to 12 minutes more, stirring occasionally. Stir in the butter, salt, and pepper. Reduce the heat to low to keep the compote warm.

7. Remove the pork chops from the smoker. Top with the compote before serving.

Recipe Note: Store leftover compote in an airtight container in the fridge for up to 1 week. You can also spoon the compote over vanilla ice cream.

3-2-1 Pork Shanks

These are some meat sticks of tasty goodness! Pork shanks are loaded with deliciousness. Big and meaty, these are a feast for the hungry. Ask your butcher for whole pork shanks that are skinless, about 2 pounds (1kg) each, and about 8 inches (20cm) long.

Prep Time	Smoker Temp	Smoke Time
20 minutes	235°F (115°C)	6 hours

wood suggestions: hickory, maple, or apple

8 cups **Basic Brine** (page 91), plus more

2 (12oz [350ml]) bottles of beer, plus more

4 meaty pork shanks (about 2lb [1kg] each), rind removed

4 tbsp vegetable oil

4 tbsp barbecue seasoning rub

½ cup maple syrup

1 cup barbecue sauce

4 tbsp light brown sugar

4 tbsp butter

1. In a large bucket or pot, combine the brine and beer. Add the pork shanks and add more brine or beer as needed to ensure the shanks are completely covered. Weigh the shanks down to keep them submerged. Refrigerate for 24 hours.

2. Remove the shanks from the brine. Rinse with cold running water and pat dry with paper towels. Place the shanks on a smoker rack and refrigerate for 24 hours.

3. Preheat the smoker per to 235°F (115°C). Use hickory, maple, or apple wood.

4. Rub the pork shanks all over with the vegetable oil and press the seasoning rub into the meat. Insert a thermometer probe into the thickest part of one shank–close to the bone but not touching the bone.

5. Place the rack in the smoker and smoke the shanks until the internal temperature reaches 160°F to 170°F (70°C to 80°C), about 3 hours. Spritz with a little beer as needed. If you get to that temperature range quickly, individually wrap the shanks in butcher paper or aluminum foil.

6. Remove the shanks from the smoker and remove the probe. Place each shank on a double sheet of aluminum foil. Drizzle each shank with a little beer and 2 tablespoons of maple syrup. Top each shank with ¼ cup of barbecue sauce. Add 1 tablespoon of brown sugar and 1 tablespoon of butter to each shank. Tightly wrap the aluminum foil.

7. Return the shanks to the smoker and smoke until the internal temperature reaches 195°F to 200°F 90°C to 95°C). Use the thermometer probe to check the temperature. Remove the shanks from the smoker and allow to rest for 10 minutes.

8. Preheat the grill to 400°F to 500°F (205°C to 260°C). Unwrap the shanks and reserve the liquids left in the foil.

9. Place the shanks on the grill and cook until lightly charred and the sauce is caramelized. Occasionally turn the shanks and baste them with the reserved syrup and beer sauce.

10. Remove the shanks from the grill and serve immediately—with lots of napkins.

Apple & Cinnamon Rack of Pork

I made this recipe one Saturday afternoon at Toronto's best barbecue event: the Dickson's SmokeShow. The folks from Dickson rock the Great White North when it comes to barbecue. I used a Slow 'N Sear kamado smoker/grill—and it made some tasty pork that day. Now you can recreate this recipe in your own smoker.

Prep Time	Smoker Temp	Smoke Time
20 minutes	235°F (115°C)	2½ hours

wood suggestions: apple and maple

1 (6-bone) frenched rack of pork (about 3 to 4lb [1.4 to 1.8kg])

1 quart (1 liter) apple cider (unsweetened recommended)

1 quart (1 liter) cold water

3 tbsp kosher salt, divided

1 cinnamon stick (3 inches [7.5cm] long), broken into pieces

2- to 3-inch [5 to 7.5cm] piece of fresh ginger, sliced

10 sprigs of fresh sage, divided

1 tsp black peppercorns

whole cinnamon sticks

1 tbsp fresh coarsely ground black pepper

2 tsp ground ginger

2 tsp granulated garlic

1 tsp ground cayenne

2 tbsp vegetable oil

4 apples (Gala, Honeycrisp, or Empire recommended), cut lengthwise into 3 or 4 equally thick slices (about ½ inch [1.25cm] thick)

honey

1. Pat dry the pork with paper towels. Place the rack in a large pot or a resealable plastic bag. Add the apple cider and water.

2. Dissolve 1 tablespoon of salt in a little warm water and add this mixture to the pork. Add the cinnamon, ginger, 2 sprigs of sage, and black peppercorns. Seal the bag, gently massage the ingredients into the pork, and refrigerate for 24 hours.

3. Preheat the smoker to 235°F (115°C). Use apple and maple woods. You can also add a few cinnamon sticks to boost the cinnamon flavor of the roast.

4. Remove the pork from the brine and discard the liquid and ingredients. Pat dry the pork with paper towels.

5. In a small bowl, combine the remaining 2 tablespoons of salt, pepper, ground ginger, garlic, and cayenne. Rub the pork all over with the vegetable oil. Press the seasonings into the meat. Insert a thermometer probe into the pork—close to the bone but not touching the bone.

6. Tightly arrange the apple slices in an even layer in the smoker. Place a layer of cinnamon sticks over the apples and top with the remaining 8 sprigs of sage.

7. Place the pork on top of the sage and smoke until the internal temperature reaches 145°F (65°C), about 2½ hours.

8. Remove the pork from the smoker and baste with honey. Allow the pork to rest for 10 minutes. Carve the pork before serving.

Pork & Cheese Meatball Burgers

Along with pork and either cheddar or mozzarella cheese, this recipe also features a sweet chili mustard sauce and an onion slaw. These mighty tasty jawbreaker meatball burgers might require you to have a flip-top head!

Prep Time	Smoker Temp	Smoke Time
15 minutes	235°F (115°C)	90 minutes

wood suggestions: hickory, apple, maple, pecan, or mesquite

2lb (1kg) ground pork

1 cup crispy fried onions

1 medium white onion, finely diced

6 garlic cloves, minced

1 green onion, chopped

¼ cup chopped fresh thyme or parsley leaves

3 tsp kosher salt

2 tsp freshly ground black pepper

pinch of ground cayenne

3 tbsp cornstarch or potato starch

1 cup diced or cubed smoked cheddar or mozzarella cheese

1 to 2 medium red onions, sliced into ½-inch-thick (1.25cm) rounds

8 tbsp roasted garlic aioli or mayonnaise

8 soft hamburger buns, toasted

8 slices of smoked bacon, crisply cooked and coarsely chopped

for the mustard sauce

¼ cup yellow mustard

1 tbsp Dijon mustard

¼ cup Thai sweet red chili sauce

splash of rice vinegar or apple cider vinegar

for the onion slaw

1 medium red onion, thinly sliced

1 tbsp chopped fresh chives

kosher salt, to taste

freshly ground black pepper, to taste

splash of rice vinegar or apple cider vinegar

1. In a large bowl, combine the ground pork, fried onions, onion, garlic, green onion, thyme, salt, pepper, cayenne, cornstarch, and cheese. Mix until well combined. Form the mixture into eight equally sized balls. Place the balls on a baking sheet and refrigerate for 1 hour.

2. Preheat the smoker to 235°F (115°C). Use hickory, apple, maple, pecan, or mesquite wood.

3. Evenly space the onion slices on a flat work surface. Press one meatball onto each slice. Place each stack on a smoker rack.

4. In a small bowl, make the sweet chili mustard sauce by combining the yellow mustard, Dijon mustard, red chili sauce, and rice vinegar. Mix well to combine.

5. Place the rack in the smoker and smoke the burgers for 30 minutes. Evenly baste the burgers with the mustard sauce. Continue to smoke for 1 hour more, basting every 15 minutes.

6. In a large bowl, make the onion slaw by combining the red onion, chives, salt, pepper, and rice vinegar. Mix well to combine.

7. Remove the rack from the smoker. Spread the aioli on the bottom buns and top with the meatball and onion stacks. Baste the burgers with mustard sauce and top with the onion slaw and bacon. Brush the underside of the top buns with mustard sauce before placing them atop the burgers.

Recipe Note: Try a variety of different ground meats with this recipe: chicken, turkey, or even fish or seafood (such as halibut or scallops).

Spare Ribs

This is a pretty simple recipe for smoking whole spare ribs. When purchasing spare ribs, look for a heavier/meatier rack weighing about 4 pounds (1.8kg). Spare ribs have the breast bone attached—called "rib tips"—and in my opinion, this is the tastiest part of the rib.

Prep Time	Smoker Temp	Smoke Time
10 minutes	225°F (110°C)	4 to 5 hours

wood suggestion: hickory

1 rack of whole spare ribs (about 4lb [1.8kg])

4 tbsp lard or vegetable shortening, softened

1 cup barbecue seasoning rub, plus more

apple juice

barbecue sauce (optional)

1. Preheat the smoker to 225°F (110°C). Use hickory wood.

2. Remove the membrane from the back of the ribs. (See page 181 for instructions on how to do this.) Press the lard into the ribs, especially the tips and sides. (This layer of fat helps keep the ribs juicy during the smoke.)

3. Press the seasoning rub into the ribs. Insert a thermometer probe into the meatiest part of the ribs—between bones but not touching any bones. Fill a spritz bottle with apple juice.

4. Place the ribs in the smoker and smoke until the internal temperature reaches 200°F to 205°F (95°C to 100°C) and the bones wiggle but stay intact, about 4 to 5 hours. Spritz with the apple juice every hour.

5. Remove the ribs from the smoker. Lightly cover with aluminum foil and a kitchen towel. Allow the ribs to rest for 15 minutes.

6. Brush the ribs with barbecue sauce (if using) and sprinkle seasoning rub over the top (if desired). Slice the ribs between every bone before serving.

Fireball Ribs with Smoked Honey Glaze

These ribs have sweet and spicy kicks from cinnamon, chipotle, apple juice, honey, and hot sauce—all enhanced by the smoke.

Prep Time	Smoker Temp	Smoke Time
40 minutes	200°F (95°C)	6 to 8 hours

wood suggestions: hickory, oak, maple, or mesquite

4 racks of pork back ribs (about 2½lb [1.2kg] each)

1 cup plus 1 tsp **Chipotle & Cinnamon Rub** (page 122)

2 cups apple juice

1 cup cold water

½ cup cinnamon schnapps liqueur

¼ cup hot sauce

1 cup **Cold-Smoked Honey** (page 331)

1. Remove the membrane from the bone side of each rack. (See page 181 for instructions on how to do this.) Rub 1 cup of the chipotle rub into both sides of each rack. Place the ribs in a large container, cover, and refrigerate for 24 hours.

2. Preheat the smoker to 200°F (95°C). Use hickory, oak, maple, or mesquite wood.

3. Use a funnel to fill a spray bottle with the apple juice, water, cinnamon schnapps liqueur, and hot sauce. Shake to mix well. (Store in the fridge for up to 1 week.)

4. Remove the ribs from the fridge. Insert a thermometer probe into the meatiest part of the ribs—between bones but not touching any bones.

5. Place the ribs in the smoker and smoke until the internal temperature reaches 185°F (85°C) and the bones wiggle but stay intact, about 6 to 8 hours. Spritz with the apple juice mixture every hour.

6. Remove the ribs from the smoker. Brush the ribs with the smoked honey and sprinkle the remaining 1 teaspoon of chipotle rub over the top. Serve immediately—with lots of napkins.

Recipe Note: Because the spritz is a bit spicy, make sure you don't spritz into the wind. You can also use this spritz on poultry, pork ribs, pork chops, fish, and seafood.

Maple-Smoked Bacon

The quest to smoke my own bacon started years ago because I was tired of buying commercial bacon that's injected with a ton of water and just splatters all over my kitchen. I started using a ready cure, but it's packed full of unnatural ingredients to preserve the bacon and give it that beautiful pink color we all know and love so much. I wanted something more natural, even if it meant losing the pink color. So I developed a cure without all the scary nitrates and nitrites to use on fresh pork bellies. This bacon doesn't last as long as the commercial stuff and it has a grayish hue instead of pink, but it tastes great and you can feel good about eating it.

Prep Time	Smoker Temp	Smoke Time
30 minutes	85°F (30°C)	24 to 36 hours

wood suggestions: maple, oak, or hickory

3 cups kosher salt

1 cup firmly packed dark brown sugar

1 cup maple syrup

½ cup **Basic Barbecue Rub** (page 115)

2 tsp pure vanilla extract

1 fresh pork belly of uniform thickness (about 10 to 12lb [4.5 to 5.4kg]), rind removed

1. In a medium bowl, combine the salt, brown sugar, maple syrup, barbecue rub, and vanilla extract. Mix until well combined. (Store in an airtight container in the refrigerator for up to 6 months.)

2. Cut the pork belly into three 10-inch-long (25cm) pieces. Rinse under cold water and pat dry with paper towels. Rub about ½ cup of the maple cure all over each piece of pork belly in an even layer. Sprinkle a handful of the cure on the bottom of a large (not metal) container and place a piece of pork belly on top. Sprinkle the top of that piece with another handful of cure, rubbing the cure into the flesh. Add another pork belly piece and repeat this process until all the pieces have been seasoned with the maple cure.

3. Cover the container and refrigerate for 5 to 10 days depending on the thickness of the pork belly and how salty you like it. I find that about 6 to 7 days works well. Every day, spoon the liquid that's accumulated in the bottom of the container over the pork belly.

4. Remove the pork belly from the container and pat dry with paper towels. Place the pork pieces on a wire rack on a rimmed baking sheet and refrigerate for 3 to 4 days or until good and dry.

5. Preheat the smoker to 85°F (30°C) for cold-smoking. Use maple, oak, or hickory wood. Remove the sheet from the fridge and insert a thermometer probe into the center of one of the pieces of pork belly.

6. Place the sheet in the smoker and smoke the pork until the internal temperature reaches 145°F (65°C) and the flesh is firm and has a rich, brownish-red color, about 24 hours. If you prefer double-smoked bacon, preheat the smoker temperature to 135°F (60°C) and smoke until the internal temperature reaches 150°F to 160°F (65°C to 70°C), about 8 hours more.

7. Remove the sheet from the smoker and allow the pork belly to cool completely. Wrap in cheesecloth or butcher's paper and refrigerate until ready to serve. Don't wrap in plastic wrap because the plastic will promote moisture and cause your bacon to spoil. Store in a vacuum-sealed bag in the fridge for up to 2 weeks or in the freezer for up to 3 months.

Recipe Note: Store the bacon as large pieces and cut slices as needed. This will prevent mold. If mold spores start to appear, simply cut them off and replace the wrapping.

Bologna

This might seem abnormal to you, but trust me when I say there's just something so comforting about smoked bologna. Food doesn't always have to be fancy and smoking is definitely all about flavor, even with something this simple. The folks in Arkansas call this an Ozark sirloin, but here in Canada, we call it a Newfie roast.

Prep Time	Smoker Temp	Smoke Time
5 minutes	250°F (120°C)	1½ to 2 hours

wood suggestion: hickory

3lb (1.4kg) pork bologna log (about 4 inches [10cm] wide and 8 inches [20cm] long)

2 tbsp vegetable oil

2 tbsp **Memphis Rib Rub** (page 119)

½ cup hickory-smoked barbecue sauce

¼ cup honey

1. Preheat the smoker to 250°F (120°C). Use hickory wood.

2. Use the tip of a sharp knife to score a ¼ inch-deep (0.5cm) and 1-inch-wide (2.5cm) diamond pattern into the entire surface of the bologna. Brush the bologna with the vegetable oil. Sprinkle the rib rub over the entire surface. Insert a thermometer probe into the center of the log.

3. In a small bowl, combine the barbecue sauce and honey. Mix well.

4. Place the bologna in the smoker and smoke until the internal temperature reaches 165°F (75°C), about 1½ to 2 hours. Baste with the honey barbecue sauce every 15 minutes after the first 45 minutes.

5. Transfer the bologna to a cutting board and slice into rounds before serving.

Recipe Note: My favorite way to serve this is thinly sliced on top of a grilled cheese sandwich with pickled onions and a drizzle of ketchup! I also like to use my meat slicer to shave the smoked bologna paper-thin, stack it high on a toasted bun, and drizzle it with extra honey barbecue sauce.

Cold-Smoked Spam

You might think smoking spam is weird, but it's really a great vehicle for smoke, taking on a sweet, smoky flavor that adds a new dimension to this popular canned meat. I've pan-fried spam with eggs for breakfast; added spam to grilled cheese sandwiches; grilled spam to make a quick and easy burger; and deep-fried little cubes of spam until crispy to use as croutons in salads and soups. And now I'm smoking spam!

Prep Time	Smoker Temp	Smoke Time
2 minutes	85°F (30°C)	3 hours

wood suggestion: hickory

2 (12oz [340g]) tins of classic spam,
  chilled in the fridge for 24 hours

1. Preheat the smoker to 85°F (30°C) for cold-smoking. Use hickory wood.

2. Open the tins and carefully remove the spam in one piece. Rinse under cold water and pat dry with paper towels. Use the tip of a knife to score a ¼-inch-deep (0.5cm) and ½-inch-wide (1.25cm) diamond pattern into the entire surface of each block. Place the spam on a smoker rack.

3. Place the rack in the smoker and smoke the spam until slightly golden brown, about 2 to 3 hours. Remove the rack from the smoker and refrigerate the spam until chilled. Slice before serving.

Recipe Note: Did you know the state of Hawaii sells more tins of spam than any other state in the United States and that South Korea is the second-largest consumer of spam in the whole world behind the United States?

Polish Sausage

Also known as kielbasa (as all sausage in Poland is called), Polish sausage is made from pork mixed with fresh garlic and marjoram. For this recipe, I've slightly modified the classic recipe by adding some hot pepper flavors for a bit of heat. I like my sausage to bite back!

Prep Time	Smoker Temp	Smoke Time
2 hours	125°F (55°C)	5 to 6 hours

wood suggestions: oak or maple

5lb (2.3kg) boneless pork butt (80% lean), cut into 1-inch (2.5cm) chunks

8 large garlic cloves, minced

1 tbsp pickling salt

2 tsp freshly ground black pepper

2 tsp granulated garlic

2 tsp dried marjoram leaves

1 tsp crushed red pepper flakes

½ tsp ground cayenne

2 tbsp cold water

1 cup finely crushed ice

hog or collagen sausage casings, soaked in cold water

1. Place the pork chunks on a baking sheet lined with parchment paper. Cover with plastic wrap and freeze for 30 minutes or until very cold but not frozen.

2. Grind the pork using the medium plate on a meat grinder. Transfer the ground pork to a large bowl. Lightly cover the bowl with plastic wrap and refrigerate for 30 minutes. (Tip: Clean your meat grinder now—it saves time and aggravation later.)

3. In a medium bowl, combine the garlic, pickling salt, black pepper, granulated garlic, marjoram, red pepper flakes, and cayenne. Mix until well combined.

4. Remove the pork from the fridge and sprinkle the spice mixture evenly over the surface. Add the cold water and crushed ice. Mix thoroughly with your hands until all the ingredients are evenly distributed.

5. Use a sausage stuffer to portion the pork mixture into the hog casings. (You can decide the length of the sausages. I like them about 6 to 7 inches [15.25 to 17.5cm] long.) Arrange the sausages on a baking sheet lined with parchment paper or butcher paper. Cover the sheet with plastic wrap and refrigerate for 1 to 5 hours.

6. Preheat the smoker to 125°F (50°C) for cold-smoking. Use oak or maple wood.

7. Hang the sausage from hooks if you have them (this ensures even smoking and doesn't cause rack markings) or evenly space them on a smoker rack. Place the hooks or rack in the smoker. Close the smoke vents for 30 minutes to allow the sausages to dry without smoke. Insert a thermometer probe into the center of one of the sausages.

8. Open the vents to start adding the smoke and maintain the 125°F (50°C) temperature. Smoke the sausages until the internal temperature reaches 165°F (75°C), about 2 hours. Raise the smoker temperature to 165°F (75°C) and continue to smoke until the internal temperature reaches 180°F (85°C), about 3 to 4 hours more. Remove the sausages from the smoker and allow to cool completely. Transfer the sausages to an airtight container. Refrigerate for up to 2 days or wrap in plastic wrap and freeze for up to 2 months.

9. To serve, preheat the grill to medium heat. Place the sausages on the grill and cook until heated through and lightly charred, about 3 to 5 minutes per side.

10. Remove the sausages from the grill and serve with your favorite condiments. (I like mayonnaise, hot mustard, sauerkraut, and red onion as well as a crispy, garlicky dill pickle on the side.)

Recipe Notes: You're going to need a meat grinder with a medium grinding plate and a sausage stuffer. If you don't have this equipment, see if you can borrow them. Your butcher should sell sausage casings, but you can also get them at specialty food service operations as well as at specialty food stores. Also, if you know your butcher really well, you can ask them to prepare a meat mixture for sausages using a spice recipe you like. But you have to ask really nicely!

Craft Beer Sausages

Like beer, sausages take on the unique flavors of local ingredients and traditions. As should be pretty obvious by now, I like to play with my food and I like beer. This is my take on a craft beer sausage. Feel free to use your favorite craft beer, and once you're comfortable with making sausages, you too can play with seasonings. Make sure the beer you use in this recipe is as cold as the meats to keep everything similar in temperature when grinding.

Prep Time	Smoker Temp	Smoke Time
1 hour	225°F (110°C)	2 hours

wood suggestions: mesquite, hickory, or oak

3lb (1.4kg) cubed pork shoulder meat

2lb (1kg) cubed veal shoulder meat

¾lb (340g) cubed pork fat

½lb (225g) double-smoked bacon, diced

1 medium white onion, minced

4 garlic cloves, minced

1 cup icy-cold craft beer (stout or IPA recommended), divided

4 tsp kosher salt

3 tsp freshly ground black pepper

3 tsp granulated garlic

2 tsp granulated onion

2 tsp celery salt

2 tsp ground cayenne

1 tsp ground ginger

½ cup chopped flat-leaf parsley leaves

½ tsp pink curing salt (Prague powder)

hog casings

hot dog rolls

1. Place the pork shoulder, veal shoulder, pork fat, and bacon on a baking sheet. Freeze for 20 to 30 minutes.

2. Grind the meats using a grinding plate with ¼-inch (0.5cm) holes. In a large bowl, combine the ground meats, onion, garlic, ½ cup of beer, salt, pepper, granulated garlic, granulated onion, celery salt, cayenne, ginger, and parsley. Add the pink curing salt and mix well. Cover the bowl and refrigerate for 2 to 3 hours.

3. Soak the hog casings in cold water for about 30 minutes. Rinse and slide one end onto a sausage stuffer nozzle. Tie a knot at the other end.

4. Use the sausage stuffer to stuff the sausage meat mixture into the casings. Tie each sausage link off at about 6 inches (15.25cm) long and about 1½ to 2 inches (3.75 to 5cm) thick. Be careful not to overstuff the casings because they might burst when smoking. Place the sausages on a baking sheet lined with parchment paper. Cover with plastic wrap and refrigerate for 24 hours.

5. Preheat the smoker to 225°F (110°C). Use mesquite, hickory, or oak wood. Insert a temperature probe into one of the sausages. Fill a spritz bottle with the remaining ½ cup of beer.

6. Place the sausages in the smoker and smoke until the internal temperature reaches 160°F (75°C), about 2 hours. Spritz with the beer after the first 30 minutes.

7. Remove the sausages from the smoker and slice before serving. (You can also allow the sausages to cool and then serve.)

Recipe Note: If you can hang the sausages in the smoker, this makes for a more even cook. I like to use my drum smoker to smoke sausages.

Lamb & Wild Game Recipes

Chapter 12

A lot of people are afraid to cook lamb. I think they have this idea that it's difficult to cook, so they don't want to experiment with an expensive cut of meat because they could screw up and waste their money. Well, even though I'm a chef, I can tell you that lamb is one of the easiest meats for the average home chef to cook. No kidding. There's really nothing more straightforward than slathering some garlic, mustard, and maybe some rosemary all over a boned leg, tying it up in a roll, and throwing it on the grill. You just have to sear it first and then move it to indirect heat—and 45 minutes later, your family thinks you're a god. It really is that easy.

Guess what? It's no harder to smoke lamb—and it's certainly worth the time. More than any other meat, lamb comes with its own built-in baste: Lamb fat is dense and sweet. If you've cooked any lamb at all, you know how quickly that fat will set up (harden) away from heat. But it melts just as fast, especially in the heat of the smoker, where it keeps that young meat moist, tender, and über juicy.

My favorite ways to prepare lamb include marinating and grilling a leg of lamb on the rotisserie, smoking a boneless leg, or—my absolute favorite—smoking a whole baby lamb. I remember one occasion in my backyard when the aroma from the lamb in the smoker just completely overwhelmed us. We began picking at it "just for a taste," and suddenly, we were like wild animals—pulling the lamb apart by hand and grabbing rolls to sandwich the meat and sop up the juices. By the time we got ourselves back under control, there wasn't much left but a pile of bones. Forget carving it properly to put it on the table and eat like human beings. That fragrant lamb demanded we dive in right then and there—and we weren't sorry!

Domestic vs. Imported Lamb

New Zealand and Australia are major exporters of lamb to North America. Most American lamb is raised in Texas, California, Wyoming, South Dakota, Colorado, and Utah. North American lamb is often marketed as having a milder flavor than imported because it's fed a combination of mixed grains and mixed grasses, whereas imported breeds are fed only grass, which gives the meat a stronger flavor. It's really only noticeable in older imported lamb because young imported lamb is similar to most North American lamb. The choice is totally personal—both are good—but I have to say I don't want to eat lamb that's been disguised to taste like beef. What's the point?

Assorted Lamb Cuts

Just like with any other animal, it's essential to know where the cuts come from to determine how to prepare them and what flavors to use. The following figure and table detail the different cuts of lamb.

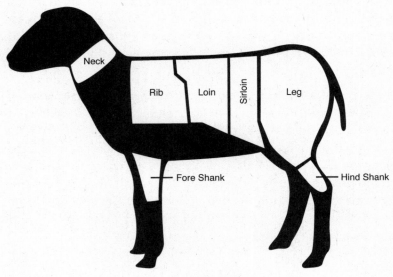

Cuts of lamb

Cut	Characteristics
Breast	Because this has a lot of cartilage and other connective tissues, it's one of the few cuts that should be cooked with moist heat. Lamb breast is also used to make ground lamb. It definitely lends itself to smoking methods: A slow-smoked breast can make sensational pulled lamb.
Flank	As with beef flank, lamb flank can be tough unless cooked with moist heat. Lamb flank is also used for making ground lamb.
Leg	A leg of lamb can be cut into leg chops, although more frequently, it's prepared whole. Roasted leg of lamb is one of the most common preparations, although braised leg of lamb is also popular in some cuisines. As smoking continues to gain in popularity, lamb legs will remain in high demand.
Loin	This is where we get the loin roast and the loin chops—tender cuts that are best prepared using dry heat. You can also grill the entire loin.
Neck	Another tougher cut with a lot of cartilage, the lamb neck is best used for making lamb stew or smoked for pulled lamb.
Rib	Sometimes called a "hotel rack," this primal cut is where we get rib chops, crown roast, and rack of lamb. Depending on the size of the ribs, a lamb chop might actually have two ribs on it. A rack prepared in the smoker will quite literally show you what "melts in your mouth" means.
Shank	The shank is the lower section of the animal's leg, and because it's extremely tough and full of connective tissue, the best cooking method for this cut is braising. Lamb has a fore shank and a hind shank, which come from the fore saddle and hind saddle, respectively. Hind shanks are just a bit meatier. Braising lamb shanks in the smoker combines two great techniques, creating an amazing texture and smoky flavor.
Shoulder	Sold with or without the bones and often used for roasts, lamb shoulder becomes incredibly tender when it's slowly smoked. Square-cut lamb shoulder is a square-shaped cut containing arm, blade, and rib bones. Ask your butcher to order it for you and then have them cut it into chops.
Sirloin	This is sometimes considered part of the leg primal cut, but it can also be prepared separately. It's frequently cut into chops or steaks.

Lamb & Wild Game Basics

We all know that a lamb is a young sheep, but there are rules around what can officially be called lamb. Lamb shouldn't be older than 1 year. A younger lamb is milder in flavor and has more tender meat than older lamb. The lamb commonly found in supermarkets is anywhere from 6 weeks to 1 year old. After 1 year, it becomes mutton and begins to take on a stronger, almost gamey flavor.

Many people only think of two cuts when they think of cooking lamb: rack of lamb and leg of lamb. But just about every cut of lamb is pretty tender because the animal wasn't alive long enough to develop old, tough meat. Because lamb is so tender, most cuts of lamb can be cooked using dry heat, even when the corresponding cut of beef or pork might not. You can apply any cooking method to lamb that you would to beef or pork, but just remember: It isn't going to take as long because the meat is younger. There's a recipe for lamb shoulder in this chapter and you'll notice it has the same steps the pork shoulder and even the beef brisket do, but the smoking time is way less. The main goal with smoking lamb is to achieve a great smoky flavor and not overcook the meat until it's too dry. A lamb can be slowly smoked to 145°F (65°C), which will give you a glorious medium-rare meat.

Because lamb meat has almost no marbling, the fat tends to encase it and not run through it like its older sibling, mutton. Lamb meat can definitely benefit from a good 6 to 8 hours of marinating before you rub it, but it doesn't really need brining. Take it easy on really strong flavors that can overpower the mild meat. Trust me, people who say lamb tastes really strong have probably been eating mutton and didn't know it.

The same can't be said of game. Game tends to have a strong earthy flavor and must be cooked accordingly. While the venison and bison cuts we see in the marketplace come from farmed animals, they still have true game flavor because of the way they're raised. Their feed is controlled, which makes the gamey flavor a bit more mild, but they're allowed to run as free as they would in the wild. This means they get a good amount of exercise, which results in their meat having very little fat. Bison is actually one of the healthiest meats you can eat. It's much leaner and higher in protein than beef. By the way, "gamey" flavor is really just a blanket term for a strong meat flavor. You'll see in my recipes that my standard method for preparing game is to marinate, rub, and cook game meats over low and slow smoke.

Because the basic forms of bison and venison are identical to that of beef, check out Chapter 10 for information on the various cuts. You can use the same general techniques as you would on beef when you're experimenting with different cuts of game meat. Just remember to multiply by at least 50% for everything—for example, a longer marinade time, a longer sit with the rub, and a longer smoke time. Additionally, the flavors you use can be stronger than you'd pair with beef.

To me, smoking game is one of the very best ways to prepare and eat it. It's also a good way to introduce it to someone who's never tasted it. In addition to smoked lamb ribs, I've given you rib recipes for venison and bison. Once you've nailed the recipes in this chapter, don't be afraid to spread your wings and try other cuts on your own.

Rack of Lamb with Goat Cheese

This recipe uses classic flavors that blend beautifully with lamb: garlic, Dijon mustard, and rosemary—a perfect example of "If it ain't broke, don't fix it"! Serve this lamb with hot-smoked creamy goat cheese and this recipe is sure to be a hit.

Prep Time	Smoker Temp	Smoke Time
30 minutes	200°F to 250°F (95°C to 120°C)	1 hour

wood suggestions: oak, maple, or pecan

½ cup unsalted butter (1 stick)

4 tbsp Dijon mustard, divided

1 tbsp chopped fresh rosemary leaves

2 garlic cloves, minced

1 cup panko breadcrumbs

¼ cup grated parmesan cheese

3 tbsp olive oil

3 tbsp chopped fresh parsley leaves

kosher salt, to taste, plus more

freshly ground black pepper, to taste, plus more

4 frenched lamb racks (about 1½lb [680g] each)

4oz (110g) creamy goat cheese

1. In a medium saucepan on the stovetop over medium heat, combine the butter, 2 tablespoons of Dijon mustard, rosemary, and garlic. Cook until the butter has melted. Lower the heat to low and keep the mixture warm.

2. In a medium bowl, combine the panko breadcrumbs, parmesan, olive oil, parsley, and the remaining 2 tablespoons of Dijon mustard. Mix until well combined. Season with salt and pepper. Set aside, stirring occasionally.

3. Preheat the smoker to 200°F to 250°F (95°C to 120°C). Use oak, maple, or pecan wood.

4. Season the lamb all over with salt and pepper. Evenly space the lamb on a smoker rack. Insert a thermometer probe into the thickest part of one of the racks of lamb without touching bone.

5. Place the rack in the smoker and smoke until the internal temperature reaches 125°F (55°C). Baste with the butter mixture every 15 minutes. Once the internal temperature has been reached, baste again with the butter mixture and coat each rack in a thin layer of the breadcrumb mixture. Continue to smoke until the internal temperature reaches 140°F (60°C).

6. Place the goat cheese in a freezer-safe bag and freeze for 20 minutes. After that time, line a smoker rack or a baking sheet with aluminum foil and place the goat cheese on top. Place the rack in the smoker and smoke during the last 30 minutes of the lamb smoke. The cheese is ready when it begins to melt and starts to take on a golden brown color. The cheese should be soft to the touch but not fluid. Transfer the cheese to a large bowl and whisk until smooth. Keep warm.

7. Remove the smoker rack from the smoker. Loosely tent the racks of lamb with aluminum foil and allow to rest for 5 minutes. Cut the racks into single-bone chops and top with a dollop of warm goat cheese before serving.

Recipe Note: Once you cut the lamb rack into chops, serve the chops in a variety of ways. Arrange 2 to 3 chops on a bed of mashed potatoes or creamy polenta (with the cheese drizzled over the chops) for an impressive entrée. Or arrange them on a platter (with the cheese offered as a dip) and pass that around at a cocktail party as an elegant hors d'oeuvre—often called "lamb lollipops" because the frenched bone resembles a long, white candy stick.

Owensboro Lamb Shoulder

My inspiration for this recipe comes from Owensboro, Kentucky, known as the barbecue mutton capital of the United States. Mutton is pretty strongly flavored, and because it can also be tough, I opted to use spring lamb for this recipe. It has a much sweeter flavor that's usually more appealing. My favorite way to serve this is piled high on warm crusty rolls with a tall glass of sweet Kentucky bourbon!

Prep Time	Smoker Temp	Smoke Time
45 minutes	200°F to 230°F (95°C to 110°C)	2½ to 3 hours

wood suggestions: oak wood or oak bourbon barrel staves (chips or chunks)

- ½ cup plus 3 tbsp freshly ground black pepper, plus more
- ¼ cup plus 3 tbsp firmly packed light brown sugar
- ¾ cup Worcestershire sauce, divided
- 6 tbsp kosher salt, divided, plus more
- 3 tbsp olive oil
- 12 garlic cloves, minced
- 2 tsp ground allspice
- 1 tsp ground cayenne

- 2 square-cut, bone-in lamb shoulder roasts (about 4 to 5lb [1.8 to 2.3kg] each)
- 2 cups lamb or beef stock
- 1 (12oz [350ml]) bottle of strong dark beer
- 1 cup white vinegar
- 2 tbsp crushed red pepper flakes
- 1 cup (2 sticks) unsalted butter
- 15 sprigs of fresh rosemary, tied together to form a brush

1. In a medium bowl, combine the ½ cup of black pepper, ¼ cup of brown sugar, ¼ cup of Worcestershire sauce, 3 tablespoons of salt, olive oil, garlic, allspice, and cayenne. Mix until well combined.

2. Use a sharp knife to score a 1-inch-thick (2.5cm) and ¼-inch-deep (0.5cm) diamond pattern into the fat cap of each roast. Rub the paste all over each roast, pushing the seasonings into the cuts. Transfer the roasts to a large pan and cover with plastic wrap. Refrigerate for 24 hours. Remove the roasts from the fridge and allow them to come to room temperature.

3. In a large saucepan on the stovetop over high heat, combine the lamb stock, dark beer, white vinegar, red pepper flakes, the remaining 3 tablespoons of black pepper, the remaining 3 tablespoons of brown sugar, the remaining ½ cup of Worcestershire sauce, and the remaining 3 tablespoons of salt. Bring to a rolling boil, then remove the saucepan from the heat. Whisk in the butter 1 tablespoon at a time until well combined. Reserve 1 cup of this mixture.

4. Preheat the smoker to 200°F to 230°F (95°C to 110°C). Use oak wood or oak bourbon barrel staves (chips or chunks). Insert a thermometer probe into the thickest part of one of the roasts.

5. Place the pan in the smoker and smoke the roasts until the internal temperature reaches 200°F (95°C) and the bones move freely, about 2½ to 3 hours. Use the rosemary brush to baste with the lamb stock mixture every 30 minutes.

6. Remove the pan from the smoker and allow the roasts to cool just enough to handle. Pull out the bones and discard them or reserve them for another use, such as a smoky lamb stock. Remove and discard any big hunks of fat if preferred. (Or leave in some fat based on how rich you'd like the final dish to be.)

7. Place the roasts in a large serving bowl. Use your fingers or two forks to shred the meat into thin strands. Stir in enough of the reserved lamb stock mixture to moisten. Season with salt and black pepper before serving.

Recipe Note: Place a aluminum foil pan under the roasts while smoking to catch the drippings. Add the drippings to the shredded meat and lamb stock mixture before serving for extra lamb goodness.

Lamb Ribs with Garlic, Ginger, Lemon & Soy Sauce Baste

Because lamb ribs can be very fatty, I use a tart and salty rub and basting mixture to cut the richness. The flavors of soy sauce, garlic, ginger, and lemon juice help balance the dish but don't mask the flavor of the lamb.

Prep Time	Smoker Temp	Smoke Time
30 minutes	235°F (115°C)	4 to 5 hours

wood suggestions: oak or hickory

¼ cup freshly ground black pepper

¼ cup molasses

12 garlic cloves, minced

5 tbsp olive oil, divided

4 tbsp soy sauce, divided

4 tbsp freshly squeezed lemon juice, divided

1 tbsp chopped fresh rosemary leaves

2 tsp minced ginger, divided

1 tsp crushed red pepper flakes

½ tsp kosher salt

8 racks of lamb ribs (about 12 to 16oz [340 to 450g] each), silver skin, sinew, and fat trimmed

1 tsp sambal oelek (red chili sauce)

1 green onion, minced

1. In a medium bowl, combine the black pepper, molasses, garlic, 3 tablespoons of olive oil, 2 tablespoons of soy sauce, 2 tablespoons of lemon juice, rosemary, 1 teaspoon of ginger, red pepper flakes, and salt. Mix until well combined. Rub this mixture all over the ribs. Place the racks in a large container and cover. Refrigerate for 24 hours, turning and spooning pooled liquids over the ribs every couple of hours.

2. Preheat the smoker to 235°F (115°C) with a moist humidity level. Use oak or hickory wood.

3. Evenly space the ribs on a smoker rack. Place the rack in the smoker and smoke the ribs until the bones move fairly freely, about 3 hours.

5. Transfer the ribs to a heatproof work surface. Brush the ribs all over with the remaining 2 tablespoons of olive oil. Tightly wrap the ribs in two layers of heavy-duty aluminum foil.

6. Return the smoker rack to the smoker and continue to smoke until the bones pull away cleanly from the meat, about 2 hours more. Remove the rack from the smoker and allow the ribs to cool slightly.

7. Preheat the grill to 350°F to 400°F (180°C to 205°C). Cut the rib racks into 2- to 3-bone portions.

8. In a medium bowl, combine the sambal oelek, green onion, the remaining 2 tablespoons of soy sauce, the remaining 2 tablespoons of lemon juice, and the remaining 1 teaspoon of ginger. Mix until well combined.

9. Place the ribs on the grill and cook until lightly charred and heated through, about 3 to 4 minutes per side. Baste once or twice per side with the green onion mixture.

10. Remove the ribs from the grill and serve immediately.

Recipe Note: Lamb ribs can be quite fatty and that can cause flare-ups during grilling. You can prevent these by searing the ribs over high heat and then finishing and basting them over indirect heat until they're caramelized rather than scorched.

Leg of Lamb

This recipe is always a crowd-pleaser for my family. Marinating the leg of lamb for 24 hours is key to getting maximum flavor penetration from the spices.

Prep Time	Smoker Temp	Smoke Time
30 minutes	235°F (115°C)	4 to 5 hours

wood suggestions: oak or maple

1 leg of lamb (about 5 to 6lb [2.3 to 2.7kg])

2 tbsp Montreal-style steak spice, plus more

25 plump garlic cloves, minced

1 tbsp chopped fresh ginger

¼ cup chopped fresh rosemary leaves

¼ cup chopped fresh mint leaves

2 tbsp Dijon mustard

3 tbsp olive oil

1 lemon

1 (12oz [350ml]) can of ginger ale

3oz (90ml) gin (something strong and herbaceous recommended)

sprigs of fresh rosemary

1. Use a sharp knife to score a 1-inch-wide (2.5cm) and ¼-inch-deep (0.5cm) diamond pattern into the leg of lamb. Rub the steak spice all over the leg and place the leg in a large pan that's deep enough for the leg to lay flat.

2. In a large bowl, combine the garlic, ginger, rosemary, mint, Dijon mustard, and olive oil. Cut the lemon in half and squeeze the juices over the garlic mixture. Coarsely dice the lemon and add to the garlic mixture.

3. Stir in the ginger ale and gin. Mix well. Pour this mixture over the leg of lamb, rubbing it into the slashes to ensure it's well coated. Cover the bowl and refrigerate for 24 hours, turning and massaging the leg every 8 hours.

4. Preheat the smoker to 235°F (115°C). Use oak or maple wood.

5. Remove the lamb from the marinade. Remove and discard the marinade. Season the lamb with a little more steak spice. Insert a thermometer probe into the thickest part of the leg.

6. Place the lamb in the smoker and cover with the rosemary. Smoke until the internal temperature reaches 165°F (75°C), about 3 hours.

7. Remove the leg from the smoker and wrap tightly in a double sheet of aluminum foil or butcher paper. Return the leg to the smoker and continue to smoke until the internal temperature reaches 205°F to 210°F (95°C to 100°C). The leg bone should pull cleanly from the meat and the meat should be moist and tender.

8. Remove the leg from the smoker and allow to rest for 30 minutes before serving.

Recipe Notes: I'd serve this on toast with shaved raw yellow onions and a schmear of creamy goat cheese. Use a strong, herbaceous gin to bring out a nice flavor in the lamb.

Veal Chops with Blackberry Butter

The key to this recipe is to quickly smoke the veal chops to keep them moist and succulent as well as allow the richness to stand out. Because this is one place you definitely don't want to overcook anything, keep a close eye on the thermometer. When buying veal, look for milk-fed veal because it's more tender and moist compared with grain-fed veal, which is a little tougher. Also, ask your butcher to french the veal chops for you, which means they clean the bones and leave them nice and long for an elegant presentation.

Prep Time	**Smoker Temp**	**Smoke Time**
30 minutes	200°F to 250°F (95°C to 125°C)	90 minutes

wood suggestions: pecan and oak or maple and cherry

4 milk-fed, bone-in veal chops (about 1½ to 2 inches [3.75 to 5cm] thick and 12 to 16oz [340 to 450g] each)

2 cups buttermilk

1 sprig of fresh thyme

2 tsp freshly cracked black peppercorns, divided

1 cup brandy

1 cup water

2 cinnamon sticks (3 inches [7.5cm] long each)

1 cup fresh blackberries

½ tsp granulated sugar

pinch of kosher salt

4 tsp freshly ground black pepper, divided

1 tsp chopped fresh thyme leaves

½ cup unsalted butter (1 stick), softened

pinch of ground cinnamon

1. In a large resealable plastic bag, combine the veal chops, buttermilk, thyme, and black peppercorns. Seal the bag, squeezing out as much air as possible, and refrigerate for at least 6 hours or up to overnight.

2. Use a funnel to add the brandy and water to a spray bottle. Add the cinnamon sticks and shake well. Refrigerate until needed.

3. In a small bowl, combine the blackberries, sugar, and salt. Toss well. Allow to rest for 15 minutes.

4. Mash the blackberry mixture until almost smooth. Add 1 teaspoon of black pepper, thyme, butter, and cinnamon. Mix until well combined. Refrigerate until needed. (Store this mixture in the fridge for up to 2 weeks.)

5. Preheat the smoker to 200°F to 250°F (95°C to 125°C). Use a blend of pecan and oak woods or maple and cherry woods.

6. Remove the chops from the marinade and pat dry with paper towels. Discard the marinade. Season all the sides with the remaining 3 teaspoons of black pepper. Evenly space the chops on a smoker rack. Insert a thermometer probe into the thickest part of a chop without touching bone.

7. Place the rack in the smoker and smoke until the internal temperature reaches 135°F to 145°F (60°C to 65°C) for medium-rare to medium doneness, about 90 minutes. Spritz with the brandy mixture every 15 to 20 minutes.

8. Remove the rack from the smoker and transfer the chops on a serving platter. Loosely tent with aluminum foil and allow to rest for 5 minutes. Serve with a dollop or two of the blackberry butter.

Recipe Note: The blackberry butter is just fantastic with so many things: Try it as a garnish for your favorite grilled or smoked chicken recipes; spread it on toast for breakfast; or enjoy it with pancakes and waffles.

Bison Short Ribs with Black Currant & Barbecue Sauce

The combination of red wine, cinnamon, and black currants works really well with the strong bison flavor. First you marinate, then you rub, and then you smoke—that's a lot of flavor layers!

Prep Time	Smoker Temp	Smoke Time
30 minutes	200°F (95°C)	6 hours

wood suggestions: oak or wine barrel

2½ cups Shiraz wine

¼ cup Concord grape juice

6 garlic cloves, minced

3 tbsp chopped fresh herbs (such as rosemary, thyme, and parsley leaves)

3 tbsp olive oil

3 tbsp balsamic vinegar

2 tbsp firmly packed light brown sugar

1 tbsp fresh coarsely ground black pepper

1 tbsp horseradish

1 tsp Worcestershire sauce

1 cup fresh black currants, blueberries, or blackberries

¼ cup granulated sugar

¼ cup cassis (black currant liqueur), plus more

2 tbsp hot red pepper jelly

6 racks of bison short ribs (about 1½lb [680g] each)

¼ cup **Chipotle & Cinnamon Rub** (page 122)

1. In a medium bowl, combine the wine, grape juice, garlic, herbs, olive oil, balsamic vinegar, brown sugar, pepper, horseradish, and Worcestershire sauce. Mix until well combined. (Store in an airtight container in the fridge for up to 1 week.)

2. In a medium saucepan on the stovetop over medium heat, combine the black currants, granulated sugar, cassis, and red pepper jelly. Bring to a boil, then reduce the heat. Simmer until the currants are extremely soft, about 20 minutes, stirring occasionally. Use a hand mixer to purée the mixture until smooth. Add another splash of cassis if the sauce is too thick.

3. In a resealable plastic bag, combine the bison short ribs and wine marinade. Seal the bag, removing as much air as possible, and refrigerate for 24 hours.

4. Preheat the smoker to 200°F (95°C). Use oak or wine barrel staves.

5. Remove the ribs from the marinade and pat dry with paper towels. Discard the marinade. Remove or score the membrane in ½-inch (1.25cm) diamond pattern. (See page 181 for instructions on how to remove the membrane.) Rub the chipotle rub all over the ribs. Evenly space the ribs on a smoker rack. Insert a thermometer probe into the thickest part of one of the racks of ribs without touching bone.

6. Place the rack in the smoker and smoke the ribs for 4 hours. Transfer the ribs to a heatproof surface and baste with the black currant sauce. Tightly wrap the ribs in two layers of heavy-duty aluminum foil. Place the ribs back on the rack.

7. Raise the smoker temperature to 235°F (115°C). Return the rack to the smoker and smoke the ribs until the internal temperature reaches 205°F (100°C) and the bones move freely, about 2 hours.

8. Remove the ribs from the smoker and carefully open the foil pouch. Serve immediately with any remaining black currant sauce.

Variation: Replace the bison ribs with beef short ribs, venison, or elk ribs.

Recipe Notes: Select a good-quality Shiraz for the marinade, but it doesn't have to be anything super pricey. Just pick something you'd want to drink with the meal you smoked. You can also use the marinade with chicken, turkey, fish, shellfish, pork, or beef.

Venison Ribs with Grape Jelly Glaze

Sweet flavors from grape jelly and brown sugar mixed with the sharpness of a Cajun rub and Thai chili sauce make for a delicious glaze for these meaty ribs. If you aren't the hunting sort, you can find venison and other game ribs in specialty meat shops. This recipe also works well with elk or bison ribs.

Prep Time	Smoker Temp	Smoke Time
30 minutes	200°F to 230°F (95°C to 110°C)	8 hours

wood suggestions: oak, hickory, maple, pecan, or cherry

4 racks of venison or elk ribs (about 1½ to 2lb (680g to 1 kg] each)

6 tbsp **Cajun Rub** (page 116)

½ cup Thai sweet red chili sauce

½ cup grape jelly

2 tbsp ketchup

2 tbsp light brown sugar

1 tbsp apple cider vinegar

2 (12oz [350ml]) bottles of fruit-infused craft beer

1. Use a sharp knife to remove the membrane from the back of the ribs or score the backside in a diamond pattern. Rub the Cajun rub all over the ribs. Place the ribs on a baking sheet, cover with plastic wrap, and refrigerate for 24 hours.

2. Preheat the smoker to 200°F to 230°F (95°C to 100°C). Use oak, hickory, maple, pecan, or cherry wood.

3. In a medium saucepan on the stovetop over medium heat, combine the chili sauce, grape jelly, ketchup, brown sugar, and apple cider vinegar. Cook until heated through and well combined, about 5 to 10 minutes. Remove the pan from the heat and set aside. (Store in the fridge for up to 2 weeks.)

4. Pour the beer into two glasses and let stand until flat. Stir to remove a few of the bubbles. Use a funnel to transfer the beer to a spray bottle.

5. Evenly space the ribs bone side down on a smoker rack. Insert a thermometer probe into the meatiest portion of one of the ribs without touching bone.

6. Place the rack in the smoker and smoke the ribs until the internal temperature reaches 160°F to 170°F (75°C to 80°C), about 2 to 3 hours. Baste with the grape jelly mixture and spritz with the beer 2 or 3 times.

7. Remove the rack from the smoker. Baste the ribs again and wrap tightly in two layers of aluminum foil or butcher paper.

8. Return the rack to the smoker and continue to smoke the ribs until the internal temperature reaches 205°F (100°C) and the bones can slightly wiggle away from the meat.

9. Remove the rack from the smoker and unwrap the foil. Baste the ribs one last time. Cut the ribs into 2-bone portions before serving.

Recipe Note: Don't worry if this or any other rib recipe makes a bit more than you need for one meal. Just refrigerate leftovers. To reheat, place the ribs on a hot grill and cook until lightly charred and heated through. Baste with the remaining grape jelly mixture once or twice.

Stuffed Deer Heart

Deer or venison heart happens to be one of my favorite meats. I'm a big fan, and when I get a fresh deer heart, my own heart starts thumping! When it comes to deer heart or any heart for that matter, it's important to make sure it's cleaned of all blood. Rinse the heart thoroughly, especially through the arteries.

Prep Time	Smoker Temp	Smoke Time
30 minutes	275°F (135°C)	2 hours

wood suggestions: apple, maple, peach or cherry

1 fresh deer heart (about 1 to 1½lb [450 to 680g])

4 tbsp olive oil, divided

pinch of crushed red pepper flakes

2 tbsp chopped fresh sage leaves

3 garlic cloves, minced

1 cup finely diced yellow onions

½ cup chopped dried dates

1 cup crushed Italian-style amaretti cookies (about 1 dozen)

kosher salt, to taste, plus more

freshly ground black pepper, to taste

2 tbsp balsamic glaze

1. To a resealable bag, add the heart and cover with cold water. Refrigerate for 24 hours, changing the water every 8 hours.

2. In a small skillet on the stovetop, heat 2 tablespoons of olive oil over medium-high heat. Add the red pepper flakes and sage. Sauté for about 30 seconds, stirring often. Add the garlic and onions. Sauté until the onions are tender, about 1 to 2 minutes more. Remove the skillet from the heat and stir in the dates and cookies. Season to taste with salt and pepper. Mix well.

3. Drain the heart and pat dry with paper towels. Butterfly the heart from top to bottom and splay it open to expose the inner muscle. Use a sharp knife to carefully remove any veins and thick artery material. Season the heart with salt.

4. Evenly spread the cookie mixture over the entire cut side of the heart. Roll up the heart and tie with butcher's twine. Rub the heart with the remaining 2 tablespoons of olive oil. Season liberally with salt and black peppers. Loosely cover with plastic wrap and refrigerate for 1 hour.

5. Preheat the smoker to 275°F (135°C). Use apple, maple, peach, or cherry wood. Insert a thermometer probe into the meatiest portion of the heart.

6. Place the heart in the smoker and smoke until the internal temperature reaches 145°F (65°C) for medium doneness, about 2 hours.

7. Remove the heart from the smoker. Remove the twine and brush the heart with the balsamic glaze. Thinly slice before serving.

Rabbit Lettuce Wraps

This is one of my favorite recipes in this book. I'm a huge rabbit fan. My favorite parts are the heart and kidney—very sweet and tasty! Smoking rabbit is pretty easy: brine, rub, smoke, and pull. It's that simple!

Prep Time	Smoker Temp	Smoke Time
30 minutes	235°F to 250°F (95°C to 115°C)	3 to 4 hours

wood suggestions: maple, apple, or hickory

1 whole rabbit (about 3 to 3½lb [1.4 to 1.6kg])

sea salt, to taste

freshly ground black pepper, to taste

for the wraps

1 large head of green leaf lettuce or iceberg lettuce leaves

½ cup julienned carrots

½ cup julienne daikon

3 tbsp rice wine vinegar

1 tsp granulated sugar (optional)

pinch of kosher salt

½ cup thinly sliced red onions

½ cup julienned cucumbers

¼ cup thinly sliced radishes

2 green onions, thinly sliced

1 tart apple, thinly sliced and julienned

big handful of bean sprouts

½ bunch of cilantro, coarsely chopped

for garnishing

¼ cup hoisin sauce

¼ cup sriracha hot sauce

¼ cup soy sauce

¼ cup fish sauce

½ cup crushed cashews

1 lime wedge

1. Preheat the smoker to 235°F to 250°F (95°C to 115°C). Use maple, apple, or hickory wood.

2. Season the rabbit inside and out with salt and pepper. Place the rabbit on a smoker rack. Stretch the legs out from the body so the rabbit has relatively the same thickness. This will help with even smoking.

3. Place the rack in the smoker and smoke the rabbit until the internal temperature reaches 185°F to 190°F (85°C to 90°C), about 3 to 4 hours.

4. Soak the lettuce leaves in icy-cold water for 10 to 15 minutes. This will help crisp the leaves. Drain and pat dry with paper towels. Roll the leaves in a kitchen towel and refrigerate until needed.

5. In a large bowl, combine the carrot, daikon, rice vinegar, sugar (if using), and salt. Mix well and set aside.

6. In a separate large bowl, combine the red onions, cucumbers, radishes, green onions, apple, bean sprouts, and cilantro. Refrigerate until needed.

7. Remove the rack from the smoker and allow the rabbit to rest for 10 to 15 minutes. Use gloved hands or a pair of tongs to peel the cooked rabbit meat off the bones. Pull the meat into thin strips and strands.

8. Place the lettuce leaves on a serving platter. Top each leaf with some of the carrot and daikon mixture. Add a few pinches of the red onion mixture. Top with a handful of pulled rabbit and drizzle with your choice of sauce. Garnish each with a sprinkle of cashews and a squeeze of fresh lime. Fold the leaves to form wraps. Serve immediately.

Recipe Note: Save the smoked rabbit bones to make a tasty stock for later use.

Veal Tongue

Tongue is a delicious meat. Some people freak out about it, but when it's done right, it's oh so good. Smoked tongue requires a bit of preparation, but it's well worth it.

Prep Time	Smoker Temp	Smoke Time
30 minutes	235°F (115°C)	2 hours

wood suggestions: maple, oak, or hickory

1 large veal tongue (about 1½ to 2lb [680g to 1kg])

2 quarts (2 liters) beef stock, plus more

1 medium yellow onion, chopped

4 garlic cloves

1 tbsp freshly ground black pepper, plus more

2 tbsp kosher salt

spicy mustard

white onions, sliced

pickles

1. In a large pot on the stovetop over high heat, combine the tongue and beef stock. Add more beef stock as needed to ensure the tongue is completely covered. Add the onion, garlic, and pepper. Bring to a boil, then reduce the heat to low. Simmer until the internal temperature of the tongue reaches 185°F (85°C), about 2 hours. (To check the internal temperature, insert a probe into the thickest part of the tongue.)

2. Preheat the smoker to 235°F (115°C). Use maple, oak, or hickory wood.

3. Remove the tongue from the pot and allow to cool for 5 minutes. Return the beef stock mixture to a rolling boil. Remove the pot from the heat, strain the stock, and cool. (Use this stock for other recipes, such as soups and sauces. Store in an airtight container in the fridge for up to 1 week. Or freeze in ice cube trays [to use for flavoring sauces] for up to 1 year.)

4. Peel the thick membrane from the tongue and discard. (Use a tip of a sharp small knife to assist if needed.) Season the tongue with salt and pepper. Insert a thermometer probe into the thickest part of the tongue.

5. Place the tongue in the smoker and smoke until the internal temperature reaches 200°F (95°C), about 2 hours.

6. Remove the tongue from the smoker. Thinly slice before serving with spicy mustard, onions, and pickles.

Chicken & Other Poultry Recipes

Is there anything you can't do with chicken? I know people who only eat chicken, and while it's not my chosen lifestyle, I can appreciate the loyalty. It's one of the most versatile proteins—as is all poultry.

Chicken & Poultry Basics

I like to buy whole birds—chickens, turkeys, or ducks—because then I can cut them the way I like. Quail, pheasant, and other game birds are usually only available whole. If I want a "suprême of chicken," I don't have to explain what that is to a grocery store butcher. When you're choosing poultry to smoke, consult the following table for the characteristics that will ensure you have not only a great smoke but also a great meal.

Area	Desired Characteristics
Overall	Look for nice, plump birds. No pin feathers or broken bones should be sticking out.
Smell	Fresh chicken shouldn't have an odor. You should have to put your face close to the bird to catch the slightly sweet, clean fragrance. Don't buy or keep a bird that has a sour or "off" odor.
Breasts	They should have broad, well-formed breasts that are even on both sides.
Thighs	These should be plump.
Flesh	Use a finger to press down on the flesh—it should feel firm, not soft.
Skin	The skin should be tight and strong with no discolorations or blemishes.
Fat	Make sure there isn't too much fat clinging to the pope's nose (the stubby knob at the rear where the tail feathers were) or under the thigh skin. A little is okay, but pulling big clumps of fat from the body cavity is annoying—and who wants to pay for fat and extra skin instead of meat?

Review the safe handling and storage information in Chapter 6 before you start preparing poultry. Raw chicken is notorious for food safety issues because of bacterial contamination from such microorganisms as listeria and salmonella. You can avoid these if you take the proper precautions. Wash your hands and all items used with raw foods in hot, soapy water before and after preparation. And never carve a cooked chicken on the same board on which you've handled raw chicken!

As with most things to do with the smoker, thorough preparation ensures success. All poultry will need a bit of work to get it ready for the smoker. First, you want to trim excess fat from the bird, but leave a little bit because this is like a built-in baste that will keep the meat moist during smoking. Next, you'll brine the bird and cut it into pieces or truss it if you're keeping it whole. Trussing ensures the bird is nice and snug and that nothing gets overly crispy. Then it's time to add more flavor by either rubbing it with a seasoning mixture or placing it in a brine or marinade.

Make sure that whatever recipe you have in mind matches the type and cut of bird you intend to use it with because you don't want to dry out the meat. If you're using pieces instead of a whole bird, remember that leaner cuts (such as breasts) will need special attention to prevent them from drying out. Indirect heat—that's the trick! Use a smoker that has the wood box off to the side or if you're smoking in your grill, set the pieces over indirect heat. This means only one side is lit and the chicken is on the other side. This will create great smoke and not burn the tips. It's wise to periodically move the chicken pieces around to take advantage of hot and cool spots. Moving the chicken also promotes even browning and picture-perfect chicken!

And possibly most importantly, make sure the fire is nice and low. This advice is even more important when it comes to duck, where very low and very slow is what's going to get you success. Duck has a large amount of fat under the skin, which can't be removed without taking off all the skin—and who wants to do that? If you have the right temperature and the patience to take your time, the fat will render at the perfect rate, getting absorbed by the meat and not causing flare-ups.

Combined with a sweet sauce and high heat, fatty skin is a "recipe" for disastrously crispy (charred) skin. Don't apply your sauce until the last quarter of the smoking/cooking time. The sauce only needs to warm up and to stick to the meat—thus no more than 2 to 3 minutes before the end of the smoke. When you can gently twist the drumstick and it comes away from the bird easily, it means the bird is done! Congratulations, you've just found what I like to call a bird's "sweet spot." But when it comes to doneness, because nothing is as accurate as a thermometer, always double-check to ensure the meat is fully cooked. (See Chapter 6 for more.)

Air-Chilled vs. Water-Chilled Birds

Two types of poultry are available commercially: air-chilled and water-chilled. Air-chilled birds are cooled by blasting them with cold air. Their surfaces are dried out a bit from the fans, but the natural flavors are maintained. Water-chilled birds are processed in one of two ways: For the natural method, the birds are tumbled in a water tank filled with crushed ice and cold water. For the more broadly used method, they're tumbled in very cold chlorinated water. The USDA considers both methods safe, but in both methods, tumbling causes damage to the birds. It also washes away a lot of the natural flavors and the birds add 5 to 7% to their body weight, making the meat a bit waterlogged. This is why air-chilled is preferred by many. But again, buy the best you can afford.

Assorted Poultry Cuts

The following figure and table detail all the major parts of poultry that are best suited for smoking. These cuts apply to chicken, turkey, and duck, although the fat-to-meat and meat-to-bone ratios vary for each bird.

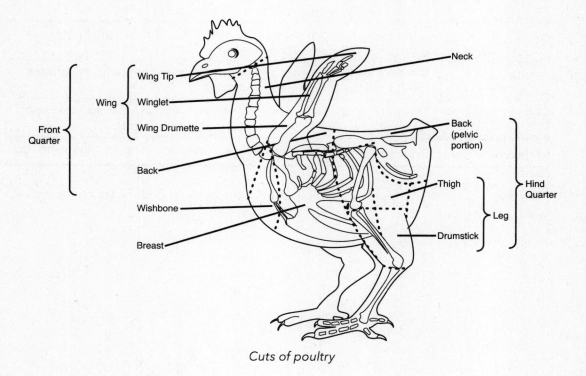

Cuts of poultry

Cut	Characteristics
Breast	This is the meat portion separated from the wing at the shoulder, from the neck by cutting through the 12th neck bone, and from the back by cutting through the ribs just above the thigh.
Breast fillet	Commonly called the tenderloin and generally removed from the breast in retail cuts, this is a thin strip of meat.
Drumstick	This is the bottom section of the leg—from the knee to the shin.
Front quarter (breast quarter)	This includes the whole breast and the wing.
Hind quarter (leg quarter)	This includes the drumstick and thigh, with the back attached.
Leg	This portion between the natural seam through the hip to the knee includes the thigh and the drumstick.
Neck	This includes the bones from the top of the shoulder to the last vertebra under the beak.
Thigh	This is the top section of the leg from the hip to the knee.
Whole back	Although this might include parts of the vertebral spine, the back is typically the neck, vertebrae, pelvic bones, and tail.
Wing	Because a whole wing is severed at the shoulder joint, it includes the drumette, winglet, and wing tip.
Wing drumette	This part resembles a drumstick and it connects the shoulder joint to the elbow joint, where the winglet is separated.
Winglet	This is the part of the wing between the drumette and the wing tip.

Now that you know and understand the basics of chicken and poultry, let's get smoking with some recipes.

Ted's Smoked Chicken Stock

I like to smoke my chicken bones before making chicken stock. It intensifies the stock, resulting in a richer flavor. You can still freeze your chicken scraps from various smoking projects until you have enough for a good stock, but this recipe works smoked or not.

Prep Time	Smoker Temp	Smoke Time
10 minutes	275°F (135°C)	1½ to 2 hours

wood suggestion: hickory

2lb (1kg) chicken wings or chicken bones (backs, necks, bones, legs)

8 garlic cloves, smashed

1 large yellow onion, chopped

2 medium carrots, peeled and chopped

2 celery stalks, chopped

8 peppercorns

2 sprigs of fresh thyme

2 sprigs of fresh parsley

2 sprigs of fresh sage or rosemary

2 bay leaves

1. Preheat the smoker to 275°F (135°C).

2. Place the wings on a smoker rack. Place the rack in the smoker and smoke the wings until golden brown, about 1½ to 2 hours, turning and shaking the rack to keep the wings from sticking. Remove the rack from the smoker.

3. In a large stockpot on the stovetop over high heat, combine the wings, garlic, onion, carrots, celery, peppercorns, thyme, parsley, sage, and bay leaves. Cover with cold water. Bring to a rolling boil, then reduce the heat to medium-low. Simmer for 1½ to 2 hours, skimming the top of the liquid as needed.

4. Remove the pot from the heat. Strain, then transfer the stock to an airtight container and refrigerate until needed. Use the stock in soups, sauces, casseroles, and anything else that requires stock.

Apple-Smoked, Bacon-Wrapped, Sausage-Stuffed Chicken Thighs

This is a pretty easy way to impress your friends and jazz up boneless, skinless chicken thighs. Remove your favorite fresh sausage from their casings, add some cheese, stuff this into the thighs, and wrap in bacon. Once smoked, the thighs will simply ooze with deliciousness.

Prep Time	Smoker Temp	Smoke Time
30 minutes	275°F (135°C)	1 hour

wood suggestions: hickory or apple

- 12oz (340g) fresh pork sausage (mild or hot Italian or bratwurst sausages recommended)
- ⅓ cup small-diced mozzarella cheese
- ½ cup crispy fried onions
- 1 green onion, chopped
- 1 cup diced fresh apples (tart and crisp varieties recommended)
- 1 tsp dried sage or 1 tbsp fresh chopped sage leaves
- 1 tsp freshly ground black pepper
- kosher salt, to taste
- 1 tbsp barbecue seasoning rub, plus more
- 12 boneless, skinless chicken thighs (about 2 to 3lb [1 to 1.4kg] total)
- 12 slices of store-bought bacon
- ½ cup grape jelly
- ¼ cup Thai sweet red chili sauce
- ¼ cup gourmet-style barbecue sauce

1. Slice, peel, and discard the sausage casings. In a large bowl, combine the sausage, mozzarella, fried onions, green onion, apples, sage, and pepper. Season with the salt. (The sausage will have already had some seasoning added.)

2. Rub the barbecue seasoning all over the chicken thighs. Place the thighs skin side down on a clean surface. Evenly spread a ½-inch-high (1.25cm) layer of the sausage mixture over each thigh. Roll up the thighs into tight oval bundles. (Reserve any leftover filling to make sliders.) Place the thighs on a baking sheet lined with parchment paper. Cover with plastic wrap and refrigerate for 30 minutes.

3. Place the bacon slices on a clean work surface. Firmly run your finger over each slice to stretch its length by half. Tightly wrap a bacon strip around the center of each thigh to create a bacon "belt." Season the thighs with a little more barbecue seasoning rub. Cover with plastic wrap and refrigerate for 1 hour more.

4. Preheat the smoker to 275°F (135°C). Use hickory or apple wood. Remove the thighs from the fridge and insert a probe into the thickest part of one of the thighs.

5. In a small bowl, whisk together the grape jelly, chili sauce, and barbecue sauce. Whisk until smooth.

6. Place the thighs in the smoker and smoke until the internal temperature reaches 180°F (85°C) and the bacon is crispy, about 60 minutes. Baste liberally with the grape jelly sauce mixture 2 to 3 times.

7. Remove the thighs from the smoker and baste with any remaining grape jelly mixture before serving.

Recipe Note: Prepare these little bundles the day before and pack them in a picnic lunch. They're also equally delicious served cold.

Barbecue Pulled Chicken

When we think about pulling meat, pork is traditionally what comes to mind. But pulling a whole smoked chicken—seasoned with a sauce—makes a perfect meal!

Prep Time	Smoker Temp	Smoke Time
20 minutes	235°F (115°C)	3 to 4 hours

wood suggestions: maple, hickory, apple, pecan, or peach

1 whole chicken (about 4 to 5lb [1.8 to 2.3kg])

8 cups **Basic Brine** (page 91), chilled, plus more

2 tbsp vegetable oil

1 tbsp **Basic Barbecue Rub** (page 115), plus more

3 to 4 tbsp honey

3 tsp butter, softened

½ cup barbecue sauce

1. Place the chicken in a resealable bag or large pot. Add the brine, making sure to completely cover the chicken. Refrigerate for 24 hours.

2. Remove the chicken from the brine and pat dry with paper towels. Discard the brine. Rub the chicken all over with the vegetable oil and barbecue rub.

3. Preheat the smoker to 235°F (115°C). Use maple, hickory, apple, pecan, or peach wood. Insert a probe into the thickest part of the chicken without touching bone.

4. Place the chicken in the smoker and smoke until the internal temperature reaches 185°F (85°C), about 3 to 4 hours. Remove the chicken from the smoker and allow to rest for 10 minutes.

5. Peel and remove the skin from the chicken. Pull the meat from the bones and shred into ½-inch-thick (1.25cm) strands/chunks.

6. In a large bowl, combine the chicken, honey, butter, barbecue sauce, and more barbecue rub to taste. Mix well to combine. Serve immediately piled high on toasted buns.

Bacon-Wrapped Drumstick Lollipops

This is such an easy recipe, but it offers outstanding results.

Prep Time	Smoker Temp	Smoke Time
30 minutes	225°F (110°C)	1 to 2 hours

wood suggestions: maple, apple, and oak

12 plump chicken drumsticks (about 2 to 3lb [1 to 1.4kg] total)

2 tbsp **Memphis Rib Rub** (page 119), plus more

12 slices of store-bought bacon

¼ cup barbecue sauce

¼ cup maple syrup

¼ cup sriracha hot sauce

1. Preheat the smoker to 225°F (110°C). Use maple, apple, or oak wood.

2. Use a sharp knife to cut off the end of each drumstick—just under the knuckle joint. Push the meat down—away from the knuckle end of the exposed bone—to form a lollipop handle with the bone. Rub the rib rub into the drumsticks.

3. Place the bacon flat on a work surface. Rub your fingers along each slice, pressing firmly to stretch its length by half.

4. Starting at the bottom of each drumstick, tightly wrap a slice of bacon around the drumstick until you reach the top of the meat. Secure the bacon with a toothpick. Wrap the knuckle end of each drumstick with a small piece of aluminum foil. Insert a probe into the thickest part of one of the drumsticks without touching bone. Season the bacon with more rib rub.

5. In a small bowl combine the barbecue sauce, maple syrup, and sriracha.

6. Place the chicken lollipops in the smoker and smoke until the internal temperature reaches 145°F (65°C), about 1 to 2 hours. Raise the smoker temperature to 325°F (165°C) and continue to smoke until the internal temperature reaches 185°F (85°C). Brush the drumsticks with the maple barbecue sauce.

7. Remove the drumsticks from the smoker and serve immediately.

Chicken Thighs

This is the perfect recipe for starting in the world of smoking chicken. This dish is easy to make—and quite a delicious meal to serve on any occasion.

Prep Time	Smoker Temp	Smoke Time
10 minutes	235°F (115°C)	3 hours

wood suggestions: maple, apple, or oak

12 plump skin-on, bone-in chicken thighs (about 4 to 5lb [1.8 to 2.3kg total)

4 cups **Basic Brine** (page 91), plus more as needed

4 tbsp Basic Barbecue Rub (page 115), plus more

barbecue sauce

1. Use paper towels to pat dry the chicken thighs. Place the thighs in a resealable plastic bag and add the brine. Refrigerate for 24 hours.

2. Preheat the smoker to 235°F (115°C). Use maple, apple, or oak wood.

3. Remove the thighs from the brine and pat dry with paper towels. Peel back the skin, but make sure to leave it attached on one side. Trim any excess clumps of fat from the underside of the skin. Rub the barbecue rub all over the thighs. Pull the skin tightly around the meat and season with a little more barbecue rub.

4. Evenly space the thighs on a smoker rack. Insert a thermometer probe into the thickest part of one of the thighs without touching bone.

5. Place the rack in the smoker and smoke the thighs until the internal temperature reaches 170°F (80°C), about 2 hours. Raise the smoker temperature to 275°F to 300°F (135°C to 150°C). Continue to smoke until the internal temperature reaches 185°F to 190°F (85°C to 90°C).

6. Remove the thighs from the smoker and serve immediately with your favorite barbecue sauce on the side.

Recipe Note: Thighs are hard to screw up. You can't really overcook them. Thigh meat is very forgiving and inexpensive—great for smoking and experimenting.

Buffalo Wings with Blue Cheese

Who doesn't love a good chicken wing? Flats or drums? What's your choice? I like 'em both as long as they're crispy and spicy!

Prep Time	Smoker Temp	Smoke Time
10 minutes	220°F (105°C)	2 to 2½ hours

wood suggestions: hickory

5lb (2.3kg) jumbo split chicken wings

7 tbsp **Cajun Rub** (page 116), divided

1 (12oz [230ml]) bottle of beer, divided

1 cup buffalo wing sauce

3 tbsp vegetable oil

2 tbsp butter

¾ cup crumbled blue cheese (optional)

1. In a large bowl, combine the chicken wings and 3 tablespoons of rub. Toss until evenly coated. Stir in 6 ounces (175 milliliters) of beer and ½ cup of wing sauce. Cover the bowl and refrigerate for 24 hours.

2. Preheat the smoker to 220°F (105°C). Use hickory wood.

3. Remove the wings from the fridge and pat dry with paper towels. Discard the brine. Add the vegetable oil and the remaining 3 tablespoons of rub. Toss to evenly coat. Place the wings on a smoker rack. Insert a thermometer probe into the meatiest portion of a large chicken wing without touching bone.

4. Place the rack in the smoker and smoke the wings until the internal temperature reaches 170°F (80°C), about 2 to 2½ hours.

5. Preheat the grill to 350°F (180°C). Transfer the wings to the grill. Season with the remaining 1 tablespoon of rub. Grill until lightly charred, about 10 to 15 minutes.

6. Transfer the wings to a large bowl. Add the remaining ½ cup wing sauce, butter, and blue cheese (if using). Toss until the wings are evenly coated and the blue cheese and butter have melted. Serve immediately.

Variation: Not a fan of blue cheese? Try this recipe with parmesan or goat cheese.

Chicken & Cheese Dogs

These hot dogs aren't your conventional store-bought wieners. These require some work, but you don't need a meat grinder or a sausage stuffer to make them. The filling is moist and delicious, and the hot dogs are topped with a cheese stick that becomes ooey and gooey in the smoker!

Prep Time	Smoker Temp	Smoke Time
2 hours	240°F (115°C)	2 to 2½ hours

wood suggestions: maple, apple, and hickory woods

6 boneless, skinless chicken breasts (about 4oz [100g] each)

1lb (450g) ground chicken

8oz (225g) boneless, skinless chicken thighs, coarsely chopped

3 tbsp crispy fried onions

2 tbsp plus 1 tsp mixed fresh herbs (such as sage, thyme, or parsley leaves), divided

1 green onion, chopped

2 garlic cloves, minced

1 tsp Dijon mustard

2 tbsp cornstarch or potato starch

kosher salt, to taste

freshly ground black pepper, to taste

6 mozzarella cheese sticks

pinches of **Memphis Rib Rub** (page 119)

2 cups **Spiced Rum & Apple Spritz** (page 142)

½ cup **Apple Butter Barbecue Glaze** (page 140)

1. Use a sharp knife to butterfly the breasts by slicing through the middle about three-fourths of the way to open them like a book. Place each breast between two sheets of plastic wrap. Use a meat mallet to pound the chicken into a rectangular shape that's about ¼ inch (0.5cm) thick. Set aside.

2. In a large bowl, gently combine the ground chicken, chicken thighs, fried onions, 2 tablespoons of mixed fresh herbs, green onion, garlic, Dijon mustard, and cornstarch. Mix until well combined. Season with salt and pepper.

3. On each of six 12-inch (30.5cm) squares of plastic wrap, place a flattened chicken breast, one-sixth of the ground chicken mixture in an even layer at the longest end of the breast, and a mozzarella stick. Use the plastic to tightly roll each breast into a sausage-shaped log to securely enclose the filling. Twist the ends of the plastic wrap to compact the log. Each log should be about 6 inches (15.25cm) long by 2 inches (5cm) in diameter. Refrigerate for 1 hour.

4. Preheat the smoker to 240°F (120°C). Use maple, apple, and hickory woods.

5. Remove the plastic from the logs and season each with the rib rub. Evenly space the logs on a smoker rack. Insert a thermometer probe into the center of one of the chicken logs. Warm the apple butter glaze.

6. Place the rack in the smoker and smoke the logs until the internal temperature reaches 165°F (75°C), about 2 to 2½ hours. Before the cook completes, brush the glaze all over the logs.

7. Remove the chicken dogs from the smoker and serve immediately on toasted buns with your favorite hot dog condiments.

Recipe Note: Freeze the mozzarella sticks for 1 hour prior to use. This will keep the ground meat cool during the first stages of smoking as well as keep the cheese from oozing out too early.

Cinnamon-Smoked Chicken Halves

If you've never smoked a chicken before, this is a great recipe to start with. This dish also has a ton of flavor. The cinnamon sticks create a sweet, pepper-like smoke. The chicken is best served hot from the smoker.

Prep Time	Smoker Temp	Smoke Time
15 minutes	180°F (85°C)	3½ to 4½ hours

wood suggestions: soaked hickory chips or chunks

8 cups **Basic Brine** (page 91), plus more as needed

24 cinnamon sticks (3 inches [7.5cm] long each), divided

2 whole chickens (about 3 to 4lb [1.4 to 1.8kg] each)

¼ cup granulated sugar

2 tsp ground cinnamon

1 tsp freshly ground black pepper

⅓ cup olive oil

3 tbsp caramel sauce, room temperature

1 tbsp gourmet-style barbecue sauce

1. Once you've made the brine, add 4 cinnamon sticks as soon as you remove the pan from the heat.

2. Wash the chickens in cold water and pat dry with paper towels. Place the chickens breast side down on a clean cutting board. Use kitchen shears to remove the backbone from each chicken by cutting down either side of the spine. (Save the backbones for stock.) Turn each chicken over and press firmly on the breastbone to flatten the chicken. Use a large French knife to cut the chickens in half. You now have 4 half chickens with no breast bone

3. To a large pot, add the chickens and brine. Place a heavy plate on top of the chickens to keep them submerged. Cover the pot and refrigerate for 24 hours.

4. Remove the chickens from the brine. Discard the brine. Rinse the chickens inside and out with cold water and pat dry with paper towels. Arrange the chickens on a large tray and refrigerate for 1 to 2 hours or until completely dry.

5. Preheat to 180°F (85°C). Use soaked hickory chips or chunks.

6. In a small bowl, combine the sugar, ground cinnamon, and pepper. Whisk in the olive oil until well combined. (Because the sugar will settle to the bottom of the bowl, be sure to stir the mixture each time before basting.)

7. Remove the chickens from the fridge and brush with the cinnamon mixture. Evenly space the chickens cut side down on a smoker rack. Insert a thermometer probe into the thickest part of one of the thighs without touching bone.

8. Place the rack in the smoker and smoke the chickens until the internal temperature reaches 165°F (75°C) and the skin is slightly sticky to the touch, about 30 minutes. (This woodless smoke will dry out the chickens, which is what you want.)

9. Add the wood smoke and a few of the remaining cinnamon sticks. Smoke the chickens until the internal temperature reaches 165°F (75°C), about 3 to 4 hours. Replenish the wood and cinnamon sticks as needed. Occasionally baste with the cinnamon mixture.

10. In a small microwave-safe bowl, combine the caramel sauce and barbecue sauce. Microwave until warm but not bubbling, about 30 to 45 seconds.

11. Remove the rack from the smoker. Drizzle the caramel and barbecue sauce over the top of the chickens before serving.

Recipe Note: Shred the smoked meat to use for sandwich fillings, pizza toppings, and taco fillings as well as for garnishing soups and chowders. I like to toss smoked chicken into my pasta dishes and serve them with a sun-dried tomato cream sauce.

Cornish Game Hens

A trip to Memphis isn't complete without a trip to the Cozy Corner for their tasty smoked Cornish game hens. As I recall, they used an aquarium-style smoker to cook their Cornish hens. That was the first time I'd tasted smoked food from this style of smoker. Here's my version of this tasty treat.

Prep Time	Smoker Temp	Smoke Time
45 minutes	200°F to 230°F (95°C to 110°C)	2½ to 3 hours

wood suggestions: apple, a blend of apple and maple, or a blend of apple, maple, and hickory

4 Cornish game hens (about 1½lb [680g] each)

12 cups **Apple & Honey Brine** (page 92)

½ cup **Memphis Rib Rub** (page 119)

¼ cup apple butter

1oz (30ml) Tennessee whiskey

2 tbsp ketchup

2 tbsp honey

1 tsp freshly squeezed lemon juice

1. To a large pot, add the game hens and brine. Place a heavy plate on top of the hens to keep them submerged. Cover the pot and refrigerate for 12 to 18 hours.

2. Preheat the smoker to 200°F to 230°F (95°C to 110°C). Use apple wood, a blend of apple and maple woods, or a blend of apple, maple, and hickory woods.

3. Remove the hens from the brine. Discard the brine. Rinse the hens inside and out under cold water. Pat dry with paper towels.

4. Place the hens breast side down on a clean cutting board. Use kitchen shears to remove the backbone from each bird by cutting down either side of the spine. (Save the backbones for stock.) Turn the hens breast side up and firmly press down on the breastbone of each hen to flatten.

5. Insert two skewers into each hen—from the breast to the opposite leg—to create an X. Rub the hens with the rib rub, pressing the spices into the meat. Insert a thermometer probe into the thickest part of the breast of one of the hens.

6. In a medium bowl, combine the apple butter, Tennessee whiskey, ketchup, honey, and lemon juice. Stir until smooth.

7. Evenly space the hens cut side down in the smoker and smoke until the internal temperature reaches 165°F (75°C), about 2½ to 3 hours. Occasionally baste with the apple butter mixture.

8. Remove the hens from the smoker and allow to rest for 5 minutes before serving.

Recipe Note: For added flavor, lift the skin from the flesh of the game hens and rub your favorite barbecue seasoning directly onto the meat under the skin. This will ensure the flavor of the rub gets into the meat, not just on the skin. (You can also do this with chicken, duck, and turkey.)

Turkey Drumsticks

I remember the first time I had a smoked turkey drumstick. It was at the Taste of Chicago and Manny's Deli served up these whopping, meaty, smoked turkey drumsticks. In this version, the turkey starts in a citrus brine and gets its smoked flavor from fruitwood.

Prep Time	Smoker Temp	Smoke Time
30 minutes	230°F to 250°F (110°C to 120°C)	3 to 4 hours

wood suggestions: soaked fruitwood chunks as well as apple, pear, peach, apricot, citrus (orange or grapefruit), or maple

6 turkey drumsticks (about 1½ to 2lb [680g to 1kg] total)

8 cups **Mango & Citrus Brine** (page 93)

¾ cup **Cajun Rub** (page 116), divided

½ cup honey

1. Rinse the drumsticks with cold water and pat dry with paper towels. In a large resealable plastic bag, combine the drumsticks and brine, turning the drumsticks to ensure they're coated. Seal the bag, squeezing out as much air as possible, and refrigerate for 24 hours.

2. Preheat the smoker to 230°F to 250°F (110°C to 120°C). Use soaked fruitwood chunks as well as apple, pear, peach, apricot, citrus (orange or grapefruit), or maple wood.

3. Remove the drumsticks from the brine and pat dry with paper towels. Discard the brine. Use your fingers to loosen the skin from each drumstick and roll the skin down the leg from the wide end to the knuckle. Sprinkle ¼ cup of the rub on the turkey meat. Pull the skin back over the drumstick and press another ¼ cup of Cajun rub into the skin. Insert a thermometer probe into the thickest part of a drumstick without touching bone.

4. Evenly space the drumsticks in the smoker and smoke until the internal temperature reaches 185°F (85°C), about 3 to 4 hours.

5. Warm the honey in the microwave on medium-high for 10 to 15 seconds. Remove the drumsticks from the smoker and brush the drumsticks all over with honey and sprinkle the remaining ¼ cup of Cajun rub over the top. Serve immediately.

Recipe Note: Shredded smoked turkey meat is great for hot or cold sandwiches. It's also nice as a garnish for soups and chowders.

Turkey with Smoked Butter Injection

The key to keeping your turkey moist 'n' juicy is to first brine it, then inject it with melted butter—or, in this case, smoked butter! Trust me: #itbetasty!

Prep Time	Smoker Temp	Smoke Time
30 minutes	230°F (110°C)	6 to 8 hours

wood suggestions: apple or maple

1 fresh turkey (about 12 to 15lb [5.4 to 6.8kg]), thawed if frozen

1lb (450g) butter, frozen

for the brine

1 quart (1 liter) boiling water

1 cup kosher salt

2 gallons (4 liters) cold water

3 (12oz [350ml]) cans of craft hard cider

1 tbsp whole black peppercorns

1 cup maple syrup

1 quart (1 liter) apple cider

3 to 4 sprigs of fresh sage

for the rub

2 tbsp kosher salt

1 tbsp freshly ground black pepper

1 tbsp granulated garlic

½ tsp ground cayenne

1. In a small bowl, begin to make the brine by combining the boiling water and salt. Stir until the salt dissolves. In a large bucket, combine the salted water, cold water, hard cider, peppercorns, maple syrup, apple cider, and sage. Stir until well mixed.

2. Rinse the turkey under cold running water and pat dry with paper towels. Place the turkey in the bucket and place a heavy plate on top to keep it submerged. Cover the bucket and refrigerate for 24 hours or up to 36 hours for a much larger turkey.

3. Remove the turkey from the brine. Discard the brine. Rinse the turkey under cold running water and pat dry with paper towels. Return the turkey to the bucket and refrigerate for 2 to 4 hours.

4. Preheat the smoker to 230°F (110°C). Use apple or maple wood.

5. In a small bowl, make the rub by combining the salt, pepper, granulated garlic, and cayenne.

6. Remove the turkey from the fridge. Rub the garlic and cayenne mixture on the inside and outside of the turkey. Place the turkey on a smoker rack, including the neck and giblets. Insert a thermometer probe into the thickest part of a turkey thigh without touching bone.

7. Place the rack in the smoker and smoke the turkey for 4 to 6 hours depending on the size of your turkey.

8. Place the butter in a metal bowl or container. Place the bowl in the smoker and smoke until the butter has melted. (Freezing prevents the butter from melting too rapidly, allowing the smoke to infuse into the butter a layer at a time to give you a sweet, smoky butter.) Fill an injection syringe with the melted butter and inject the turkey in a variety of spots. (I suggest 3 to 4 injections per breast and thigh.)

9. Continue to smoke the turkey until the internal temperature reaches 165°F (75°C).

10. Remove the rack from the smoker. Loosely cover the turkey with aluminum foil and allow it to rest for 10 to 20 minutes. Carve as desired before serving.

Holiday-Flavored Turkey Breast with Bacon, Apple & Apricot Stuffing

I'm always reminded of my dad when it comes to the holiday season and turkey. He always roasted a whole turkey, but it was sometimes a little overdone. For this recipe, I decided to change things up a bit. Instead of a whole bird or even a spatchcocked (butterflied) bird, I decided to break down the turkey into its primal parts: boneless breasts, thighs, drumsticks, wings, and giblets. This makes for a quicker cook, especially during those cold holiday smoking sessions, and allows you to stuff the breasts with your traditional bread stuffing.

Prep Time	Smoker Temp	Smoke Time
45 to 60 minutes	275°F (135°C)	3 to 4 hours

wood suggestions: oak, apple, maple, hickory, or pecan

1 fresh turkey (about 19lb [8.6kg]), thawed if frozen

2 tbsp kosher salt

1 tbsp fresh coarsely ground black pepper

1 tbsp granulated garlic

4 tbsp olive oil

2 Granny Smith or Honeycrisp apples, sliced into ¼-inch (0.5cm) rounds

2 oranges, sliced into ¼-inch (0.5cm) rounds

8 sprigs of fresh sage

for the brine

1 quart (1 liter) plus 1 gallon (4 liters) cold water, divided

1¼ cups kosher salt

½ cup granulated sugar

2 quarts (2 liters) craft beer (honey brown lager recommended)

1 large Granny Smith or Honeycrisp apple, smashed

1 large orange, chopped

1 head of garlic, cut in half crosswise through the middle to expose all the cloves

2 medium yellow onions, chopped

½ leek, chopped

4 sprigs of fresh sage

2 tbsp black peppercorns

1 tsp ground allspice

for the stuffing

1lb (450g) sliced bacon, cut into 1-inch (2.5cm) pieces

½ cup butter, cubed

1 medium yellow onion, diced

2 celery stalks, diced

½ leek, diced

½ cup chopped apricots

1 tart apple, cored and diced

¼ cup beer

1 tbsp ground savory

2 tbsp chopped fresh sage leaves

1 tsp freshly ground black pepper

12 slices of day-old white bread, grilled or toasted, cut into 1-inch (2.5cm) cubes

kosher salt, to taste

1. In a small saucepan on the stovetop over medium heat, begin to make the brine by bringing 1 quart (1 liter) of water to a rolling boil. Add the salt and sugar, and stir until they dissolve. Remove the pan from the heat and allow the water to fully cool.

2. In a large bucket, combine the salted water, the remaining 1 gallon (4 liters) of cold water, beer, apple, orange, garlic, onions, leek, sage, peppercorns, and allspice. Stir to combine. Set aside and keep cool.

3. Remove the neck and giblets from the cavity of the turkey. Set aside.

4. Rinse the turkey under cold running water and pat dry with paper towels. You want to eliminate as much moisture as possible. This will make cutting the turkey much easier for breaking it down into its primal parts (breasts, thighs, drumsticks, and wings). (Breaking down a turkey can seem like a daunting task, but I know you can do it. If not, ask your local butcher to do this for you. But you can have some satisfaction in cutting up the turkey yourself.)

5. Place the turkey on a cutting board, with the cavity facing away from you and the breasts up. Pull each wing away from the body and cut between the flat and drumette portion. Place the flats with tips into the beer brine.

6. Rotate the turkey to face the cavity toward you. Cut through the skin between the breast and the leg of the turkey, cutting almost to the bone where the thigh meets the hip joint. Repeat on the other side of the leg.

7. Flip the turkey over onto its breast and grab one leg and pull firmly upward toward the back, dislocating the thigh bone from the joint. (You should hear a pop when you dislocate the bone.) Repeat with the other leg.

8. Use the tip of a sharp knife to cut the legs away from the body. Find the joint between the thigh and drumstick. Cut through this joint to separate the thigh from the drum. Repeat with the other leg. Place the drumsticks and legs in the brine.

9. To debone the breasts, flip the turkey onto its back and rotate the turkey to face the cavity away from you. Start at the top of the breast at the cavity end (the pointy part of the breast). Use your fingertips to feel for the keel bone that separates the two breasts. Cut along one side of the keel bone, following it from the tip to the top of the neck. Carefully slice along the entire breast plate, keeping as close to the bone as possible. Cut the wing tip from the body, leaving the wing bone attached to the boneless breast. Repeat on the other side.

10. Place the carcass and boneless breasts into the brine, making sure all the turkey parts are fully submerged. Cover the bucket and refrigerate for 24 hours.

11. In a heavy-bottomed pan on the stovetop over medium-high heat, begin to make the stuffing by sautéing the bacon until just crisp, about 5 to 6 minutes, stirring often. Remove the pan from the heat and drain off the fat, reserving 3 tablespoons.

12. Return to the pan to the heat. Add the reserved bacon fat and butter. Stir until melted. Add the onion, celery, and leek. Sauté until tender, about 2 to 3 minutes, stirring often. Add the apricots, apples, and ¼ cup of beer.

13. In a large bowl, combine the bread cubes, savory, sage, and pepper. Add the bacon and the apricot mixture. Season with the salt and mix well. The stuffing should be a little moist and sticky. Set aside to fully cool.

14. Remove all the turkey parts from the brine and pat dry with paper towels. Discard the brine.

15. French each wing drumette bone by using a sharp knife to cut around the base of the wing bone, pull the meat back over the knuckle, and cut the meat off. Scrape the bone to remove the excess meat and sinew.

16. Flip the breast onto its skin side to expose the under portion. Remove the tenderloin from the breast, trim the white tendon from the meat, and butterfly the tenderloin lengthways. Lightly pound the tenderloin to flatten. Repeat with the other breast.

17. Use a sharp knife to cut a large pocket about 1 to 2 inches (2.5 to 5cm) deep from the top of each breast to the bottom. Use the tip of the knife to cut horizontally to

make a pocket. Use your fingers to push the meat aside to make the pocket cavity as large as possible.

18. Pack half the stuffing into each breast cavity, pressing firmly to get as much in as you can. Place the flattened tenderloin into and over the opening, firmly pressing and tucking in the edges to make a tight seal. Place the breasts skin side up on a baking sheet. Cover with plastic wrap and refrigerate for 1 hour.

19. Preheat the smoker to 275°F (135°C). Use oak, apple, maple, hickory, or pecan.

20. In a small bowl, combine the salt, pepper, and garlic. Rub the turkey breasts all over with some of the olive oil and season liberally with some of the garlic mixture.

21. On a smoker rack, layer the apple slices, orange slices, and sage sprigs. Place the stuffed breasts on top. Insert a thermometer probe into the thickest part of one of the breasts.

22. Season the remaining turkey parts (wings, thighs, and drumsticks) with the remaining olive oil. Season with the remaining garlic mixture. Place these parts on a second smoker rack.

23. Place the carcass, neck, giblets, and tail piece on a third smoker rack.

24. Place the racks in the smoker in this order: breasts on top, parts in the middle, and carcass and remaining pieces on the bottom. Smoke until the internal temperature reaches 165°F (75°C).

25. Remove the racks from the smoker. Loosely cover the breasts with aluminum foil and allow them to rest for 10 to 15 minutes. Carve the thighs and legs, and set aside the meat for sandwiches later. (Save the carcass, neck, and giblets for making stock and gravy.) Carve the breasts before serving.

Recipe Notes: To smash the apple, cut it into chunks, cover with plastic wrap, and smash with a heavy pan. Ground savory is a spice that usually consists of dried parsley, sage, rosemary, thyme, and marjoram. Using apple, orange, and sage as a base for the breasts will provide extra flavor and moisture into the turkey as it smokes, helping keep your breasts moist and juicy.

Dry-Cured Turkey Breast

Dry-curing a turkey breast removes excess moisture from the meat, allowing it to become firmer. This makes it easier to slice thinly. This turkey recipe is best served on a hot or cold sandwich.

Prep Time	Smoker Temp	Smoke Time
30 minutes	85°F (30°C)	11 to 12 hours

wood suggestions: hickory, mesquite, a blend of pecan and oak, or a blend of apple and maple

1 large boneless, skin-on turkey breast (about 8 to 9lb [3.6 to 4.1kg])

4 cups roughly chopped fresh parsley leaves

1 cup roughly chopped fresh sage leaves

1 cup **Aromatic Cure** (page 109), divided

1. Rinse the breast under cold water and pat dry with paper towels. Line a baking sheet with plastic wrap.

2. In a medium bowl, combine the parsley and sage. Evenly sprinkle ⅓ cup of the cure down the center of the sheet. Evenly sprinkle about one-third of the herb mixture over the cure. Place the turkey breast skin side down on the herb mixture. Fold the thin end of the breast under to create an even thickness.

3. Evenly sprinkle the remaining herb mixture and the remaining ⅔ cup of the cure over the breast, making sure all the meat is coated. Cover with plastic wrap. Place a second baking sheet on top of the breast. Weigh this sheet down with a foil-covered brick or a large can of tomatoes. Refrigerate for 3 days.

4. Remove the breast from the fridge. Rinse under cold water and pat dry with paper towels. Wrap the breast in a paper towel or a kitchen towel and refrigerate for 2 hours to dry out completely. Insert a thermometer probe into the thickest portion of the breast.

5. Preheat the smoker to 85°F (30°C) for cold-smoking. Use hickory, mesquite, a blend of pecan and oak, or a blend of apple and maple woods.

6. Place the breast in the smoker and smoke for 5 hours.

7. Raise the smoker temperature to 150°F (70°C) and smoke for 3 hours more.

8. Raise the smoker temperature to 185°F (85°C) and add a pan of hot water near the fuel source to add humidity to the smoker. Smoke until the internal temperature reaches 165°F (75°C), about 3 to 4 hours more.

9. Remove the turkey breast from the smoker and allow to cool completely. Refrigerate for 24 hours. Slice thinly and use in a sandwich with your favorite garnishes and accompaniments. When vacuum-packed, the sliced turkey will last for 2 weeks in the fridge.

Recipe Note: Use a meat slicer to shave the smoked turkey into thin, deli-style slices.

Maple-Cured Duck Breasts

Curing duck breasts not only imparts great flavor but also reduces the moisture in the meat, making it much faster to smoke. This allows for a better texture and gives the duck a longer life when refrigerated.

Prep Time	Smoker Temp	Smoke Time
30 minutes	125°F (55°C)	3 hours

wood suggestions: maple, a blend of hickory and maple, or a blend of apple and maple

½ cup chopped fresh parsley leaves

½ cup chopped fresh sage leaves

½ cup chopped fresh thyme leaves

4 cups **Maple & Whiskey Brine** (page 94), divided

4 large boneless duck breasts (about 12oz [340g] total)

2 tsp fresh coarsely ground black pepper

¼ cup maple syrup

1. In a medium bowl, combine the parsley, sage, and thyme.

2. To a nonreactive 3-inch (7.5cm) pan, add 1 cup of the brine. Sprinkle half the herb mixture over the top. Evenly space the duck breasts skin side down in a single layer. Press firmly on the breasts to ensure the herbs adhere to the meat. Evenly sprinkle the remaining herb mixture over the breasts and top with the remaining 3 cups of the brine. Cover with plastic wrap and top with a heavy plate to keep the breasts submerged. Refrigerate for 2 days.

3. Preheat the smoker to 125°F (55°C) for cold-smoking. Use maple, a blend of hickory and maple, or a blend of apple and maple woods.

4. Remove the breasts from the fridge. Rinse under cold water and pat dry with paper towels. Rub the pepper all over the breasts. Insert a thermometer probe into the thickest portion of a breast.

5. Evenly space the breasts skin side up in the smoker and smoke until the internal temperature reaches 135°F (60°C), about 3 hours.

6. Remove the breasts from the smoker and baste with the maple syrup. Refrigerate for 2 hours. Store in an airtight container in the fridge for up to 1 week or up to 6 months if vacuum-sealed.

7. Slice the breasts thinly before serving.

Recipe Note: Check on the breasts daily while in the cure to ensure they're not drying out completely. You still want to maintain some moisture for the succulence factor.

Wine-Brined Duck

A good hot smoke helps render the fat on duck, making the skin crispy and the meat super succulent.

Prep Time	Smoker Temp	Smoke Time
30 minutes	275°F (135°C)	3 to 4 hours

wood suggestions: hickory, oak, or maple

1 whole duck (about 4 to 5lb [1.8 to 2.3kg])

gourmet-style barbecue sauce

for the brine

1 bottle (25oz [750ml]) of Riesling white wine

3 cups water

¼ cup kosher salt

2 tbsp honey

1 medium orange, juiced

2 sprigs of fresh sage

2-inch (5cm) piece of fresh ginger, chopped

8 garlic cloves, chopped

1 medium white onion, chopped

2 tbsp black peppercorns

2 cinnamon sticks (3 inches [7.5cm] long each)

for the rub

2 tbsp kosher salt

1 tbsp freshly ground black pepper

1 tbsp granulated garlic

½ tsp ground cinnamon

1. In a large pot, make the brine by combining the wine and water. Stir in the salt and honey until the salt dissolves. Add the orange juice. Chop the orange rinds and add them to the pot.

2. Add the sage, ginger, garlic, onion, peppercorns, and cinnamon sticks. Mix well to combine. Place the duck in the brine and place a plate over the top to keep the duck submerged. Cover the pot and refrigerate for 24 hours.

3. Remove the duck from the brine and pat dry inside and out with paper towels. Discard the brine. Place the duck on a smoking rack and refrigerate for 4 hours or overnight.

4. In a small bowl, make the rub by combining the salt, pepper, granulated garlic, and cinnamon. Rub the duck inside and out with the rub. Insert a thermometer probe into the thickest part of a thigh without touching bone.

5. Preheat the smoker to 275°F (135°C). Use hickory, oak, or maple wood.

6. Place the duck back side down into the smoker and smoke until the internal temperature reaches 185°F (85°C), about 3 to 4 hours.

7. Remove the duck from smoker and allow to rest for 10 minutes. Carefully remove the skin and thinly slice into julienne strips. Pull the meat off the bones. Use your hands or two forks to shred the meat into little strips.

8. In a large bowl, combine the shredded meat, julienned skin, beer, and just enough barbecue sauce to moisten the mixture. Serve immediately.

Recipe Note: Use the reserved duck bones to make a poultry stock.

Cold-Smoked Foie Gras

Foie gras is one of my favorite decadences. Fattened goose or duck liver is loaded with flavor. And it doesn't take long to add a little smoky goodness to the liver.

Prep Time	Smoker Temp	Smoke Time
30 minutes	160°F (75°C)	2 hours

wood suggestions: maple, oak, wine barrel, or whiskey barrel

4 cups kosher salt

½ cup brandy or cognac, plus more

4 to 6 bushy sprigs of fresh thyme, divided

1 lobe of goose or duck liver (about 1½ to 2lb [680g to 1kg]), kept refrigerated until ready to use

1. In a small bowl, combine the salt and brandy. Pour one-third of this mixture on a baking sheet lined with parchment paper. Place 2 to 3 thyme sprigs on the brandy.

2. Place the goose liver on the thyme. Top the liver with the remaining thyme sprigs and pour the remaining brandy mixture over the top. Spread the brandy mixture to completely cover the liver. Drizzle a little more brandy over the top. Cover with plastic wrap and refrigerate for 3 days.

3. Remove the liver from the fridge and brush as much of the salt from the liver as you can. Rinse with a little more brandy. Place the liver on a smoker rack.

4. Preheat the smoker to 160°F (75°C) for cold-smoking. Use maple, oak, wine barrel, or whiskey barrel wood.

5. Place the rack in the smoker and cold-smoke the liver for 2 hours.

6. Remove the rack from the smoker and refrigerate the liver until ready to serve.

Recipe Notes: Spread the foie gras on toasted brioche and season with some sea salt and black pepper. Or slice into ½-inch-thick (2.5cm) slices and quickly pan-fry. Then serve with grilled steak. You can also make a terrine (similar to pâté) or a torchon (wrapped in cheesecloth and poached). The Internet has great recipes for both.

Goose Breasts with Gin & Tonic Cure

These breasts require a 36- to 48-hour dry-cure and a low-and-slow cold smoke.

Prep Time	Smoker Temp	Smoke Time
45 minutes	160°F (75°C)	2 to 3 hours

wood suggestions: maple or oak

6 boneless, skinless goose breasts (about 1 to 2lb [450g to 1kg] total)

6oz (175ml) herbaceous gin

4oz (120ml) tonic

2 tbsp freshly ground black pepper, plus more

3 cups kosher salt

¾ cup granulated sugar

6 sprigs of fresh thyme, divided

2 cups chopped fresh dill, divided

1. In a large container, combine the goose breasts, gin, and tonic. Allow the breasts to soak for 4 to 6 hours. Remove the breasts from the brine. Reserve ½ cup of the brine and discard the rest. Press the pepper into the breasts.

2. In a small bowl, combine the salt and sugar. Line a baking sheet with parchment paper. Place one-third of the salt and sugar mixture in an even layer on the paper. Place 3 thyme sprigs and 1 cup of dill on top of this mixture.

3. Place the breasts on top of the herbs. Add the remaining 3 sprigs of thyme, the remaining 1 cup of dill, and the remaining two-thirds of the salt and sugar mixture. Make sure to completely cover the goose breasts. Drizzle the reserved ½ cup of brine over the top. Cover with plastic wrap and refrigerate for 36 to 48 hours.

4. Preheat the smoker to 160°F (75°C) for cold-smoking. Use maple or oak wood.

5. Remove the breasts from the cure. Rinse under cold water and pat dry with paper towels. Place the breasts on a smoker rack.

6. Place the rack in the smoker and cold-smoke the breasts until they're dark in color and firm to the touch, about 2 to 3 hours.

7. Remove the rack from the smoker and refrigerate the breasts until ready to serve.

8. Thinly slice the breasts and serve atop grill toasted crostini. Top with a slice of brie, slices of fresh pear, and freshly ground black pepper.

Fish & Shellfish Recipes

Smoking seafood is probably one of the oldest cooking methods. This is a great way to get your feet wet (pun intended) in the smoking world without having to spend a whole bunch of time and money to get set up. You can smoke just about any kind of fish you like, but denser-fleshed fish like tuna, fatty fish like mackerel, and, of course, salmon are ideal for the smoker. You can also smoke shellfish, such as shrimp, scallops, lobster tails, oysters—the works! You can even smoke crab cakes using a plank. You'll need to marinate some seafood, such as octopus and calamari, before smoking, but I promise, once you've tried it, you'll never do it any other way.

Fish & Seafood Basics

Choosing your fish and seafood requires just as much thought as if you were choosing any cut of meat. First, buy the freshest fish you can. Right off the boat is always best, but because that's not always an option, find a great fish market or grocery store that takes pride in their fish department. You should keep the following in mind when selecting which fish you're going to buy:

- Eyes on a whole fish should be clear. The cloudier the eyes, the older the fish.

- Fish shouldn't smell like fish. They should smell like nothing. If it has a strong fishy odor, it isn't fresh.

- The flesh should be firm to the touch, not mushy.

- Scales should be intact.

Get to know your fishmonger and ask these questions about the fish before buying:

- When did the fish come in? How old is the fish?

- Where's the fish from?

- Was the fish or shellfish previously frozen? (What often looks fresh actually arrived frozen and was thawed for display.)

With all the hard work you're going to do to smoke your fish and shellfish, you should buy the freshest ingredients possible. Your dish can only be as good as your ingredients. This is very important.

Make sure the day you're buying the fish is the same day you'll start the recipe process. First-day fresh is always the best! Once you get your fish home, get to a quick cleaning and start the preparations. Cure it, brine it, rub it, or marinate it—and then smoke it as soon as it's ready.

Because seafood can make you very sick if abused, make these food safety habits a part of every smoking experience:

- Keep everything chilled. Seafood should never sit out of the fridge for longer than a few minutes before it goes in the smoker.

- Ensure the shells on mussels, clams, and oysters are tightly closed before cooking. Discard any that aren't closed. You can try pressing the open shells together, but if they don't snap shut, it means it's dead and no longer safe to eat. Throw it away!

- Always marinate in the fridge.

- Never put cooked fish on any surface that previously had raw fish on it.

Cold- & Hot-Smoked Fish

You have two ways to smoke fish: cold-smoked and hot-smoked. Cold-smoking is basically smoking below 200°F (95°C) with the smoke a long distance from the heat. Those paper-thin slices of translucent smoked salmon that everyone loves were cold-smoked. A properly cold-smoked fish is considered preserved and it will keep nicely in the refrigerator or freezer for a long time. But then again, it'll probably get eaten up before you need to worry about storing it!

The cold-smoked salmon product you get depends on the species of salmon you're planning to use. Atlantic salmon are fattier than Pacific salmon (sockeye or pink). These fish are much leaner and thus the texture of the smoked salmon will be different from the Atlantic salmon. The Atlantic salmon has a higher fat content, making it a bit moister than the others when cold-smoked. The Pacific salmon has a beautiful color and it absorbs the flavor of wood extremely well—try a blend of alder with about 15% cedar added in—but it has a slightly dryer texture than the Atlantic. Don't get me wrong: They're both delicious and it's ultimately up to you to choose the type of salmon you want to work with. I'm an Atlantic salmon fan, but that's probably because I was raised on it: My dad was a Newfoundlander with a passion for fly-fishing for Atlantic salmon.

Cold-smoking requires some fairly specialized equipment and probably shouldn't be embarked upon until you're feeling fairly accomplished in your other smoking techniques. Hot-smoking is much easier to master and is suitable for all kinds of fish. With hot-smoking, you are, in fact, cooking the fish. The texture will be different from a cold-smoked fish, but both methods produce delicious results. Because hot-smoking cooks the fish rather than preserving it, you should eat it right away. Leftovers will keep for a few days in the fridge and about a month in the freezer if wrapped well.

The Right Fish for the Right Recipe

Like all other proteins with various cuts, you need to keep in mind that not all fish is the same and therefore won't cook the same. Smoking something with a firm flesh, such as halibut or fatty mackerel, is pretty straightforward because the dense flesh is sturdy enough to stand up to the smoking process.

A more delicate fish, such as sole, perch, or tilapia, is going to require more attention and much less time in the smoker than other fish. Because these are delicate loose-fleshed fish, you need to handle them gently. They cook quickly and they'll have a milder smoke flavor. The same goes for adding flavor: Delicate fish need more delicate flavors so you don't overpower the taste of the fish. If you're not sure what category the fish you want to work with falls into, just ask your fishmonger for advice. At the end of the day, you're just cooking, so relax, be patient, and have fun with it! That said, let's get to the recipes.

Irish Whiskey Salmon

The key to making good smoked salmon is to cure it properly, allowing the cure to remove all excess moisture. Next, a long and cold smoke makes sure that all the sweet smoke permeates the salmon.

Prep Time	Smoker Temp	Smoke Time
30 minutes	125°F (55°C)	5 hours

wood suggestions: alder, maple, hickory, pecan, or whiskey barrel

7oz (205ml) Irish whiskey, divided

1 skin-on Atlantic salmon fillet
   (about 1½ to 2lb [680g to 1kg])

2 tbsp freshly ground black pepper

2 cups fresh dill fronds

¾ cup kosher salt

½ cup firmly packed light brown sugar

½ cup granulated sugar

1. Line a large roasting pan with plastic wrap. Add 6 ounces (175 milliliters) of Irish whiskey. Place the salmon skin side up in the pan. Refrigerate for 2 hours.

2. Turn the salmon over. Gently rub the pepper into the salmon flesh. Evenly scatter the dill fronds over the salmon. Drizzle the remaining 1 ounce (30 milliliters) of whiskey over the dill.

3. In a small bowl, combine the salt, brown sugar, and granulated sugar. Sprinkle evenly over the salmon. Cover the fish with plastic wrap. Place a baking sheet over the top and weigh it down with a foil-wrapped brick or a heavy can. Refrigerate for 48 hours.

4. Remove the salmon from the fridge. Remove the plastic wrap and scrape away the salt, sugars, and dill. Rinse the salmon under cold water and pat dry with paper towels. Place the salmon on a clean baking sheet. Cover with plastic wrap and refrigerate for 12 hours.

5. Preheat the smoker to 125°F (55°C) for cold-smoking. Use alder, maple, hickory, pecan, or whiskey barrel wood.

6. Place the salmon on a smoking rack or insert a meat hook through the tail section of the fillet, then hang the hook in the smoker. This ensures a more even smoke and allows any excess fat to drip off.

7. Allow the salmon to dry in the smoker for 1 to 1½ hours before adding the smoke. This helps remove excess moisture from the fish. Add the smoke and cold-smoke the salmon until the flesh is firm to the touch, about 4 hours.

8. Remove the rack from the smoker. Use a very sharp, flexible slicing knife to thinly slice the salmon on a sharp angle. Serve chilled with your favorite smoked salmon garnishes. Store in an airtight container in the fridge for up to 1 week or in the freezer for up to 2 months.

Variation: Try a different liquor to change the flavor of your smoked salmon. You can replace the Irish whiskey with a variety of other whiskeys (Tennessee, bourbon, Canadian, rye, or Scotch) as well as dark rum, cognac, Armagnac, brandy, or tequila.

West Coast Candied Salmon

Making candied salmon takes a few days, but the result is well worth the work. These tasty morsels of salmon cured with sweet maple and whiskey are addictive! You can either cold-smoke or hot-smoke the salmon.

Prep Time	Smoker Temp	Smoke Time
30 minutes	cold: 60°F (15°C)	6 to 7 hours (for cold-smoking)
	hot: 180°F (85°C)	3 to 4 hours (for hot-smoking)

wood suggestions: alder or maple

2 boneless, skinless fresh wild sockeye salmon fillets (about 2 to 3lb [1 to 1.4kg] total)

1 cup light brown sugar

2 cups warm water

2oz (30ml) bourbon

3 tbsp soy sauce

½ cup honey

½ cup maple syrup, plus more

1 tbsp minced fresh ginger

2 tbsp fresh coarsely ground black pepper

2 tsp crushed red pepper flakes

1. Cut the salmon into strips that are about 2 to 3 inches (5 to 7.5cm) long and 1 to 2 inches (2.5 to 5cm) wide. Place the salmon strips on a large flat-bottomed dish.

2. In a medium bowl, combine the brown sugar and warm water. Stir until the brown sugar dissolves. Add the bourbon, soy sauce, honey, maple syrup, ginger, black pepper, and red pepper flakes. Mix well to combine. You should now have a sweet, sticky slurry. Pour this over the salmon and gently mix. Refrigerate for 24 hours, turning the fish 3 to 4 times a day.

3. Remove the salmon from fridge and wipe off the cure. Evenly space the salmon strips on a wire rack. Place the rack on a baking sheet. Refrigerate until the fish is tacky, about 24 to 36 hours, turning every 8 hours.

4. To cold-smoke the salmon, preheat the smoker to 60°F (15°C). Use alder or maple wood. I like to use a pellet smoking tray—a zigzag trough you fill with smoking pellets and ignite on one end. It burns slowly, creating a small amount of smoke and adding no significant amount of heat to the smoker. It's the easiest way to cold-smoke. Brush the salmon with a little maple syrup and smoke until firm to the touch and tacky, about 6 to 7 hours.

5. To hot-smoke the salmon, preheat the smoker to 180°F (85°C). Use alder or maple wood. Brush the salmon with a little maple syrup and smoke until the internal temperature reaches 145°F (65°C), about 3 to 4 hours. To check the internal temperature, insert a thermometer probe into several fillets.

6. Remove the salmon from the smoker. Refrigerate overnight before serving.

Plank-Smoked Salmon

Plank-smoking salmon is an easy, hot, and fast way to add the sweet flavor of cedar wood to salmon with no need to cure it beforehand. It's absolutely delicious and super simple—and you can also do it on a gas grill!

Prep Time	Grill Temp	Smoke Time
30 minutes	350°F (180°C)	25 to 30 minutes

wood suggestions: cedar, maple, or oak

plank needed: western red cedar (2 feet [0.5m] long and ½ inch [1.25cm] thick), soaked in water for 1 hour

1 tbsp plus 1 tsp kosher salt, divided

¼ cup firmly packed light brown sugar

2 tbsp freshly ground black pepper

½ tsp cracked coriander seeds

½ tsp cracked mustard seeds

½ tsp granulated garlic

½ tsp granulated onion

1 skin-on salmon fillet (about 2 to 3lb [1 to 1.4kg])

½ medium orange

1. Preheat the grill to 450°F to 550°F (235°C to 290°C). Remove the plank from the water and dry with paper towels.

2. Place the plank on the grill and season with 1 tablespoon of salt. Close the lid and heat the plank until it begins to crackle and smoke, about 3 to 4 minutes.

3. In a large bowl, combine the brown sugar, pepper, coriander seeds, mustard seeds, granulated garlic, granulated onion, and the remaining 1 teaspoon of salt. Mix until well combined. Rub the mixture all over the top of the salmon.

4. Place the salmon skin side down on the plank. Close the lid and reduce the heat to 350°F (180°C). Smoke until the salmon is just cooked through and opaque in the center, about 25 to 30 minutes, occasionally checking for flames.

5. Remove the plank from the grill and squeeze the orange over the salmon. Serve immediately.

Recipe Note: Use leftover plank-smoked salmon in your favorite salmon salad recipe for an awesome sandwich filling.

Salmon-Wrapped Scallops

Large scallops wrapped in salmon belly—tinged with Himalayan pink salt—not only enhance the flavor of both seafoods but also create a mouthwatering delight that you didn't realize was missing from your menu.

Prep Time	Smoker Temp	Smoke Time
45 minutes	180°F to 200°F (85°C to 95°C)	1½ to 2 hours

wood suggestions: maple, oak, alder, or hickory

- 8 jumbo sea scallops (U-10 count), patted dry with paper towels
- 8 strips of fresh salmon belly (5 to 6 inches [12.5 to 15.25cm] long and ½ inch [1.25cm] thick) (page 274)

- coarsely ground Himalayan pink salt, to taste
- fresh coarsely ground black pepper, to taste
- 3 tbsp melted butter
- 1 tbsp chopped fresh chives

1. Tightly wrap each scallop with a strip of salmon belly. Secure with a toothpick. Place on a smoker rack and refrigerate uncovered for 1 to 2 hours.

2. Preheat the smoker to 180°F to 200°F (85°C to 95°C). Use maple, oak, alder, or hickory wood.

3. Remove the salmon-wrapped scallops from the fridge and season with the Himalayan pink salt and pepper.

4. Place the rack in the smoker and smoke until the scallops are opaque and just firm to the touch, about 1½ to 2 hours.

5. Transfer the scallops to a serving platter. Brush with the butter and garnish with the chives. Serve immediately.

Variation: You can use slices of smoked salmon or slices of partially cooked bacon instead of salmon belly.

Soy & Sesame Salmon

For this recipe, I place cinnamon sticks across my smoker rack and then place the salmon on top. The cinnamon permeates the salmon with a sweet, smoky flavor. Make sure you don't oversmoke or overcook this dish. It's best when the salmon is served medium, which is a warm coral-colored center.

Prep Time	Smoker Temp	Smoke Time
30 minutes	250°F (125°C)	30 minutes

wood suggestion: maple

20 cinnamon sticks (6 inches [15.25cm] long each)

1 skin-on salmon fillet (about 1½ to 2lb [680g to 1kg])

1 tsp fresh coarsely ground black pepper

¼ cup soy sauce

2 tbsp mirin (rice wine)

2 tbsp rice wine vinegar

2 tbsp firmly packed light brown sugar

1 tsp sambal oelek (red chili sauce)

1 tsp freshly grated ginger

1 tsp toasted sesame seeds

1 tsp black sesame seeds

½ tsp wasabi powder

1 small lemon, zested and juiced

¼ cup chopped fresh cilantro leaves

2 green onions, finely chopped

kosher salt

freshly ground black pepper

1. Place the cinnamon sticks on a baking sheet lined with aluminum foil. Place the salmon over the top and evenly sprinkle the black pepper over the salmon. Loosely cover with plastic wrap and refrigerate for 1 hour.

2. Preheat the smoker to 250°F (125°C). Use maple wood.

3. In a large bowl, combine the soy sauce, mirin, rice wine vinegar, brown sugar, sambal oelek, ginger, toasted sesame seeds, black sesame seeds, wasabi powder, and lemon zest and juice. Mix until well combined. Stir in the cilantro and green onions.

4. Remove the salmon from the fridge. Season with salt and pepper. Evenly brush some of the soy sauce mixture over the salmon. Insert a thermometer probe into the thickest part of the salmon. Use the aluminum foil to help transfer the salmon to a smoker rack.

5. Place the rack in the smoker and smoke the salmon until the internal temperature reaches 150°F (70°C) for medium, about 30 minutes.

6. Remove the rack from the smoker and transfer the salmon to a serving platter. Liberally spoon the remaining soy sauce mixture over the salmon before serving.

Recipe Note: Always ensure your fish and seafood are icy cold before putting them in the smoker. This helps them stay firm and hold in the natural juices.

Salmon with Bay Scallop Stuffing

This is far from an easy recipe, but if you're up to the challenge, the end results will blow your mind with deliciousness!

Prep Time	Smoker Temp	Smoke Time
30 minutes	180°F (85°C)	2 to 3 hours

wood suggestions: maple, alder, or apple

1 boneless, skinless fresh salmon
(about 2 to 3lb [1 to 1.4kg])

2 tbsp fresh coarsely ground black
pepper

1 bunch of fresh dill

½ cup kosher salt

½ cup plus ¼ cup maple syrup, divided

¼ cup dark rum

kosher salt, to taste

freshly ground black pepper, to taste

for the stuffing

2 cups bay scallops (U-10 count),
thawed if frozen

2 green onions

kosher salt, to taste

freshly ground black pepper, to taste

1 small lemon

¼ cup maple syrup

1. Trim the salmon by cutting off the head and tail ends to square it up. Trim and reserve the belly flesh. (See page 271 for a recipe for the salmon belly.)

2. Place the salmon skin side down in a large pan. Push the salmon flesh together to plump it up. Liberally rub the top with the pepper, pushing the seasoning into the fish. Place the dill atop the salmon.

3. In a small bowl, combine the salt and the ½ cup of maple syrup. Drizzle this mixture and the dark rum over the salmon. Cover the salmon with plastic wrap. Place another pan over the top and add something heavy to weigh that pan down. Refrigerate for 24 hours.

4. Remove the salmon from the fridge. Remove the dill and salt mixture from the salmon. Rinse under cold water and pat dry with paper towels. Place the salmon on a clean large pan and refrigerate uncovered for 2 to 3 hours.

5. Preheat the smoker to 180°F (85°C). Use maple, alder, or apple wood.

6. To make the stuffing, add the bay scallops to a large bowl. Use the flat side of a knife or a rolling pin to smash the green onions. (This brings out the sweet onion juices.) Coarsely chop and add to the bowl. Season with salt and pepper.

7. Use a rasp or grater to zest the lemon. Add the zest to the bowl. Squeeze the lemon juice over the scallops. Mix well to combine.

8. Remove the salmon from the fridge. Use a sharp knife to make an incision the length of the salmon, starting on one side. You want to butterfly the salmon to make a large pocket. Place the salmon on a smoker rack. Stuff the scallop mixture into the salmon. Fold over the top, pressing firmly to form a log. Season the salmon with salt and pepper.

9. Place the rack in the smoker and smoke until the internal temperature reaches 155°F (70°C) and the salmon and scallops are just cooked through, about 2 to 3 hours. Brush the salmon with the ¼ cup of maple syrup during the last 30 minutes.

10. Remove the rack from the smoker and allow the salmon and stuffing to rest for 5 minutes. Slice the salmon before serving.

Recipe Notes: U-10 refers to the total weight of the scallops. These guys are so big, you only get about 10 per pound. Be sure to remove the connective muscle found on the side of each scallop. This piece of flesh is tough and it's not meant to be eaten.

Cold-Smoked Halibut Gravlax

Although salmon is often used for gravlax—a cured dish that involves herbs—the sweet taste of halibut works well in this recipe. Brown sugar, beer, and dill—which meets the herb requirement for gravlax—help enhance the fish's flavor. You can serve this Nordic dish as a main meal or as an appetizer.

Prep Time	Smoker Temp	Smoke Time
30 minutes	75°F (25°C)	90 minutes

wood suggestion: maple

1 skin-on, boneless, scaled halibut fillet (about 1½ to 2lb [680g to 1kg])

2 tbsp fresh coarsely ground black pepper

¾ cup kosher salt

¾ cup light brown sugar

1 bunch of fresh dill

2oz (60ml) beer

1. Place the halibut skin side down on a 2-inch-deep (5cm) baking sheet. Rub and press the pepper into the flesh.

2. In a small bowl, combine the salt and brown sugar.

3. Evenly spread the dill over the halibut. Drizzle about 2 ounces (60 milliliters) of beer over the top. Evenly sprinkle the salt mixture over the halibut, making sure to cover the entire fish. Drizzle a little more beer over the top. Cover with plastic wrap. Place another baking sheet on top of the fish and weigh it down with a heavy can or a brick. Refrigerate for 24 hours.

4. Remove the halibut from the fridge. Unwrap and scrape away the salt, brown sugar, and dill. Quickly rinse the halibut under cold water and pat dry with paper towels. Place on a clean baking sheet and refrigerate uncovered for 8 hours or overnight.

5. Preheat the smoker to 75°F (25°C) for cold-smoking. Use maple wood.

6. Remove the halibut from the fridge. Run a meat hook through the tail section of the halibut and let it hang in the smoker. This ensures a more even smoke and allows any excess fat to drip off the fish.

7. Place the halibut in the smoker and cold-smoke for 90 minutes.

8. Remove the halibut from the smoker and transfer to an airtight container. Refrigerate until ready to serve. Store in the fridge for up to 1 week or in the freezer for up to 2 months.

Diver Scallops & Lobster

What can be better than butter-infused scallops wrapped inside a cocoon of lobster, chives, and a snap of lemon juice?

Prep Time	Smoker Temp	Smoke Time
30 minutes	250°F (125°C)	1 hour

wood suggestion: maple

12 jumbo fresh scallops (U-10 count), uniform in size

sea salt, to taste

freshly ground black pepper, to taste

½ cup melted butter

1 cup cooked lobster or crab meat

4 tbsp softened butter

2 tbsp chopped fresh chives

2 tbsp freshly squeezed lemon juice

2 tbsp olive oil

1. Pat dry the scallops with paper towels. Season with salt and pepper. Place the scallops on a baking sheet lined with parchment paper. Cover with plastic wrap and freeze for 10 minutes.

2. Fill an injector syringe with the melted butter. Carefully plunge the needle into the center of each chilled scallop and inject with a little butter, being careful to slowly push the plunger to keep the butter in the scallops. Place the scallops on a clean baking sheet lined with parchment paper. Cover with plastic wrap and refrigerate for 1 hour.

3. Preheat the smoker to 250°F (125°C). Use maple wood.

4. In a large bowl, combine the lobster, softened butter, chives, lemon juice, and olive oil. Season with salt and pepper.

5. Remove the scallops from the fridge and place them on a fine-mesh wire rack to keep them flat. Cover the scallops with the lobster mixture.

6. Place the rack in the smoker and smoke the scallops until the flesh is golden brown and a little opaque, about 1 hour.

7. Remove the rack from the smoker. Drizzle the scallops with any remaining melted butter before serving.

Rainbow Trout

This is a very easy hot-smoking recipe and it doesn't take a lot of time to prepare.

Prep Time	Smoker Temp	Smoke Time
15 minutes	235°F (115°C)	2 to 3 hours

wood suggestions: alder, maple, or pecan

4 skin-on rainbow trout fillets (about 8 to 10oz [225 to 285g] each)

8 tbsp light brown sugar

2 tsp sea salt

2 tsp fresh coarsely ground black pepper

pinch of ground cayenne

1. Preheat the smoker to 235°F (115°C). Use alder, maple, or pecan wood.

2. Rinse the trout fillets under cold water and pat dry with paper towels. Place the fillets skin side down on a smoker rack.

3. In a small bowl, combine the brown sugar, salt, pepper, and cayenne. Mix well. Rub the spices into the meat side of the fillets.

4. Place the rack in the smoker and smoke the fillets until the internal temperature reaches 145°F (65°C), about 2 to 3 hours. To check the internal temperature, insert a thermometer probe into a thick spot.

5. Remove the rack from the smoker. Serve the fillets hot or allow them to cool completely and use in other recipes, such as dips and salads.

Cold-Smoked Mackerel with Maple Syrup & Dark Rum

Mackerel is quite an oily fish, which makes it perfect for smoking. The fattier the fish, the less likely it will be to dry out during the smoking process.

Prep Time	Smoker Temp	Smoke Time
30 minutes	145°F (65°C)	4 to 6 hours

wood suggestions: maple, oak, apple, hickory, rum barrel, or whiskey barrel

4 whole fresh mackerel (about 1½lb [680g] each), head, rib bones, and backbone removed, cleaned and butterflied

9 tbsp maple syrup, divided

2 tsp fresh coarsely ground black pepper

½ cup flaked sea salt

3 tbsp firmly packed light brown sugar

4oz (120ml) good-quality dark rum, divided

1. Evenly space the mackerel skin side down on a baking sheet lined with parchment paper. Brush 6 tablespoons of the maple syrup on the cut sides of the mackerel. Evenly sprinkle pepper over the top.

2. In a small bowl, combine the salt and brown sugar. Evenly sprinkle this mixture over the fish. Drizzle 3 ounces (90 milliliters) of dark rum over the top. Cover the fish with plastic wrap and top with a heavy plate. Refrigerate for 2 hours.

3. Remove the mackerel from the fridge. Use a pastry brush to remove as much of the salt mixture as possible without damaging the flesh. Rinse under cold water and pat dry with paper towels. Arrange the mackerel skin side down on a clean baking sheet lined with parchment paper. Refrigerate uncovered for 2 to 3 hours.

4. Preheat the smoker to 145°F (65°C) for cold-smoking. Use maple, oak, apple, or hickory wood or use rum or whiskey barrel staves.

5. In a small bowl, combine the remaining 3 tablespoons of maple syrup and the remaining 1 ounce (30 milliliters) of dark rum. Remove the mackerel from the fridge and brush the fish with this mixture.

6. Place the mackerel skin side down in the smoker and cold-smoke until the flesh is golden brown and flakes easily with a fork, about 4 to 6 hours.

7. Remove the mackerel from the smoker and serve immediately. You can also completely cool the mackerel to use in recipes for dips, salads, or other dishes.

Recipe Note: Smoked mackerel makes a great dip when combined with cream cheese, green onions, and fresh dill. Serve this with crackers and chips. It's also really tasty when flaked into a white wine cream sauce and served over fresh pasta.

Whitefish Dip

Along with the moistness of the smoked fish, this dip shines with pungent flavors from apple cider vinegar, red onions, and fresh dill as well as a velvety consistency from cream cheese and mayonnaise.

Prep Time	Smoker Temp	Smoke Time
15 minutes	180°F (85°C)	2 to 3 hours

wood suggestions: alder, maple, or pecan

2 cups warm water

2 tsp kosher salt

1 tsp granulated sugar

2 skin-on fresh whitefish fillets
(about 8 to 12oz [225 to 340g] total)

for the dip

1½ cups softened cream cheese

3 tbsp mayonnaise

1 tsp apple cider vinegar

¼ cup finely chopped red onions

1 tbsp chopped fresh dill

2 green onions, finely chopped

sea salt, to taste

freshly ground black pepper, to taste

1. In a small bowl, combine the water, salt, and sugar. Stir until the salt and sugar dissolve. Place the fish fillets in a resealable plastic bag and pour the salt brine over the top. Seal the bag, squeezing out as much air as possible, and refrigerate for 24 hours.

2. Remove the fish from the brine. Discard the brine. Place the fillets skin side down on a smoker rack. Cover with plastic wrap and refrigerate for 6 hours or overnight.

3. Preheat the smoker to 180°F (85°C). Use alder, maple, or pecan wood.

4. Place the rack in the smoker and smoke the fish until the internal temperature reaches 145°F (65°C), about 2 to 3 hours. To check the internal temperature, insert a thermometer probe into the meatiest part of one of the fillets.

5. Remove the rack from the smoker and allow the fish to cool completely.

6. Remove and discard the skin and any bones from the whitefish. Flake the fillets into ½-inch (1.25cm) pieces. Place the flaked fish into a medium bowl.

7. In a large bowl, make the dip by combining the cream cheese, mayonnaise, and apple cider vinegar. Mix until smooth. Add the red onions, dill, green onions, and whitefish. Season with salt and pepper. Gently mix to incorporate.

8. Transfer the dip to a serving dish. Cover and refrigerate for 1 hour. Serve with crackers and fresh bread.

Recipe Note: Try this recipe with haddock, halibut, salmon, mackerel, or trout. All work well and make for a tasty dip.

Honey & Hoisin Oysters

Smoking oysters is a bit of a process—and it requires some patience. First, you need to choose the right-sized fresh oysters, which is a bit of a Goldilocks-type experience. They can't be too large (they get too mushy when smoked) and they can't be too small (they get too shriveled when smoked). The next key is to not rush the smoke—it'll all be worth it in the end!

Prep Time	Smoker Temp	Smoke Time
30 minutes	125°F (55°C)	4½ hours

wood suggestions: maple, alder, oak, or cherry

4 quarts (4 liters) water

3 dozen large fresh oysters

1oz (30ml) sake

1 tbsp firmly packed light brown sugar

1 tbsp honey

2 tsp hoisin sauce

1½ tsp low-sodium soy sauce, divided

½ tsp freshly ground black pepper

2 cups kosher salt, divided

1 tsp sesame seeds

1 green onion, finely chopped

¼ tsp sambal oelek (red chili sauce)

2 tbsp peanut oil

1. Add the water to a large pot and place a steamer basket in the pot. Place the pot on the stovetop over high heat and bring the water to a boil. Working in batches, place 12 oysters in the basket and steam until the shells pop open, about 5 to 8 minutes. Discard any unopened shells.

2. Use an oyster knife to carefully shuck the oysters. Transfer the oysters to a large bowl and reserve the shells. Gently pat dry the oysters with paper towels.

3. In a medium bowl, combine the sake, brown sugar, honey, hoisin sauce, ½ teaspoon of soy sauce, and pepper. Mix until well combined. Pour this over the oysters. Cover the bowl with plastic wrap and refrigerate for 12 hours.

4. Preheat the smoker to 125°F (55°C) for cold-smoking. Use maple, alder, oak, or cherry wood.

5. Evenly spread 1 cup of salt on each of two baking sheets. Arrange the shell bases in the salt so they're all level. Spray the shells with nonstick cooking spray. Drain the oysters and pat dry with paper towels. Place one oyster in each shell.

6. Place the sheets in the smoker and dry the oysters for 90 minutes, turning the oysters every 30 minutes.

7. Get some smoke going and smoke the oysters for 1 hour. Raise the smoker temperature to 140°F (60°C) and continue smoking for 1 hour more. Raise the smoker temperature again to 160°F (75°C) and continue to smoke until the gills have begun to shrivel and dry, about 1 hour more.

8. Remove the sheets from the smoker and allow the oysters to cool completely. Cover with plastic wrap and refrigerate until chilled through, about 2 hours.

9. Transfer the oysters to a large bowl and add the sesame seeds, green onion, and sambal oelek. Gently stir to combine.

10. In a small skillet on the stovetop, heat the peanut oil over medium-high heat until smoking, about 1 to 2 minutes. Pour the sizzling oil over the oysters and drizzle the remaining 1 teaspoon of soy sauce over the top. Gently stir. Serve immediately.

Recipe Note: Chop about 6 smoked oysters and stir them into a cream cheese-based dip for a delicious appetizer or snack.

Hot Curry Tilapia with Cilantro & Lime Butter

This recipe stands out because of its pings of hot curry powder and ground ginger, but the tilapia bites back with a cilantro and lime butter.

Prep Time	Smoker Temp	Smoke Time
30 minutes	275°F (135°C)	45 to 60 minutes

wood suggestions: maple or alder wood, rum barrel staves, coconut shells, and/or cinnamon sticks

4 large tilapia fillets (about 1½ to 2lb [680g to 1kg] total), thawed if frozen

2 tbsp hot curry powder

2 tsp ground ginger

2 tsp kosher salt

2½ tsp freshly ground black pepper, divided

3 tsp granulated sugar

½ cup unsalted butter (1 stick), softened

1 cup chopped fresh cilantro leaves

3 medium limes, divided

1. Pat dry the tilapia fillets with paper towels. Refrigerate until ready to smoke.

2. In a large bowl, combine the hot curry powder, ground ginger, salt, 2 teaspoons of pepper, and sugar. Mix until well combined. Sprinkle the mixture all over the tilapia. Arrange the fillets skin side down on a baking sheet lined with parchment paper. Refrigerate for 2 hours.

3. In a small bowl, combine the butter, cilantro, and the remaining ½ teaspoon of pepper. Add the juice from 1 lime. Mix well to combine. Cover the bowl and refrigerate until ready to serve.

4. Preheat the smoker to 275°F (135°C). Use maple or alder wood, rum barrel staves, coconut shells, and/or cinnamon sticks.

5. Evenly space the fillets on a smoker rack. Insert a thermometer probe into the thickest part of one of the fillets.

6. Place the rack in the smoker and smoke the tilapia until the internal temperature reaches 145°F to 150°F (65°C to 70°C), about 45 to 60 minutes.

7. Remove the rack from the smoker and immediately serve the fillets with the cilantro and lime butter.

Recipe Notes: This recipe works well with a variety of seafood. Try grouper, mahi mahi, salmon, kingfish, or scallops. You can use leftovers for a smoky fish sandwich filling by just adding a little mayonnaise.

Garlic & Chili Shrimp

This is a killer easy recipe. Find the biggest shrimp you can for this dish. Look for colossal-sized shrimp (13/15)—they're plump and juicy.

Prep Time	Smoker Temp	Smoke Time
30 minutes	225°F (110°C)	45 to 60 minutes

wood suggestions: maple, alder, apple, cherry, or pecan

2lb (1kg) colossal shrimp (13/15 size)

5 tbsp sea salt

4 tbsp olive oil

1 medium orange, juiced

4 tbsp minced fresh garlic

1 tbsp minced fresh ginger

2 tsp finely chopped hot chili peppers

1 tbsp granulated onion

2 tsp fresh coarsely ground black pepper

1 tsp ground cayenne

1. Peel and devein the shrimp, leaving the tail piece attached and intact. Place the shrimp in a large bowl and add the salt. Toss to evenly coat. Allow to rest for 15 minutes. This will put a salt boost into the shrimp to give them more flavor.

2. Rinse the shrimp in cold water to remove excess salt. Drain and pat dry with paper towels. Place the shrimp in a clean large bowl.

3. Add the olive oil, orange juice, garlic, ginger, chili peppers, granulated onion, black pepper, and cayenne. Mix well. Cover the bowl and refrigerate for 1 hour.

4. Preheat the smoker to 225°F (110°C). Use maple, alder, apple, cherry, or pecan wood.

5. Remove the shrimp from the marinade and evenly space them on a smoker rack. Place the rack in the smoker and smoke the shrimp until they're opaque, pink, and firm to the touch, about 45 to 60 minutes.

6. Remove the rack from the smoker and immediately serve the shrimp.

Recipe Note: For an easy dipping sauce, in a small bowl, combine ½ cup of mayonnaise, as much or as little chipotle hot sauce as you like, a squeeze of lemon, and some chopped fresh cilantro.

Starters, Sides & Sweets

When people ask me what they shouldn't smoke, I tell them you can smoke anything. At the very least, you should give most everything a chance. I'll try anything once and usually I'll keep going until I make it work. I'm always trying to find new ways to push the culinary envelope. I've smoked a lot of foods—even a variety of bubblegums. (How did that turn out? Horrible—but not all things work.)

When it comes to food, you're only limited by your imagination. Think outside the box and smoke something different and unexpected. That's how new recipes are created. Who thought that smoked chocolate could be so mouthwatering? The recipes in these chapters use foods that aren't exactly synonymous with a smoker, but they're fantastic and I hope you give them a go. Have fun and even get a little sticky!

Vegetable & Side Dish Recipes

Your smoked protein is the star of your meal, but it needs a delicious supporting cast to really make it shine! Your side dishes should be flavorful but understated when you're presenting your masterpiece. Sides are a great way to get to know your smoker without the same time and financial commitment many smoked meats require.

That said, because side dishes shouldn't be an afterthought, plan your menu carefully. Too many "loud" dishes can overwhelm the palate and actually have the opposite effect you're going for. Plus, because not everything needs to be smoked, add some fresh steamed vegetables or only serve smoked sides with a grilled or roasted protein.

Don't be afraid to be creative and brave enough to give your ideas a shot. You can be more adventurous when it's a side dish and not the main event. In fact, look ahead in this chapter—you don't think I thought I was crazy when a few of these ideas popped in my head? But I try everything—just ask my neighbors. I'll be honest: Not everything turns out the way I thought, but more often than not, the results are delicious. The following recipes are great starting places for sides, but don't be afraid to modify them to suit your needs and desires.

Cauliflower

When it comes to smoking vegetables, I find cauliflower to be extremely receptive to the flavors of wood smoke. Give it a go!

Prep Time	Smoker Temp	Smoke Time
15 minutes	235°F (115°C)	90 minutes

wood suggestions: maple or hickory

1 medium-sized head of cauliflower

1 cup mayonnaise

½ cup softened cream cheese

2 tbsp yellow curry spice (mild or hot) or **Tandoori Rub** (page 120)

½ tsp orange zest

2 tsp freshly squeezed orange juice

kosher salt, to taste

freshly ground black pepper, to taste

½ cup finely chopped red onions

1 green onion, finely chopped

1 to 2 fresh hot red chili peppers, seeded and finely chopped (optional)

1 cup chopped fresh cilantro leaves

2 tbsp crispy fried onions

1 tbsp chopped cashews

maple syrup, to taste

1. Trim the leaves and stem from the cauliflower so it will stand upright. Rinse under cold water and place stem side down in a large microwave-safe bowl. Cover with plastic wrap and microwave on high until the cauliflower is fork-tender, about 6 to 8 minutes. Remove the bowl from the microwave and allow the cauliflower to rest for 2 minutes. Remove the plastic, drain, and allow to cool for 30 minutes.

2. Preheat the smoker to 235°F (115°C). Use maple or hickory wood.

3. In a small bowl, combine the mayonnaise, cream cheese, and yellow curry spice. Add the orange zest and juice. Season with salt and pepper. Mix until smooth.

4. Place the cauliflower on a smoker rack. Brush the curry mayonnaise all over the cauliflower, carefully and gently pushing it into the crevices between the florets.

5. Place the rack in the smoker and smoke the cauliflower for 60 minutes.

6. Raise the smoker temperature to 375°F (195°C) and continue to smoke until the cauliflower is heated through, tender, and a golden smoky color, about 30 to 45 minutes more.

7. In a small bowl, combine the red onions, green onion, chili peppers, and cilantro.

8. Remove the rack from the smoker and transfer the cauliflower to a serving bowl. Sprinkle the red onion mixture, fried onions, and cashews over the top of the cauliflower. Drizzle the maple syrup over the top before serving.

Recipe Note: You can use a vegan mayonnaise and a nondairy/vegan cream cheese spread instead.

Bacon-Wrapped Carrots with Spiced Honey

With this recipe, you might get the kids—and even some adults—to eat their carrots!

Prep Time	Smoker Temp	Smoke Time
90 minutes	235°F (115°C)	90 minutes

wood suggestions: hickory or apple

8 medium fresh carrots (1 inch [2.5cm] thick and 8 inches [20cm] long each), trimmed and peeled

1 tbsp chopped fresh dill, plus more

kosher salt, to taste

freshly ground black pepper, to taste

8 slices of bacon

for the honey

½ cup liquid honey

1 whole star anise

2-inch (5cm) cinnamon stick

5 black peppercorns

1 tsp crushed red pepper flakes

1. Rinse the carrots under cold running water and pat dry with paper towels. Season the carrots with the dill, salt, and pepper.

2. Place the bacon on a flat work surface. Use your fingers to stretch the strips to increase their length by almost half. Start at the top end of each carrot and tightly wrap a bacon strip around the entire length. Secure the bacon with a toothpick. Place the wrapped carrots on a baking sheet. Cover with plastic wrap and refrigerate for 1 hour.

3. Preheat the smoker to 235°F (115°C). Use hickory or apple wood.

4. Remove the carrots from the fridge and evenly space them on a smoker rack. Place the rack in the smoker and smoke the carrots until the bacon is crispy and the carrots are tender, about 90 minutes.

5. In a small saucepot on the stovetop over low heat, make the spiced honey by combining the honey, star anise, cinnamon stick, peppercorns, and red pepper flakes. Simmer for 45 minutes, stirring occasionally. Turn off the heat, but leave the pot on the stovetop to keep the spiced honey warm.

6. Remove the rack from the smoker and transfer the carrots to a serving platter. Drizzle the spiced honey and sprinkle more dill over the top. Serve immediately.

Blooming Onions with Cajun Remoulade Sauce

If you're a lover of onions like I am, then these will blow your mind. Serve this appetizer with your favorite grilled steak or try these blossoms alongside a tender, juicy smoked prime rib!

Prep Time	Smoker Temp	Smoke Time
30 minutes	255°F (125°C)	90 minutes

wood suggestions: apple, hickory, pecan, or peach

8 medium onions (Vidalia, Maui, or other sweet onion varieties recommended)

olive oil

kosher salt, to taste

freshly ground black pepper, to taste

4 tbsp chopped fresh herbs (such as parsley, sage, rosemary, and thyme leaves), plus more

8 slices of thick-cut bacon, cut into thin strips

8 tbsp pure maple syrup, plus more

2 cups shredded smoked cheddar or mozzarella cheese

for the remoulade

1 cup mayonnaise

2 tbsp creole mustard or grainy Dijon mustard

1 tbsp **Cajun Rub** (page 116)

1 tbsp grated dill pickles or minced capers

2 tsp horseradish

1 tsp hot sauce

kosher salt, to taste

freshly ground black pepper, to taste

1. Preheat the smoker to 255°F (125°C). Use apple, hickory, pecan, or peach wood.

2. Peel the onions, but leave the root ends intact. Stand the onions on their roots, but trim the root ends if necessary to allow the onions to stand upright. From top to bottom, make 4 slices about three-fourths of the way through each onion without cutting into the root to keep the onion together. (Once the onions start to smoke, they'll open up like blooming flowers.)

3. Evenly space the onions on a Bradley smoker tray. Drizzle the olive oil into the center of each onion. Season with the salt, pepper, and fresh herbs.

4. Place the tray in the smoker and smoke the onions until they've blossomed and have a nutty brown color, about 60 minutes.

5. In a small pan on the stovetop over medium heat, cook the bacon until just crisp. Remove the bacon from the pan and pat dry with paper towels. Cut the strips into ½-inch (1.25cm) pieces. Set aside.

6. In a small bowl, make the remoulade by combining the mayonnaise, mustard, rub, dill pickles, horseradish, and hot sauce. Season with salt and pepper.

7. Remove the tray from the smoker. Spoon the remoulade over the onion petals. Drizzle the maple syrup and sprinkle an equal amount of bacon over the top of each onion. Sprinkle ½ cup of cheese over the top of each onion.

8. Return the tray to the smoker and smoke the onions until the cheese has melted and the onions are tender, about 20 to 30 minutes more.

9. Remove the tray from the smoker and transfer the onions to a serving platter. Drizzle with more maple syrup and garnish with more herbs. Serve immediately.

Baba Ghanoush (Eggplant Dip)

Instead of grilling or roasting eggplant, I like to—you guessed it—smoke this nightshade vegetable! The smokiness really gets absorbed by the flesh, making this classic dip a bit more interesting. Salting eggplant helps draw out excess moisture and bitterness, allowing the smokiness to really come through and dance all over your taste buds.

Prep Time	Smoker Temp	Smoke Time
30 minutes	275°F (135°C)	2 to 3 hours

wood suggestions: oak, maple, mesquite, or hickory—or a blend—plus a few cinnamon sticks

2 large dark purple eggplants, halved lengthwise

2 tbsp kosher salt, plus more

2 tbsp olive oil

1 medium sweet onion, diced

4 garlic cloves, minced

1 cup whipped cream cheese

2 tbsp mayonnaise

2 tbsp crispy fried onions

2 green onions, minced

1 tbsp chopped fresh cilantro leaves

freshly ground black pepper, to taste

pinch of ground cayenne

1. Place the eggplants cut side up on a baking sheet. Sprinkle the salt over the top and allow the eggplants to rest for 1 hour.

2. Preheat the smoker to 275°F (135°C). Use oak, maple, mesquite, or hickory wood— or a blend—and a few cinnamon sticks.

3. Rinse the eggplants under cold running water and pat dry with paper towels. Use the tip of a knife to score the skins about ¼ inch (0.5cm) deep and 1 inch (2.5cm) apart. Place the eggplants cut side down on a smoker rack.

4. Place the rack in the smoker and smoke the eggplants until the skins are wrinkled and the flesh is very tender, about 2 to 3 hours. Remove the rack from the smoker and allow the eggplants to cool for 5 to 10 minutes.

5. Use a spoon to scoop the flesh from the eggplants. Discard the skins. Place the eggplant flesh in a fine-mesh sieve to drain and cool completely. Coarsely chop the eggplant. Set aside.

6. In a large skillet on the stovetop, heat the olive oil over medium-high heat. Add the sweet onion and garlic. Sauté until tender but not browned, about 3 to 4 minutes. Remove the skillet from the heat and allow the vegetables to cool.

7. In a medium bowl, whisk together the cream cheese and mayonnaise until smooth. Add the sweet onion, garlic, fried onions, green onions, and cilantro. Stir in the eggplant until well combined. Season with the salt, pepper, and cayenne.

8. Store in an airtight container in the refrigerator for at least 1 hour before serving. Serve with assorted fresh-cut vegetables, grilled pita, and assorted chips or crackers. Store in the fridge for up to 3 days.

Vidalia Onion Relish

I had a bunch of onions and thought to myself: "Self, you should smoke some of these big, juicy, sweet onions." So that's what I did. The next thing I knew, I was adding orange juice and sugar to make this sweet and delish garnish. It's great with smoked sausages and burgers.

Prep Time	Smoker Temp	Smoke Time
1 hour	230°F (110°C)	6 hours

wood suggestions: pecan, apple, oak, or hickory

8 large sweet Vidalia onions (or other varieties of sweet onion), peeled and quartered

1 cup apple cider vinegar

1 cup rice wine vinegar

¼ cup mirin (rice wine)

¾ cup freshly squeezed orange juice, divided

⅓ cup kosher salt

6 medium thick-skinned sweet oranges

1 cup granulated sugar

1 cup firmly packed light brown sugar

1 cup honey

¼ cup white grape juice

1 tbsp fresh coarsely ground black pepper

1. Preheat the smoker to 230°F (110°C). Use pecan, apple, oak, or hickory wood.

2. Place the onions on a smoker rack. Place the rack in the smoker and smoke the onions until they're smoky brown and slightly tender, about 6 hours.

3. Remove the rack from the smoker. Slice the onions into ½-inch (1.25cm) strips and place the slices in a large nonreactive container. (You should have about 8 cups of sliced onions.)

4. In a small saucepan on the stovetop over high heat, combine the apple cider vinegar, rice wine vinegar, mirin, and ¼ cup of orange juice. Bring to a boil, then stir in the salt until dissolved. Remove the pan from the heat. Pour the mixture over the onions and allow them to cool completely. Top with a heavy plate to keep the onions submerged. Cover the container with plastic wrap and refrigerate for 2 weeks, stirring well once a day.

5. Use a vegetable peeler to remove the skins from the oranges, avoiding the pith (the bitter white stuff). Juice the oranges and cut the orange peel into ¼-inch (0.5cm) strips.

6. Remove the onions from the brine and transfer them to a large saucepan on the stovetop over medium-high heat. Discard the brine. Add the orange peels, sugar, brown sugar, honey, white grape juice, and the remaining ½ cup of orange juice. Bring to a low boil, stirring occasionally, then reduce the heat. Simmer until the mixture is thick and slightly syrupy, about 30 minutes, stirring occasionally. If the mixture is too thick, add a little orange juice to thin it. Stir in the pepper. Transfer everything to a dozen 1-pint (½-liter) sterilized canning jars. Seal with sterilized lids and caps.

7. To a large pot on the stovetop over high heat, add enough water to cover the jars by 1 inch (2.5cm). Bring the water to a boil, then carefully lower the jars into the water. Process for 45 to 60 minutes. Remove the pot from the heat and allow the jars to cool. Tighten the caps. Store the jars in a cool, dark place for up to 1 year.

Recipe Note: A good-quality apple cider vinegar is tart and sweet with a bright flavor rather than just acidic. So it's worth the extra couple bucks to get the good stuff.

Beet & Pear Salad with Blue Cheese & Walnuts

This is a salad for all the senses. A smoky aroma combined with sweet, tender pears, vibrant-colored beets, creamy-textured cheese, and crunchy walnuts—it's like a sensory overload! It's as beautiful as it is tasty and it's a perfect choice to serve alongside smoked brisket or beef tenderloin.

Prep Time	Smoker Temp	Smoke Time
1 hour	125°F (55°C)	90 minutes

wood suggestions: oak, maple, or apple

- 3 large red beets, scrubbed
- 1 large golden yellow beet, scrubbed
- 3 tbsp olive oil, divided
- ½ tsp freshly ground black pepper, plus more
- pinch of kosher salt, plus more
- 3 medium pears, peeled, halved, and cored
- 2 cups plus 2 tbsp apple juice
- 2 cups water
- ¼ cup granulated sugar

- 3 cloves
- 1 bay leaf
- 1-inch (2.5cm) cinnamon stick
- ½ cup chopped toasted walnuts or candied walnuts
- ½ cup crumbled creamy blue cheese
- ¼ cup diced sweet onions
- 4 green onions, thinly sliced, divided
- 2 tbsp white balsamic vinegar
- 1 tbsp honey
- 1 tbsp chopped fresh thyme leaves

1. To a medium saucepan on the stovetop over high heat, add the red beets and yellow beet. Cover with cold water. Bring to a slow boil, then reduce the heat to medium. Simmer until the beets are fork-tender, about 20 to 30 minutes. Remove the pan from the heat. Drain and rinse the beets under cold running water. Peel and leave whole. In a large bowl, combine the beets, 1 tablespoon of olive oil, pepper, and a pinch of salt. Toss gently to coat. Set aside.

2. In a separate medium saucepan on the stovetop over medium-high heat, combine the pears, 2 cups of apple juice, water, sugar, cloves, bay leaf, and cinnamon stick. Bring to a slow boil, then reduce the heat to low. Poach the pears until they're fork-tender, about 20 to 30 minutes. Remove the pan from the heat and allow the pears to cool in the poaching liquid.

3. Preheat the smoker to 125°F (55°C) for cold-smoking. Use oak, maple, or apple wood. Evenly space the beets and pears on a smoker rack.

4. Place the rack in the smoker and smoke for 90 minutes. Remove the rack from the smoker and allow the beets and pears to cool completely.

5. Cut the beets into ½-inch (1.25cm) cubes and thinly slice the pears. In a large bowl, combine the beets, pears, walnuts, blue cheese, sweet onions, and 2 green onions.

6. In a medium bowl, whisk together the white balsamic vinegar, honey, thyme, the remaining 2 tablespoons of olive oil, the remaining 2 tablespoons apple juice, and the remaining 2 green onions. Mix until well combined. Drizzle the dressing over the top of the beet and pear mixture and gently stir to combine. Season with salt and pepper. Serve immediately.

Variation: You can replace the beets with large carrots or butternut squash.

Recipe Note: It's always a good idea to cook root vegetables on the stovetop until fork-tender before smoking them. It would just take way too long to smoke any dense vegetable without cooking it beforehand.

Corn & Creamed Corn

Smoke once, eat twice—that's how this recipe rolls! We're going to smoke more corn than we need for tonight's dinner and then use the leftover to make a smoky side dish for tomorrow's dinner. On night one, you'll have smoked corn on the cob, and on night two, you'll have smoked creamed corn. Genius and delicious!

Night 1		
Prep Time	**Smoker Temp**	**Smoke Time**
15 minutes	250°F (125°C)	2½ hours

Night 2		
Prep Time	**Oven Temp**	**Cook Time**
15 minutes	350°F (180°C)	20 to 25 minutes

wood suggestions: oak or hickory

for night 1

8 ears of unshucked fresh corn on
   the cob

for night 2

2 cups chicken stock

2 smoked cobs of corn

3 tbsp butter

1 medium yellow onion, diced

2 garlic cloves, minced

¼ cup all-purpose flour

½ cup 35% whipping cream

5 cups smoked corn kernels

2 cups shredded smoked provolone,
   smoked buffalo mozzarella, or
   smoked mozzarella cheese

1 (14oz [400g]) can of creamed corn

1 tbsp chopped fresh sage leaves

kosher salt, to taste

freshly ground black pepper, to taste

1 cup panko breadcrumbs

¼ cup grated parmesan cheese

On Night 1

1. Peel back the husk and remove as much silk as possible from each ear of corn. Pull the husk back up around the corn and soak the ears in cold water for 4 to 6 hours.

2. Preheat the smoker to 250°F (125°C). Use oak or hickory wood.

3. Evenly space the ears of corn in the smoker and smoke for 2 hours. Remove the husks from the corn and continue to smoke for 30 minutes more. Occasionally spritz the corn with water.

4. Remove the ears from the smoker. Use a sharp knife to cut the kernels from the cobs. Reserve 5 cups of kernels and 2 stripped cobs for tomorrow's dinner. Enjoy the remaining corn with tonight's meal

On Night 2

1. Preheat the oven to 350°F (180°C).

2. In a medium saucepan on the stovetop over high heat, combine the chicken stock and stripped cobs. Bring to a boil, then reduce the heat to medium. Simmer for 15 minutes. Remove the pan from the heat. Strain and discard the solids.

3. In a large saucepan on the stovetop over medium heat, melt the butter. Add the onion and sauté until tender but not browned, about 3 to 4 minutes. Add the garlic and continue to sauté until fragrant, about 2 to 3 minutes more. Stir in the flour and cook until browned, about 2 minutes more, stirring constantly.

4. Add the corncob-infused chicken stock ½ cup at a time, whisking constantly. Bring to a boil, then reduce the heat to medium-low. Simmer until thick, about 10 to 15 minutes, stirring occasionally.

5. Whisk in the whipping cream until well combined. Stir in the smoked corn kernels, mozzarella, creamed corn, and sage. Mix until well combined. Season with the salt and pepper.

6. Pour the mixture into a greased 9 × 11-inch (23 × 28cm) casserole dish. Sprinkle the breadcrumbs and parmesan over the top.

7. Place the dish in the oven and bake until the top is crisp and golden brown, about 20 to 25 minutes. Remove the dish from the oven and serve immediately.

Variation: Want to add some tasty fun to your smoked corn? Wrap each cob of corn in a slice of bacon before smoking.

Recipe Notes: Always buy fresh corn with the husks on. If you're looking for good fresh corn, it's always best straight from a roadside stand. I like to smoke either bicolor or white corn because they balance out the smoke flavor better.

Plank-Smoked Mashed Potatoes

This side dish is quite easy to prepare and it's a great way to use leftover mashed potatoes. I like to mix up the flavors depending on what they're being served with and what I have in the fridge. Try a variety of cheeses, herbs, roasted garlic, pesto, or even horseradish. If you like it, throw it in there—odds are it'll taste pretty good with the potatoes.

Prep Time	Grill Temp	Smoke Time
45 minutes	450°F to 550°F (235°C to 290°C)	45 minutes

wood suggestion: two maple planks, soaked in cold water for 1 hour

8 large Yukon gold potatoes, peeled and quartered

1 tbsp kosher salt, plus more

2 tbsp softened butter

½ cup 35% whipping cream

freshly ground black pepper, to taste

½ cup creamy goat cheese

¼ cup chopped fresh chives

1. In a large pot on the stovetop over high heat, add the potatoes and cover with cold water. Add the salt. Bring to a boil and cook until fork-tender, about 15 to 20 minutes. Drain well and return the potatoes to the pot. Reduce the heat to low. Cook the potatoes until dry, about 2 to 3 minutes, shaking the pot constantly.

2. Remove the pot from the heat. Add the butter and whipping cream. Mash the potatoes until smooth. Season with salt and pepper. Allow the potatoes to cool completely. Cover the pot and refrigerate for 24 hours.

3. Preheat the grill to 450°F to 550°F (235°C to 290°C). Remove the planks from the water and pat dry with paper towels. Spray one side of each plank with nonstick cooking spray.

4. In a large bowl, combine the mashed potatoes, goat cheese, and chives. Mix well to combine. Use a 2-ounce (60g) ice cream scoop or a ¼ dry measure cup to divide the potatoes into 24 portions. Form each portion into a firm disc. Evenly space the discs on the planks. Spray the tops of the discs with nonstick cooking spray.

5. Place the planks on the grill and close the lid. Smoke until the plank starts to crackle and smoke, about 5 to 10 minutes. Reduce the heat directly under the plank or move the plank to a cooler spot without direct heat. Continue to smoke until the potatoes are heated through and golden and crisp on the outside, about 20 to 30 minutes more.

6. Carefully remove the planks from the grill and serve the potatoes immediately.

Recipe Note: The key to plank-smoking mashed potatoes is to prepare the potatoes 24 hours in advance. This allows the starch in the potatoes to set up, which keeps the mashed potatoes from running off the plank and making a mess of the grill or smoker.

Risotto with Spinach, Prosciutto & Smoked Mozzarella

I've done a lot of experimenting with smoking various types of rice and I've found that Arborio rice absorbs the smoke flavor best. This rice has a high starch content and is porous enough to allow the smoke to penetrate the grain, adding a nice nutty, smoky flavor to this twist on classic risotto.

Prep Time	Smoker Temp	Smoke Time
30 minutes	200°F (95°C)	6 hours

wood suggestions: grapevine cuttings, oak wine barrel staves, whiskey barrel staves, or apple or olive branches

- 4 cups Arborio rice
- 8 cups chicken broth
- 3 tbsp butter
- 1 medium white onion, diced
- 2 garlic cloves, minced
- ½ cup dry white wine
- 4 cups packed baby spinach leaves
- 1 cup smoked mozzarella, shredded smoked provolone, or smoked buffalo mozzarella cheese

- ½ cup freshly grated parmesan cheese
- ¼ cup 35% whipping cream
- kosher salt, to taste
- freshly ground black pepper, to taste
- 12 very thin slices of prosciutto or smoked prosciutto
- chopped fresh parsley leaves, to taste

1. Preheat the smoker to 200°F (95°C). Use vine cuttings, oak wine barrel staves, whiskey barrel staves, or apple or olive branches. Keep the humidity level very low. Wrap a smoker rack with aluminum foil and puncture the foil with the needle of an injector to make several tiny holes.

2. Scatter the rice over the rack and place the rack in the smoker. Smoke until the rice is slightly colored, about 6 hours, stirring every hour. Remove the rack from the smoker and allow the rice to cool completely. Reserve 2 cups to prepare the risotto. Vacuum-pack the remaining rice and store for up to 6 months.

3. In a large saucepan on the stovetop over high heat, bring the chicken broth to a boil. Reduce the heat to low and keep the broth warm.

4. In a separate large saucepan on the stovetop over medium heat, melt the butter. Add the onion and sauté until translucent, about 5 minutes. Add the garlic and sauté until tender, about 2 to 3 minutes. Add the 2 cups of rice and stir until well coated and lightly toasted. Add the white wine and simmer until the wine has almost completely evaporated, about 1 minute.

5. Slowly and gently stir in the chicken broth 1 cup at a time, adding up to 6 cups total. Continue to cook the rice is tender, creamy, and a bit soupy but not gluey, about 15 to 18 minutes more. Add more broth ¼ cup at a time until the proper consistency is achieved.

6. Stir in the spinach, mozzarella, parmesan, and whipping cream. Season with salt and pepper. Spoon the risotto into serving bowls. Garnish with the prosciutto and parsley before serving.

Recipe Note: Slowly stir the risotto so the rice slowly releases its starch and doesn't make the risotto overly sticky. Risotto should be creamy and the grains of rice should still be a bit firm in the center.

Baked Macaroni & Cheese

This is a new twist on a family favorite. Mozzarella is a mild melting cheese that absorbs a lot of smoke, which enhances the simplicity of it. The white cheddar shouldn't be any older than two years. Otherwise, the strong aged flavor will compete with the smoke. Serve this as a side dish with your favorite smoked ribs or brisket.

Prep Time	Smoker Temp	Smoke Time
2 hours	85°F (30°C)	4 to 6 hours

wood suggestions: apple, maple, or a blend of apple, maple, and hickory

- 1lb (450g) part-skim mozzarella cheese balls
- 1lb (450g) white cheddar cheese (1 to 2 years old)
- 1½lb (680g) double elbow macaroni
- 6 quarts (5.5 liters) water
- 1 tbsp kosher salt, plus more
- 2 tbsp olive oil
- 3 tbsp butter

- ¼ cup all-purpose flour
- 2½ cups milk
- 1 cup 35% whipping cream
- 1 small white onion, diced
- 1 (8oz [225g]) package of cream cheese
- ½ tsp freshly ground black pepper
- 1 cup hickory-flavored potato sticks
- 4 slices of bacon, fully cooked and chopped

1. Preheat the smoker to 85°F (30°C) for cold-smoking. Use apple, maple, or a blend of apple, maple, and hickory woods.

2. Place the cheeses on a smoker rack and place the rack in the smoker directly above the ice or ice packs. Smoke for 4 to 6 hours depending on the amount of smoke flavor you're looking for. (You can go longer if you wish, but I find 4 to 6 hours to be plenty of time.) Remove the rack from the smoker and loosely wrap the cheeses in parchment paper. Refrigerate for 24 hours.

3. In a large pot on the stovetop over high, combine the elbow macaroni, water, and salt. Cook until the macaroni is just tender, about 10 minutes. Drain and allow to cool. Evenly spread the macaroni on a smoker rack lined with parchment paper.

4. Place the rack in the smoker while the cheeses smoke. Smoke the macaroni for 1 hour, stirring occasionally. (You don't want to smoke the macaroni for more than 1 hour because the smoke flavor could get too strong.) Transfer the macaroni to a resealable plastic bag and refrigerate until needed.

5. Preheat the oven to 350°F (180°C). Grease a 2- or 3-quart (2- or 3-liter) casserole dish with the olive oil. Remove the cheeses from the fridge and shred them.

6. In a large saucepan on the stovetop over medium-low heat, melt the butter. Stir in the flour until well combined and cook for 1 minute, stirring constantly. Slowly add the milk and whipping cream, whisking constantly until smooth. Add the onion and sauté until tender, about 2 to 3 minutes, stirring often. Simmer until thickened, about 10 to 15 minutes, stirring frequently.

7. Reduce the heat to low and whisk in the cream cheese and the shredded cheeses until smooth. Remove the pan from the heat. Stir in the pepper and season with salt to taste.

8. In the casserole dish, combine the cooked macaroni and cheese mixture. Stir until thoroughly combined.

9. Place the dish in the oven and bake until the cheeses bubble and are golden brown, about 20 to 30 minutes.

10. Remove the dish from the oven. Top the casserole with the potato sticks and bacon before serving.

Deviled Eggs

Having a party and want to show off your smoking skills? Try these deviled eggs with a bacon garnish.

Prep Time	Smoker Temp	Smoke Time
20 minutes	180°F (85°C)	30 minutes

wood suggestions: oak, maple, whiskey, or cherry

8 large eggs

4 tbsp mayonnaise

1 tsp Dijon mustard

2 tsp chopped fresh dill

splash of apple cider vinegar

½ tsp hot sauce

pinch of ground cayenne

kosher salt, to taste

freshly ground black pepper, to taste

4 slices of smoked crispy bacon

1 green onion, finely chopped

1 hot red chili pepper, finely chopped

1. Preheat the smoker to 180°F (85°C). Use oak, maple, whiskey, or cherry wood.

2. To a large pot on the stovetop over high, add the eggs and cover with cold water. Cover the pot and bring the water to a rolling boil. Turn off the heat, keeping the pot on the burner, and allow the eggs to cook for 8 minutes.

3. Drain and run the eggs under cold water for 10 minutes to cool. Peel and discard the shells. Place the eggs on a smoker rack.

4. Place the rack in the smoker and smoke the eggs until they're golden and smoky, about 30 minutes. Remove the rack from the smoker and refrigerate the eggs until completely cooled.

5. Cut the eggs in half lengthwise. Place the egg whites on a serving platter.

6. In a large bowl, combine the egg yolks, mayonnaise, Dijon mustard, dill, apple cider vinegar, and hot sauce. Season with the cayenne, salt, and black pepper. Mix until smooth. Spoon the yolk mixture into the egg whites. (Use a piping bag to make filling the egg whites with the deviled egg mixture a little easier.)

7. Break or cut each piece of bacon into 4 equal pieces and insert a piece of bacon in each egg. Garnish with the green onion and chili pepper before serving.

Portobello Mushrooms

These tender, smoked portobello mushrooms topped with cheese make a **perfect** side dish for that perfect grilled steak!

Prep Time	Smoker Temp	Smoke Time
15 minutes	275°F (135°C)	2 hours

wood suggestions: oak, hickory, or cherry

8 medium portobello mushroom caps (about 3 to 4 inches [7.5 to 10cm] in diameter)

3 cups hot water

3 tbsp extra-virgin olive oil, plus more

⅓ cup aged balsamic vinegar

6 garlic cloves, minced

1 tbsp chopped fresh oregano leaves

pinch of crushed red pepper flakes

kosher salt, to taste

freshly ground black pepper, to taste

¼ cup grated parmesan cheese

½ cup crumbled goat cheese

1 cup shredded smoked mozzarella cheese

½ cup panko breadcrumbs

1. Brush any dirt off the mushrooms. Remove and discard the stems. Place the mushroom caps in a large bowl and cover with the hot water. Allow the mushrooms to soak for 10 to 15 minutes. Drain and pat dry with paper towels.

2. In the same large bowl, combine the olive oil, balsamic vinegar, garlic, oregano, and red pepper flakes. Season with salt and pepper. Add the mushroom caps, turning to coat well. Cover the bowl and refrigerate for 1 hour.

3. Preheat the smoker to 275°F (135°C). Use oak, hickory, or cherry wood.

4. In a small bowl, combine the cheeses and breadcrumbs. Refrigerate until needed.

5. Place the mushrooms gill side up in the smoker and smoke for 1 hour. Flip the mushrooms to gill side down, brush with a little olive oil, and continue to smoke for 30 minutes more. Flip the mushrooms again when they're tender. Sprinkle the cheese mixture over the mushrooms and continue to smoke until the cheeses melt, about 15 to 20 minutes more.

6. Remove the mushrooms from the smoker and serve immediately.

Appetizer & Snack Recipes

Smoking isn't just about meats and vegetables. And it doesn't just belong to the main course. As I've said before, I'll smoke anything. These days, folks like to graze. A backyard gathering might not include a huge feed. Maybe it's an unexpected neighborhood drop-in or maybe it's the big game. Then again, maybe it's a big bash and starters feel right. No matter how many people you've got coming over, one of the following recipes will surely suit your needs—and wow all your guests!

Bacon-Wrapped Jalapeño Poppers

Jalapeños stuffed with a mixture of mozzarella and cream cheeses and then wrapped in bacon make for spicy treats that are sure to get any party off to a great start. Tortilla chips inside and outside the peppers help protect the cheese and enhance the flavors. This one be mighty tasty!

Prep Time	Smoker Temp	Smoke Time
1 hour	275°F (135°C)	1½ to 2 hours

wood suggestions: hickory, apple, maple, or cherry

18 jalapeños, seeds and ribs removed, cut lengthwise

½ cup shredded mozzarella cheese

¼ cup cream cheese

2½ cups finely crushed corn tortilla chips, divided

2 green onions, finely chopped

1 tbsp chopped fresh cilantro leaves

1 tsp freshly squeezed lemon juice

18 slices of smoked bacon

1 tbsp **Basic Barbecue Rub** (page 115) or your favorite rub

1. In a large bowl, combine the mozzarella cheese, cream cheese, ¼ cup of tortilla chips, green onions, cilantro, and lemon juice. Pack the cheese mixture tightly into each jalapeño half.

2. Place the remaining 2¼ cups of tortilla chips on a baking sheet. Firmly press each jalapeño filling side down into the crushed tortilla chips until completely coated.

3. Place the bacon on a clean work surface and firmly run your fingers over each slice to stretch the length by half. Cut each piece in half through the center. Tightly wrap a piece of bacon around each jalapeño, leaving no gaps to prevent the cheese from oozing out during smoking. Place the jalapeños on a tray and freeze until well chilled but not frozen, about 30 to 60 minutes.

4. Preheat the smoker to 275°F (135°C). Use hickory, apple, maple, or cherry wood.

5. Remove the tray from the freezer and season the bacon well with the barbecue rub. Place the jalapeños in the smoker and smoke until the bacon is slightly crispy and the filling is heated through, about 1½ to 2 hours.

6. Transfer the jalapeños to a serving platter and allow them to rest for 5 minutes before serving.

Variation: Change things up and add some shredded barbecue pulled pork, smoked chicken, brisket, turkey, crab meat, or shrimp to the cheese filling. Just about anything would taste good—use your imagination to create an amazing appetizer.

Recipe Note: Buy jalapeños that are large, plump, and uniform in size. This will ensure they freeze and cook at the same rate (and that no one gets more or less than someone else—that's how fistfights start!). I like big jalapeños because you can load them up.

Plank-Smoked Camembert

This recipe is a winner, a head-turner, and a crowd-pleaser. I've been plank-smoking brie and camembert cheeses for years and years. I'm 99.9% sure I'm the one who came up with this—not 100% sure but still pretty sure. I developed it for my first cookbook, *Sticks and Stones*, back in 1999. Either way, this recipe is fast, it's easy, and it will get your party started right!

Prep Time	Grill Temp	Smoke Time
10 minutes	325°F (165°C)	15 to 20 minutes

wood suggestions: ½-inch-thick (1.25cm-thick) maple, oak, pecan, or hickory plank, soaked in cold water for 1 hour

- 1 tsp kosher salt, plus more
- 1 tsp freshly ground black pepper, divided, plus more
- 6 slices of thick double-smoked bacon
- 1 small Vidalia onion, sliced
- 2 tbsp coarsely crushed cashews
- 1 tsp chopped fresh thyme leaves
- 2oz (60ml) maple syrup
- 2 (4-inch [10cm]) camembert rounds (about 5oz [150g] each)

1. Preheat the grill to 325°F (165°C). Remove the plank from the water and pat dry with paper towels. Place the plank on the grill and close the lid. Heat the plank until it begins to crackle and lightly smoke, about 3 to 5 minutes. Season the plank with salt and ½ teaspoon of pepper.

2. In a large skillet on the stovetop over medium heat, cook the bacon until lightly browned and crisp, about 7 to 10 minutes. Transfer the bacon to a plate lined with paper towels. Set aside.

3. To the same large skillet, add the onion and sauté until tender but not browned, about 5 minutes, stirring occasionally. Remove the skillet from the heat and drain the onion. Pat the onion with paper towels to remove excess bacon fat.

4. In a large bowl, combine the bacon, onion, cashews, thyme, and maple syrup. Season with salt and pepper to taste. Mix well to combine.

5. Evenly space the camembert on the plank about 1 inch (2.5cm) from the edge. Sprinkle the remaining ½ teaspoon of pepper over the cheese. Evenly divide the bacon mixture among the rounds, mounding the mixture into tall piles.

6. Close the grill lid and smoke the rounds until the topping is heated through and the cheese is bulging in the rind and golden brown, about 15 to 20 minutes. Occasionally check for flames.

7. Transfer the rounds to a serving platter or a second uncharred plank. Allow them to cool slightly. Serve with a variety of breads and crackers.

Recipe Note: Small wheels of cheese with a hearty rind are the best for plank-smoking because the rind keeps the hot, bubbly cheese in place instead of oozing everywhere.

Moink Balls

I'm not sure who first created this recipe, but I know when and where I first had it. My friend Danielle of Diva Q BBQ gave me a taste at a barbecue event when I was visiting some years ago. She calls them "mo-ink" balls—moo for the beef and oink for the pork. They're beef meatballs wrapped in bacon and smoked to mouthwatering awesomeness. Here's my version with the addition of a dunk and a crunch.

Prep Time	Smoker Temp	Smoke Time
2½ hours	275°F to 300°F (135°C to 150°C)	1 to 1½ hours

wood suggestions: hickory or a blend of hickory, maple, and apple

2 buttery croissants, cut into 1-inch (1.25cm) pieces

¼ cup whole milk

3lb (1.4kg) ground beef

1lb (450g) ground pork

½ cup finely diced white onion

4 garlic cloves, minced

3 tbsp **Basic Barbecue Rub** (page 115), divided

2 tsp Dijon mustard

1 tsp Worcestershire sauce

1½ cups diced mozzarella cheese

32 slices of hickory-smoked bacon

2 cups gourmet-style barbecue sauce

½ cup apple butter

½ cup chipotle-style hot sauce

¼ cup honey

¼ cup apple juice

1oz (30ml) bourbon (optional)

1 (8oz [225g]) bag of kettle-style potato chips, finely crushed

1. To a medium bowl, add the croissant pieces and milk. Soak until softened, about 15 minutes.

2. In a large bowl, combine the beef, pork, onion, garlic, 1 tablespoon of barbecue rub, Dijon mustard, and Worcestershire sauce. Gently mix in the mozzarella.

3. Squeeze and discard excess milk from the croissants. Add the croissants to the meat mixture. Gently mix until the meat mixture is moist and sticky but not wet.

4. Use a 2-ounce (60g) ice cream scoop or a ¼ dry measure cup to divide the meat mixture into 32 equally sized portions. Form the portions into balls.

5. Place the meatballs on a baking sheet lined with parchment paper. Refrigerate until chilled through, about 1 hour.

6. Place the bacon on a flat work surface. Use your fingers to stretch the strips to increase their length by almost half. Season one side of each slice with the remaining 2 tablespoons of barbecue rub. Tightly wrap a slice of bacon seasoned side in around each meatball until completely covered. Place the meatballs on a tray and refrigerate for 1 hour.

7. Preheat the smoker to 275°F to 300°F (135°C to 150°C). Use hickory wood or a blend of hickory, maple, and apple woods.

8. Place the meatballs on a smoking rack. Insert a thermometer probe into the center of one of the meatballs.

9. Place the rack in the smoker and smoke until the bacon starts to crisp, the meatballs are fully cooked, and the internal temperature reaches 160°F (75°C), about 1 to 1½ hours.

10. In a medium saucepan on the stovetop over medium heat, combine the barbecue sauce, apple butter, hot sauce, honey, and apple juice. Cook until the mixture comes to a boil. Stir in the bourbon (if using) and remove the pan from the heat.

11. Remove the meatballs from the smoker. Dip each meatball one at a time into the sauce and then into the potato chips until evenly coated. Serve immediately— with lots of napkins!

Recipe Note: Freeze the mozzarella before mixing it into the raw meat mixture. This is extra insurance that the cheese won't ooze from the meatballs while in the smoker.

Frittata with Grape Tomatoes & Pancetta

I was smoking some peameal bacon one morning for breakfast when I got to thinking: I've smoked hard-boiled eggs and soft-poached eggs, but I've never smoked scrambled eggs. This needed to be remedied—and fast. So here's my smoky take on the classic frittata. The egg mixture takes on the sweet smoke, adding a new dimension to your eggs.

Prep Time	Smoker Temp	Smoke Time
15 minutes	275°F (135°C)	3½ to 4½ hours

wood suggestions: apple, hickory, cherry, pecan, or oak

1 cup grape tomatoes

kosher salt, to taste

12 slices of pancetta

12 extra-large eggs

3 tbsp 35% whipping cream

2 cups shredded mozzarella cheese

2 tbsp grated parmesan cheese

1 cup crispy fried onions

handful of chopped fresh basil leaves

2 green onions, chopped

1. Preheat the smoker to 275°F (135°C). Use apple, hickory, cherry, pecan, or oak wood. Evenly space the grape tomatoes on a smoker rack lined with aluminum foil. Season with the salt.

2. Place the rack in the smoker and smoke the tomatoes until they're slightly softened and the skins are a little wrinkly, about 2 to 3 hours. Remove the rack from the smoker and allow the tomatoes to cool completely. Chop the tomatoes and set aside. Keep the smoker going.

3. In a medium skillet on the stovetop over medium-high heat, cook the pancetta until crisp, about 2 to 3 minutes per side. Remove the pan from the heat and pat dry the pancetta with paper towels. Allow the pancetta to cool before coarsely chopping. Set aside.

4. Grease a 10-inch (20cm) cast-iron pan with nonstick cooking spray.

5. In a medium bowl, whisk together the eggs and whipping cream until lightly beaten. Add the pancetta, cheeses, fried onions, basil, and green onions. Add the mixture to the pan and scatter the tomatoes over the top.

6. Place the pan in the smoker and smoke until the frittata is set and hot throughout, about 90 minutes.

7. Remove the pan from the smoker and serve the frittata immediately.

Recipe Note: While you're at it, make extra smoked tomatoes to use in smoky barbecue sauces, as salad garnishes, or for charcuterie and antipasto platters.

Steak-Wrapped Shrimp with Honey & Sriracha Barbecue Sauce

If you're like many people I know, you love steak with a side of shrimp. But what if you could have shrimp wrapped *inside* steak? This recipe helps you do just that!

Prep Time	Smoker Temp	Smoke Time
45 minutes	275°F (135°C)	1 to 1½ hours

wood suggestions: maple, cherry, or hickory

2lb (1kg) beef tenderloin

1 cup beer

1lb (450g) colossal shrimp (13/15 size), peeled and deveined

2 to 3 tbsp **Garlic & Herb Rub** (page 117)

2 to 3 tbsp vegetable oil

for the sauce

½ cup honey

¼ cup barbecue sauce

1oz (30ml) sriracha hot sauce

pinch of **Basic Barbecue Rub** (page 115)

1. Freeze the beef for 15 minutes to make it easier to slice. Soak 15 chopsticks (or bamboo skewers) in water for 1 hour. (You can also use metal skewers, which you don't need to soak.)

2. Preheat the smoker to 275°F (135°C). Use maple, cherry, or hickory wood.

3. In a small bowl, make the honey and sriracha barbecue sauce by whisking together the honey, barbecue sauce, sriracha, and barbecue rub. Set aside.

4. Fill an injection syringe with the beer and inject each shrimp with some beer. Season the shrimp with some of the barbecue rub.

5. Thinly slice the beef into 1- to 2-ounce (30 to 60g) slices. Use your fingers to gently flatten each slice. Wrap each shrimp with 1 to 2 slices of beef, pressing firmly around the middle to ensure the beef adheres.

6. Brush the steak with the vegetable oil and season with the remaining barbecue seasoning. Skewer the shrimp onto the chopsticks.

7. Place the chopsticks in the smoker and smoke until the internal temperature reaches 145°F to 160°F (65°C to 75°C), about 1 to 1½ hours. The shrimp should be cooked through, pink and opaque, and firm to the touch. The beef should be tender. To check the internal temperature, insert a thermometer probe into a meaty part without touching a chopstick. Glaze the steak with the honey and sriracha sauce during the last 20 minutes.

8. Remove the chopsticks or skewers from the smoker. Glaze the steak with extra sauce before serving.

Chicken Liver Pâté

Pâté is the quintessential appetizer. You can serve this version with grilled breads or on crackers. You can also use this pâté as part of a cheese or vegetable platter.

Prep Time	Smoker Temp	Smoke Time
15 minutes	225°F (105°C)	1½ to 2 hours

wood suggestions: maple, apple, or cherry

1lb (450g) chicken livers, trimmed

1 tbsp **Mediterranean Rub** (page 121)

1oz (30ml) cognac, brandy, or bourbon

2 tbsp olive oil

2 tsp kosher salt

1 small white onion, thinly sliced

3 sprigs of fresh thyme or sage

4 tbsp butter (or use chicken schmaltz for the truly best flavor)

1 tbsp sherry wine vinegar or red wine vinegar

pinch of ground cayenne

2 tsp kosher salt

1 tbsp honey mustard

1. In a large bowl, combine the chicken livers and rub. Toss to coat.

2. In a small bowl, combine the cognac, olive oil, and salt. Pour this over the livers. Cover the large bowl and refrigerate for 1 hour.

3. Preheat the smoker to 225°F (105°C). Use maple, apple, or cherry wood.

4. Evenly space the chicken livers on a smoker rack. Scatter the onion slices over the top. Place the thyme sprigs over the onion slices.

5. Place the rack in the smoker and smoke until the internal temperature reaches 160°F (75°C), about 1½ to 2 hours. To check the internal temperature, insert a thermometer probe into the thickest part of 2 or 3 plump livers. Remove the rack from the smoker and allow the livers and onions to cool completely. Discard the thyme sprigs.

6. In a food processor, combine the livers and onions. Blend until smooth. Add the butter, vinegar, cayenne, salt, and honey mustard. Blend until fully incorporated and smooth.

7. Transfer the pâté to a serving bowl. Cover with plastic wrap and refrigerate until ready to serve. Store for up to 3 to 4 days.

Bacon-Wrapped Onion Rings

This tasty recipe is always a crowd-pleaser. The key is to buy some mighty large onions, which makes wrapping slices of onion with bacon easier. Look for onions that are about the size of a softball.

Prep Time	Smoker Temp	Smoke Time
1 hour	235°F (115°C)	2 to 3 hours

wood suggestions: maple, apple, or hickory

4 to 6 large sweet onions, peeled

2lb (1kg) bacon (about 32 slices total)

6 tbsp **Chipotle & Cinnamon Rub** (page 122), divided

honey

1. Slice the onions into ½-inch-thick (1.25cm) rounds. (You should get about 3 to 5 slices per onion.) Carefully remove the inner layers of each onion, leaving the outer two layers together. You want to have onion rings that are two layers thick for easier bacon wrapping.

2. Place the bacon on a flat work surface. Use your fingers to stretch the strips to increase their length by almost half. Season one side of each slice with a little barbecue rub. Tightly wrap a slice of bacon around each two layers of onion, seasoning side in. Secure the bacon ends with toothpicks if necessary. Place the onion rings on a tray and season the bacon with a little barbecue rub. Cover with plastic wrap and refrigerate for 2 hours.

3. Preheat the smoker to 235°F (115°C). Use maple, apple, or hickory wood.

4. Place the onion rings on smoker racks. Place the racks in the smoker and smoke the onion rings until the bacon is crispy and the onions are tender, about 2 to 3 hours, turning once.

5. Transfer the onion rings to a serving platter. Sprinkle any remaining barbecue rub and drizzle the honey over the top before serving.

Dessert & Sweet Treat Recipes

When I was asked to make a really special dessert for an old client, I had to dig deep for a new idea. One of the criteria was that it had to be simple but also have a "wow" factor. In a moment of inspiration, it came to me: cold-smoked chocolate! So that's what I did. But I didn't stop there. I shaved it and mixed it into a homemade buttermilk ice cream. It was a huge hit–to say the least! Ever since then, I've been playing with desserts and discovering that sweet goes extremely well with smoky. They're two extreme flavors that tend to balance each other perfectly. Like I said, imagination.

Now let me tell you the story of how the smoked Twinkie was born—possibly the most weird and wonderful recipe in this book. I was tailgating with a bunch of friends, and after a good feed, one of my friends said: "So what's for dessert?" Loving a challenge as I do, I hit the gas station around the corner from the stadium and got some quick dessert provisions. Twinkies were the first thing I grabbed, then peanut butter, jam, chocolate bars, Oreos, mini marshmallows, a bottle of Tennessee whiskey, and more beer. (We *were* tailgating after all.)

So back to the parking lot I went and fired up my grill. I lined those Twinkies up on a plank, spread the peanut butter over the top, then the jam, crushed the cookies and cut up the chocolate bars to sprinkle over the top, and then added the mini marshmallows. Onto the grill they went to smoke. Let me tell you, once I injected each Twinkie with a little whiskey, we were off to the races! I actually had another tailgater offer me $25 for a single Twinkie. Easiest money I've ever made!

Smoked Maple Syrup

I use a pellet grill for smoking maple syrup. Use this to jazz up your morning pancakes and French toast or just have yourself a shot of smoky-sweet goodness.

Prep Time	Smoker Temp	Smoke Time
5 minutes	275°F (135°C)	3 to 4 hours

wood suggestion: maple

1 quart (1 liter) pure maple syrup

1. Preheat the smoker to 275°F (135°C). Use maple wood.

2. Add the maple syrup to a nonreactive pan. Place the pan in the smoker and smoke the maple syrup for 3 to 4 hours. Too much smoke will make your syrup acrid. Taste occasionally to make sure it isn't going bitter.

3. Remove the pan from the smoker and pass the syrup through a fine-mesh sieve or cheesecloth to catch any carbon particulates. Jar the syrup and refrigerate for 2 to 3 days to allow the syrup to bloom with the flavor of smoke.

Variation: Add a few dried hot chili peppers to the maple syrup and let them infuse with smoke to add a spicy kick to your syrup.

Cold-Smoked Honey

Adding smoke to honey is a real treat. It's a great way to naturally add a smoky flavor into your barbecue sauces and marinades. It's also fantastic basted on ribs!

Prep Time	Smoker Temp	Smoke Time
10 minutes	85°F (30°C)	3 to 4 hours

wood suggestions: maple and apple; oak and pecan; oak and mesquite; or maple and cherry

2 cups honey, refrigerated to harden

2 honeycomb pieces (about 2 inches [5cm] square)

1. Preheat the smoker to 85°F (30°C) for cold-smoking with low humidity. Use maple and apple; oak and pecan; oak and mesquite; or maple and cherry woods.

2. Place the honey in a nonreactive pan. Add the honeycomb and any liquid honey. Place the pan in the freezer for 10 minutes.

3. Place the pan in the smoker and smoke the honey until it takes on a smoky flavor, about 3 to 4 hours. (Taste occasionally.) Keep the smokehouse filled with smoke and the vents open.

4. Remove the pan from the smoker. Transfer the honey to a medium saucepan on the stovetop over low heat. Once the honey has melted, add the honeycomb and remove the pan from the heat. Allow the honey to cool uncovered for 2 hours. Cover the pan and leave at room temperature for 24 hours.

5. Rewarm the honey until fluid. Cut each honeycomb in half and place them in wide-mouthed 1-pint (½-liter) canning jars. Pour the warm honey over the honeycombs and seal the jars. Store at room temperature for up to 2 weeks.

Recipe Notes: Liquid honey doesn't absorb the smoke flavor as well as raw honey, which is a cloudy and thick variety that has all the pollen left in. Honeycomb is great for this purpose because it really attracts the smoke flavor, which it will continue to infuse into the honey as they sit in the jar. To easily remove raw honey from a container, just warm it for a few seconds in a bowl of hot water and turn it out into a pan to refrigerate.

Strawberry, Rhubarb & White Chocolate Crumble

Do you like strawberries and rhubarb? Have I got a dessert for you! I dare you to read this recipe and not run to the nearest grocery store for supplies!

Prep Time	Smoker Temp	Smoke Time
10 minutes	235°F (115°C)	45 minutes

wood suggestions: apple, cherry, peach, or maple

4 pints (1½kg) fresh strawberries, hulled, rinsed in cold water, and drained

3 cups rhubarb, peeled and chopped into 3-inch (7.5cm) pieces

1½ cup granulated sugar, divided

3 tbsp cornstarch

2 tbsp freshly squeezed orange juice

Grand Marnier orange liqueur

pinch of kosher salt

1 cup butter, softened

1 tsp baking powder

1 cup almond flour

2 cups rolled oats

½ cup white chocolate chips

1. Preheat the smoker to 235°F (115°C). Use apple, cherry, peach, or maple wood.

2. Place the strawberries and rhubarb onto smoker trays. Sprinkle ½ cup of sugar over the top.

3. Place the trays in the smoker and smoke the strawberries and rhubarb until they've darkened and have a smoky fragrance, about 30 to 45 minutes. Remove the trays from the smoker and allow the strawberries and rhubarb to cool.

4. Preheat the oven to 375°F (195°C).

5. Cut the rhubarb into 1-inch (2.5cm) pieces. In a large bowl, combine the rhubarb and strawberries. Add the cornstarch, orange juice, a splash of orange liqueur, and ½ cup of sugar. Gently mix. Transfer the mixture to a 10- or 12-inch (25 or 30.5cm) heavy-bottomed ovenproof pan.

6. In a large bowl, combine the butter, baking powder, almond flour, rolled oats, and the remaining ½ cup of sugar. Add another splash of orange liqueur to moisten. Mix well until it forms buttery crumbs. Scatter the butter mixture over the strawberries and rhubarb. Sprinkle the white chocolate chips over the top.

7. Place the pan in the oven and bake until the mixture is bubbling and the crumble topping is golden brown, about 35 to 45 minutes.

8. Remove the pan from the oven and allow the crumble to cool for 20 minutes. Serve with vanilla ice cream.

Smoked Martini

Who needs olives or onions or lemon zest when you can have a smoke-infused martini with a bacon garnish? Read it again if you have to, but it's going to say the same thing—we're smoking water to make a bacon-garnished martini. How could you not make this recipe?

Prep Time	Smoker Temp	Smoke Time
10 minutes	125°F (55°C)	2 to 3 hours

wood suggestions: maple, oak, hickory, or cherry

2 quarts (2 liters) cold water

1 (25oz [750ml]) bottle of vodka

12 slices of **Spicy Pig Candy** (page 339)

3 tbsp **Cold-Smoked Honey** (page 331)

freshly ground black pepper, to taste

4 tbsp ice wine

1. To a 2-quart (2-liter) milk carton (or a similar container) with the top cut off, add the water and freeze for at least 24 hours.

2. Preheat the smoker to 125°F (55°C) for cold-smoking. Use maple, oak, hickory, or cherry wood.

3. Remove the carton from the freezer and place the ice in a nonreactive metal container large enough to hold 2 quarts of liquid. Place the container in the smoker and smoke until melted and smoky, about 2 to 3 hours.

4. Remove the pan from the smoker and transfer the water to a large pot. Place the pot on the stovetop over high heat. Bring the water to a boil. After 2 minutes, remove the pot from the heat and strain the water through a paper coffee filter to remove any carbon particles. Pour the water into ice trays and freeze until solid.

5. Place the vodka bottle in the freezer and chill 4 martini or rock glasses.

6. Evenly space the spicy pig candy on a baking sheet lined with parchment paper. Brush the top of each slice with the smoked honey and season with pepper.

7. Swirl 1 teaspoon of ice wine in each frosted glass until evenly coated. Drain any excess. To each glass, add 2 to 3 ounces (60 to 90 millimeters) of chilled vodka, 2 smoked ice cubes, and 1 strip of bacon. Serve immediately.

Recipe Notes: Add smoked ice cubes to any liquor you like or in your favorite cocktails to add a smoky twist. Try them in a Caesar, mojito, sidecar, or chocolate martini. The reason I freeze the water into a huge ice block before smoking is because the heat will cause it to melt slowly, which means the water will absorb more of the smoke and create a more rounded smoke flavor. A bowl of water will only get the smoke on the top, resulting in too mild a smoke flavor to really complement a cocktail.

Chocolate & Banana Ice Cream

Smoke blends nicely with chocolate and brings out a whole new dimension of flavor than what we're used to with regular chocolate. Use any remaining smoked chocolate to make a chocolate sauce to garnish other ice creams and desserts, for *mole* and barbecue sauces, for frostings for cakes and cupcakes, or just to snack on in bed with a handful of toasted nuts.

Prep Time	Smoker Temp	Smoke Time
30 minutes	85°F (30°C)	30 minutes

wood suggestions: almond wood or coconut shells and either cherry, pecan, apple, walnut, or mesquite

1lb (450g) milk, dark, or white chocolate slab (about 1 inch [2.5cm] thick), well chilled

4 cups 35% whipping cream

2 cups 10% half-and-half

2 vanilla beans, split lengthwise

1½ cups granulated sugar

12 large egg yolks

1 cup mashed ripe bananas

1. Preheat the smoker to 85°F (30°C) for cold-smoking. Use almond wood or coconut shells and either cherry, pecan, apple, walnut, or mesquite wood. If you're using a water smoker, fill the water tray with blocks of ice or bags of ice cubes. If you're not using a water smoker, place frozen ice packs on the shelf below the chocolate to keep it cold.

2. Place the chocolate in the highest position of the smoker and as far away from the heat source as possible. Smoke for 30 minutes, being careful to maintain a cold temperature. Remove the chocolate from the smoker and let cool completely. Store wrapped in parchment paper and in an airtight container in a cool, dark place for at least 24 hours.

3. In a large heavy-bottom saucepan on the stovetop over medium heat, combine the whipping cream and half-and-half. Scrape the seeds out of the vanilla beans. Add the seeds and pods to the saucepan. Slowly bring the mixture to a boil, then remove the pan from the heat. Allow the mixture to cool slightly.

4. In a medium bowl, whisk together the sugar and egg yolks until thick and smooth. Whisking constantly, slowly pour the cream mixture into the egg mixture. Return the custard to the saucepan over medium heat. Cook until thickened enough to coat the back of a spoon, about 8 to 10 minutes, stirring constantly.

5. Remove the chocolate from the freezer and chop into small pieces. Add 12 ounces (340g) of chocolate to the saucepan. Stir until completely melted. Remove the pan from the heat and strain the mixture through a fine-mesh sieve into a large bowl.

6. Stir in the bananas until evenly distributed. Cover the surface of the ice cream with parchment paper. Refrigerate for at least 8 hours and preferably overnight.

7. Prepare the ice cream in an ice cream machine according to the manufacturer's instructions. Divide and pack the ice cream into two airtight containers (about 4 cups each). Freeze for at least 2 hours before serving. Chop the remaining smoked chocolate and sprinkle over the top before serving.

Recipe Notes: The colder the smoker temperature, the less likely it is that the chocolate will melt. Some people line their smoker rack with aluminum foil to catch any melted chocolate or smoke the chocolate in a pan. I like the challenge of maintaining the right temperature—it gives me more bragging rights! I've smoked chocolate using a variety of smokers and I've found that electric smokers produce the best results.

PB&J Plank-Smoked Twinkies

Yes, you can even smoke the humble Twinkie. These cream-filled confections are lined up on a wooden plank and topped with peanut butter, jam, chocolate, and marshmallows, then smoked until ooey and gooey. This is the best dessert for pleasing a crowd of tailgaters or just about anyone.

Prep Time	Grill Temp	Smoke Time
15 minutes	450°F (235°C)	15 minutes

wood suggestions: maple, oak, pecan, or hickory plank (about 12 inches [0.5cm] long and ½ inch [2.5cm] thick), soaked in cold water for at least 1 hour

12 Twinkies, unwrapped

1 cup smooth peanut butter

½ cup strawberry preserves

1 cup white mini marshmallows

½ cup milk chocolate chips

½ cup unsalted peanuts, crushed

3oz (90g) Tennessee whiskey (optional)

1. Preheat the grill to 450°F (235°C). Remove the plank from the water and dry with paper towels.

2. Arrange the Twinkies right next to each other on the plank. Vigorously stir the peanut butter to loosen, then evenly spread it over the Twinkies, filling any gaps. Evenly spread the preserves over the peanut butter. Sprinkle the marshmallows over the top. Sprinkle the chocolate chips and peanuts over the marshmallows.

3. Place the plank on the grill and close the lid. Smoke until the plank begins to smoke, about 3 to 5 minutes. Turn off the heat source directly under the plank and reduce the remaining burners to 300°F to 350°F (150°C to 180°C). Or you can spread out the fuel on one side and move the plank away from direct heat. Continue to smoke until the Twinkies are lightly browned and crisp and the marshmallows are warm and gooey, about 10 to 15 minutes more.

4. Transfer the plank to a heatproof work surface. Fill an injector syringe with the Tennessee whiskey (if using). Insert the needle about halfway into each Twinkie and inject with about ¼ ounce (7 milliliters) of whiskey. Serve immediately.

Recipe Notes: Leave out the Tennessee whiskey if this is a treat for the kids. And be sure to make extra—most people can't stop after just one.

Spicy Pig Candy

This truly is the best dessert: crispy smoked bacon glazed with maple syrup, chipotle hot sauce, and brown sugar. Then it's drizzled with melted chocolate. It's heavenly.

Prep Time	Smoker Temp	Smoke Time
15 minutes	275°F (135°C)	1 hour

wood suggestions: maple or fruitwoods

16 slices of thick bacon

3 tbsp **Basic Barbecue Rub** (page 115)

½ cup maple syrup

¼ cup chipotle-style hot sauce

½ cup light brown sugar, divided

1 cup melted milk chocolate or dark chocolate

1. Preheat the smoker to 275°F (135°C). Use maple or fruitwoods.

2. Season the bacon all over with the barbecue rub. Evenly space the bacon on a smoker rack.

3. In a small bowl, combine the maple syrup and hot sauce. Brush half this mixture on the top sides of the bacon strips. Sprinkle ¼ cup of brown sugar over the top.

4. Place the rack in the smoker and smoke the bacon until it starts to render its fat, about 30 minutes. Flip the bacon and brush with the remaining maple mixture. Sprinkle the remaining ¼ cup of brown sugar over the top. Continue to smoke until the bacon is well rendered of fat, firm, and a little crispy, about 30 to 45 minutes more.

5. Remove the rack from the smoker. Evenly space the bacon on a baking sheet lined with parchment paper. Drizzle the chocolate over the bacon. Allow the chocolate to cool and set before serving the bacon.

Glossary

Arborio rice Plump, short-grain Italian rice traditionally used for risotto.

bacteria Single-cell microorganisms that can contaminate food and cause foodborne illness.

balsamic vinegar A red wine vinegar produced from a specific type of grape and aged in wood barrels. It's heavier, darker, and sweeter than most vinegars.

barbecue This refers to a method of cooking over an open fire or a hot grill outdoors. It can also be used as a noun to describe the actual grilling appliance or a specific flavor profile in foods, such as sauces or cooked meats.

bark (1) The outer layer of a long, slow-cooked cut of meat, such as pork shoulder. This layer will be about ½ inch deep, dark, and somewhat tougher in texture than the meat it protects. A good bark is highly prized by barbecue enthusiasts. (2) The outer protective layer of wood.

baste A technique used to keep foods moist during cooking by spooning or brushing the meat with a sauce, marinade, or another flavored liquid.

brine A highly salted, often seasoned liquid used to flavor, add moisture, and/ or preserve foods.

brisket The cut located between the fore shank and the plate of the beef carcass. It's often cut into two halves: the flat and the point cut.

butcher paper A strong wrapping paper that resists penetration by blood or meat fluids; usually brown in color; used by butchers for wrapping meat.

Cajun cooking A style of cooking that combines French and Southern characteristics and includes many highly seasoned stews and meats. Can also refer to spice blends that might include such spices as thyme, paprika, mustard, and hot dried peppers.

capers The flavorful buds of a Mediterranean plant, ranging in size from *nonpareil* (about the size of a small pea) to larger, grape-sized berries.

cardamom A sweet-smelling, intense spice common to Indian cooking; often used in baking and coffee.

chili or **chilies**   Any one of many different hot peppers (or capsicum), dried or fresh, and ranging in intensity from relatively mild to blisteringly hot.

chili powder   A seasoning blend that includes cayenne, cumin, garlic, and oregano. Proportions vary among different versions, but all offer a warm, rich flavor.

chimney   A large, hollow, upright cylinder used to start a fire in a smoker or grill.

chipotle   A smoked jalapeño that's dark brown with a reddish tinge, wrinkled skin, and a sweet and chocolaty flavor with a kick of heat. They can be dried or pickled as well as canned in *adobo* (Mexican sauce).

churrasco   A term for a style of barbecue that originated in southern Brazil. It's a variety of meats that might be cooked on a purpose-built *churrasqueira* (a grill, often with supports for spits or skewers).

chutney   A thick condiment often served with Indian curries; made with fruits and/or vegetables, vinegar, sugar, and spices.

cilantro   A member of the parsley family, this herb is used in Mexican and Asian cuisines. The dried seed of a cilantro plant is called coriander.

cold-smoking   The process of applying smoke flavor to foods without necessarily cooking them.

cooler   Used to hold meats after smoking to help tenderize.

crispy fried onions   Typically found in Asian grocery stores, these are thinly sliced onions or shallots that are lightly dusted with starch and fried until golden brown and crisp. Sold packed in cans, jars, or plastic bags, they're ready to use in a variety of applications as a garnish or ingredient.

cumin   A smoky-tasting spice popular in Middle Eastern and Indian dishes. Cumin is a seed; ground cumin seed is the most common form used in cooking. Its flavor is best known as the predominant flavor of chili powder.

cure or **curing**   A term that refers to food preservation and flavoring processes, especially of meat or fish, by the addition of a combination of salt, nitrates, and/or sugar.

curry   Rich, spicy sauces and the dishes prepared with them. Curries involve complex seasoning bases often with 30 or more ingredients and long, slow cooking to draw out the flavors. Common to the cuisines of India, Southeast Asia, and the Caribbean.

curry powder   A ground blend of rich and flavorful spices used as a basis for curry and many other Indian-influenced dishes. Common ingredients include cayenne, nutmeg, cumin, cinnamon, pepper, and turmeric. Modern curry powder is a blend invented by the English occupiers of India to mimic the *masala* blends in a less intense fashion.

diffuser   A gas grilling accessory that helps distribute heat evenly and prevent flames from coming in direct contact with food; also known as a heat diffuser or a barbecue flame diffuser.

Dijon mustard   Hearty, spicy condiment made in the style of the Dijon region of France.

drizzle   To lightly sprinkle drops of liquid over food, often as the finishing touch to a dish.

dunk   A seasoned liquid or sauce into which a cut of meat or a vegetable is fully immersed either before cooking or before eating.

fennel seed   A fragrant, licorice-tasting spice. The bulbs have a much milder flavor and celery-like crunch, and they're used as a vegetable in salads or cooked recipes.

frenched   To cut the meat away from the end of the bone of a rib or chop so that part of the bone is exposed; done with racks of lamb, beef, and pork to make meats more pleasing to the eye.

garnish   An embellishment not vital to the dish but added to enhance the visual appeal.

ginger   Available fresh or dried, this plant adds a pungent, sweet, and spicy quality to a dish.

grilling   The act of cooking meat (or other foods) by setting it on a grate over a gas flame or hot coals.

hoisin sauce   A sweet Asian condiment similar to ketchup made with soybeans, sesame, chili peppers, and sugar.

hot-smoking   Smoking in an enclosed atmosphere in the presence of heat and smoke.

infusion   A liquid in which flavorful ingredients, such as herbs, have been soaked or steeped to extract that flavor into the liquid.

injection   A technique where you push liquid into meat in several areas with an injector to increase the internal moisture of the meat and add flavor.

kosher salt   A coarse-grained salt made without any additives or iodine.

marinate   To soak meat, seafood, or other food in a seasoned liquid, called a marinade, which is often high in acids. Its main purpose is to add flavor, although the acids in the marinade might break down the muscle tissue, helping make it tender.

mirin   A sweet, golden rice wine made from glutinous rice. It's low in alcohol and is often used in sauces and dressings. Typically found in Japanese and Asian cuisines.

mop   The action of slopping a seasoned liquid over slow-cooked meat or fish using a tool (of the same name) that resembles a miniature old-fashioned string mop.

nitrates or **nitrites**   Compounds that contain a nitrogen atom combined with either two (nitrite) or three (nitrate) oxygen atoms. They're used as food additives in cured meats to preserve color and prevent dangerous foodborne illnesses, such as botulism.

olive oil   A fragrant liquid produced by crushing or pressing olives. Extra-virgin olive oil—the most flavorful and highest quality—is produced from the first pressing of a batch of olives; oil is also produced from later pressings.

panko breadcrumbs   Coarse, airy, textured white breadcrumbs traditionally used in Japanese cuisine as a breading for seafood, poultry, and pork. Can be found in grocery and specialty food stores in the Asian ethnic food section.

parchment paper   A cellulose-based composite that's been processed to give it additional properties. Commonly used as a disposable, nonstick, grease-resistant surface; also called vegetable parchment.

paste   A thick wet mixture that's made by adding a fluid to a seasoning rub or mixture that's massaged on the surface of meat or, in the case of poultry, under the skin and is left to sit for a period of time before cooking.

peameal bacon   A Canadian tradition of curing pork loins with a solution of salt and water (brine). Traditionally injected and then rolled in cornmeal. It can be smoked, grilled, and fried.

picanha   A cut of beef taken from the top of the rump. You might also know it as a rump cover, rump cap, sirloin cap, or even culotte steak. It's triangular in shape and surrounded by a thick layer of fat called a fat cap.

pink salt   A natural, coarse-grained salt containing a high concentration of minerals. The pink coloring of this salt is derived from the mineral components held within each crystal. Harvested from ancient seabeds within the foothills of the Himalayan mountains, this salt provides a seasoning that boasts more than 60 different minerals, including the key nutrients of calcium, magnesium, potassium, copper, and iron.

portobello mushroom   A mature and larger form of the smaller cremini mushroom; it's brownish, chewy, and flavorful. Often served as whole caps, grilled, or as thin sautéed slices.

Prague powder A curing mixture used in making cured meat products that require short cures that will then be cooked, such as sausages, hot dogs, fish, and corned beef. Also called pink curing salt.

prosciutto Dry, salt-cured ham that originates from Italy.

purée To reduce a food to a thick, creamy texture, usually using a blender or a food processor.

render To cook a meat to the point the fat melts and can be removed.

reserve To hold an ingredient for another use later in the recipe.

ribs Cuts of meat from pigs, cattle, lamb, venison, and others. They're the less meaty parts of the chops and are typically cooked as a slab.

rice vinegar A condiment produced from fermented rice or rice wine, popular in Asian-style dishes. Different from rice wine vinegar.

risotto A popular Italian rice dish made by browning Arborio rice in butter or oil and slowly adding a liquid that cooks the rice, resulting in a creamy texture.

rub A blend of seasonings that's massaged on the surface of meat and, in the case of poultry, under the skin that's left to sit for a period of time before cooking.

sambal oelek A spicy condiment often used in Malaysian and Indonesian cuisines; made from crushed chili peppers, brown sugar, and salt.

shellfish A broad range of seafood, including clams, mussels, oysters, crabs, shrimp, and lobster.

shuck To remove the shells from shellfish such as oysters, clams, mussels, and scallops. Also a term used to remove the outer husk from corn on the cob.

slather To generously rub or spread a thick paste-like mixture over the surface of food, usually a cut of meat.

smoking The process of flavoring, cooking, or preserving food by exposing it for a lengthy period of time to smoke from burning or smoldering plant materials (most often wood or a wood derivative, such as charcoal).

spritz A flavored liquid or simply water placed in a spray bottle to periodically mist over meat during the cooking process to keep the surface moist and provide additional flavor.

sriracha A type of Thai hot sauce named after the coastal city of Si Racha in the Chonburi Province of central Thailand. It's a paste of chili peppers, distilled vinegar, garlic, sugar, and salt. Quite spicy and delicious as a condiment or when used in sauces, dressings, and glazes.

suprême A boneless breast of chicken or another poultry bird that still has the first joint of the wing (drumstick) attached.

tamarind A sweet, pungent flavorful fruit used in Indian-style sauces and curries; made into a sweet sauce popular in Indian dishes.

truss To secure meats and poultry with string or butcher's twine.

turmeric A spicy, pungent yellow root used in many dishes, especially Indian cuisine, for color and flavor. Turmeric is the source of the yellow color in many prepared mustards.

wasabi A fiery, pungent, horseradish-like condiment (often sold as a paste) used with many Japanese-style dishes.

zest Small, thin slivers of peel, usually from citrus fruit, such as lemon, lime, or orange.

Resources

Yes, even a seasoned, professional chef uses the books of other chefs. The following are some books and websites I'd recommend to a new smoker. They're great for providing additional information, answering questions, and getting inspiration. Smoking should be fun, and these are the words of some of the folks who prove that every day!

Books

Anderson, Warren R. *Mastering the Craft of Smoking Food.* Shrewsbury, UK: Quiller Press, 2007.

Big Green Egg. *Big Green Egg Cookbook: Celebrating the World's Best Smoker & Grill.* Kansas City: Andrews McMeel Publishing, 2010.

Browne, Rick, and Jack Bettridge. *The Barbecue America Cookbook: America's Best Recipes from Coast to Coast.* Guilford, CT: The Lyons Press, 2002.

Davis, Ardie A., and Paul Kirk. *The Kansas City Barbeque Society Cookbook, 25th Anniversary Edition.* Kansas City: Andrews McMeel Publishing, 2010.

Hasheider, Phillip. *The Complete Book of Butchering, Smoking, Curing, and Sausage Making: How to Harvest Your Livestock & Wild Game.* Minneapolis: Voyageur Press, 2010.

Jamison, Cheryl Alters, and Bill Jamison. *Smoke and Spice: Cooking with Smoke, the Real Way to Barbecue.* Rev. ed. Boston: Harvard Common Press, 2003.

Kirk, Paul. *Paul Kirk's Championship Barbecue: Barbecue Your Way to Greatness with 575 Lip-Smackin' Recipes from the Baron of Barbecue.* Boston: Harvard Common Press, 2004.

Knote, Charlie, and Ruthie Knote. *Barbecuing and Sausage-Making Secrets.* Cape Giradeau, MO: Culinary Institute of Smoke Cooking, 1992.

Lilly, Chris. *Big Bob Gibson's BBQ Book: Recipes and Secrets from a Legendary Barbecue Joint.* New York: Clarkson Potter Publishers, 2009.

Marianski, Stanley, Robert Marianski, and Adam Marianski. *Meat Smoking and Smokehouse Design.* 2nd ed. Seminole, FL: Bookmagic, LLC, 2009.

Mills, Mike, and Amy Mills Tunnicliffe. *Peace, Love, and Barbecue: Recipes, Secrets, Tall Tales, and Outright Lies from the Legends of Barbecue.* New York: Rodale Books, 2005.

Mixon, Myron, and Kelly Alexander. *Smokin' with Myron Mixon: Recipes Made Simple, from the Winningest Man in Barbecue.* New York: Ballantine Books, 2011.

North American Meat Processors. *The Meat Buyers Guide: Meat, Lamb, Veal, Pork, and Poultry.* Hoboken: Wiley, 2006.

Perry Lang, Adam. *Serious Barbecue: Smoke, Char, Baste, and Brush Your Way to Great Outdoor Cooking.* New York: Hyperion, 2009.

Reader, Ted. *Napoleon's Everyday Gourmet Grilling.* Toronto: Key Porter Books, 2008.

——. *Napoleon's Everyday Gourmet Plank Grilling.* Toronto: Key Porter Books, 2009.

——. *The Art of Plank Grilling: Licked by Fire, Kissed by Smoke.* Toronto: Key Porter Books, 2007.

Reed, John Shelton, Dale Volberg Reed, and Will McKinney. *Holy Smoke: The Big Book of North Carolina.* Chapel Hill: University of North Carolina Press, 2008.

Tarantino, Jim. *Marinades, Rubs, Brines, Cures and Glazes.* Berkeley, CA: Ten Speed Press, 2006.

Websites

- amazingribs.com
- barbecuebible.com
- barbecuetricks.com
- bbq.about.com
- bbqsmokersite.hubpages.com
- biggreenegg.com

- bradleysmoker.com
- www.fsis.usda.gov
- greatlakesgrilling.com
- grilling24x7.com
- horizonbbqsmokersstore.com
- hpba.org
- kcbs.us
- nakedwhiz.com/nwindex.htm
- nordicware.com
- proq.forumotion.com
- ribolator.com
- seriouseats.com
- smokepistol.com
- smokingmeatforums.com
- southernpride.com

Index